19 YEARS TO JOHNSTON
And The Knife Left Behind.

G. R. CARNEY

Nonfiction,
Memoir | Military History - Political.

First Edition

Self-published,
Covers by Author.

Front Cover image was photographed by Author. The
Epilogue image was approved for public release,
unlimited distribution, by the U.S. Air Force on January
5th, 2016.

19 YEARS TO
JOHNSTON

is taken from actual events. Names are changed to
protect the innocent, some words redacted for civility.

In remembrance of the brethren whom
were exiled there, especially the days…

Introduction

Once the Prologue for this story is read, postulating that the main character requires some degree of psychological therapy is reasonable. But what will he encounter pursuing such intervention at a Veterans Administration Medical Center? Will exposing a past tour of duty as what debilitates him so, be acknowledged by Its Clinical Mental Health Professionals as precipitating? Be likened to bodily harm precipitated by? Where then does he look for support, understanding or fellowship if the Government that sent him there turns Its back profiling him as a dissociated disgruntled to keep swept under the rug of obscurity that place of tour?

This Author had to do just that for the Government did just that, and nowhere were such found except in a gentleman who is long deceased that inspired me to write this story. He is identified at the end of the book.

In November of 1991, HR3236 of public record was brought before a subcommittee for the House Veterans Affairs Committee. The bill addressed the radioactive threat men in uniform faced fulfilling the foregoing tour of duty up to 1980. With evidence put forth that explicitly outlined the hazards of exposure to the widespread radiation that existed there until then, the then Senator Alan Cranston (D-Ca.) was urged to include as Atomic Veterans the personnel assigned to that place during the period from June 30, 1946 to August 31, 1980.

It did not happen. A Radiological Survey Report of the place, dated April-August 1980, (DNA-8114) produced by the Edgerton, Germhausen and Grier Energy Measurements Group, Remote Sensing Laboratory, U.S. Department of Energy, which had not been released for public consumption for almost a decade after its completion, failed to impress the legislator or enough of his cohorts to enact HR3236. Facts presented picturing the extent of exposure to atomic radiation by inhabitants as the result of nuclear assault posturing by the United States during the so-called cold war, and not be remiss to mention poisoning of surrounding sea and wildlife, were of no greater impact.

If honored, the bill would have provided the platform for us Veterans assigned duty of tour there to collectively voice illnesses to Government Officials that so far in their responsibilities show no concern for our health and wellbeing resulting from inhabitancy, the exception being those if still alive that fall within the later Congressionally gaveled six months from any Plutonium dowsing, as if were found distinguishable MD's to signoff that the place after any such timeframe was clear of radio-pathogenic outcomes to staffing who endured prolonged exposures to the remaining widespread atomic waste. To legislatively avail service connected recognition to one exposed within 180 days of nuclear contamination while refusing another for 181 is at best arbitrary, capricious and unreasonable since the half-life, the time it takes for half of the atoms of a radionuclide to undergo radioactive decay, is 432 years for Americium 241 (^{241}Am), the radioactive byproduct which is formed giving off high energy alpha particles (alpha radiation) and gamma rays from the radioactive decay of Plutonium 241 (^{241}Pu).

Until anyone of the honorable occupying a cushy office under the dome in D.C. steps up to the podium and acknowledges the sacrifice we were ignorantly made to endure, the profiling of us as dissociated disgruntles by them remains repugnant being yet psychologically and physically encumbered by that place's shameful legacy.

Table Of Contents

Prologue

Arkansas, 2013 ...during the night of
August 21st into the 22nd.

A foot away ...darkish blue-gray wall slowly going by, enough hazy light revealing. Now in the opposite direction. Does not matter how movement is along a path, nor is the head turned over either shoulder staring, just that the view of it is straight in front of the eyes ...passing only a foot away. No periphery to what spans the few inches of its width.

Now likewise the same going by, at same pace, in the other direction. Now once again in the opposite.., again opposite.., once more.., again --Then, am sinking hind end first going deep peering up at the ocean's surface gurgling muffled cries for help! ...panic!! --Suddenly am sitting upright, eyes flying open spotting the dim-lit wall ahead of the bed's end!!! Half a dozen seconds passing.., fall back into the pillow.

Gradually blinking eyes open; when later..? ...do not know or even care, for the nightmare had once more retreated into the subconscious abyss.

Hard awakening.., lying on the right side facing the windows. Though closed, light is piercing through the horizontal slits of the bedroom's subtle bay shape of three blinds a few feet away. Gazing at them.., they nearly take up the wall's entirety, a foot from the left and right edges to their adjacent corners of the small space; full-size bed occupying some three-quarters of it.

Except for slow breathing.., no additional movements are had as minutes drift by waiting for the will to roll onto the back. Maybe can just go back to sleep ...so, surrender the eyes shut. But it's happening ...like always every morning in concert with the perpetuated lack of conviction, from nil of forsaking thoughts beginning way back when ...to now the manifested level worst; "Lonely existence for the rest of my life..?"

Feelings of uncertainty are wanting to invoke another likened day. But lack of conviction, loneliness ...and that, have not yet finished off this loser, a son the reason from out of a broken home. See him just enough.

Since being discharged from the Air Force forty years ago, there has been another nightmare alternatingly dogging. In it, am standing at the edge of a docking pier and staring down to the water eight feet below ...gripped by fear seeing submerged a large dark shadow cruising slowly roundabout --Then, have fallen in! ...and cannot see it!! ...where is it at?!!

But now lying on the right side facing the windows, do out of boredom roll onto the back, lashes opening in sync. Settling.., focus on the large five-blade ceiling fan commanding in-your-face attention although it is motionless and its center-dome unlit.

There has got to be a better reason than the yesterdays to depart from the sheets and not return ...throwing them open, going for the bathroom to empty the bladder is not. Groggy ...what will the stream profess? The odor is summoning; "Why didn't I foresee somewhere along the way my life turning out like this..?" Keep on smelling the smell. Bit ironic, there is no aroma of spent alcohol blended, not a drinker. Trickle...trickle, shakti...shake; briefs going up, back to the sack.

Sometime later manage to get breakfast down and then melancholically amble through the afternoon in the one-bedroom flat searching for a reason to escape; am on SSA Disability for three Southern Cal auto accidents in the span of a year and a half, each having been highspeed rear-ended.

Now ...a minute past 5:30 p.m., turning on the 24" flatscreen and right off is...

The Syrian President has allegedly nerve-gassed his people..!
Glancing by one after another every second are images and sounds of men, women and children lying in streets and hospitals, spasming and gasping for air! Some lying motionless!!

~ III ~

FEAR!!! ...PANIC!!! ...FLASHING BACK TO THAT SPECK in the middle of the ocean whereat far distant past saw that survival film showing helpless chimps being subjected to mustard and nerve gases!!!

ANXIOUS ...rapid shallow breathing!!! ...am going to DIE!!!

TEARING UP!!! ...escaping from the sofa rushing to the front door FLEEING!!!

DOWN the flight of stairs!!! ...begin quick stepping around the apartment complex!!!

Halfway.., FRANTICALLY START SENSING THE RADIATION FROM THERE..!!!

Carrying no ID if found dead..!!!

APPROACHING the apartment and can't get a grip ...so, another trip around!!! ...then slowing, another!! ...slower, another!

Finally back.., am standing in front of the door hesitant to enter! ...ISOLATION, RADIATION, GASES..!

Vertical the other side of it with back pressed against, sounds from the television are no longer moans of torment ...so, slowly close to the sofa. Sit stoic for hours as darkness edges in. Eventually fall over passing out, left to believe am on the evil side of creation.

Waking lying flat-out, remote control wedged between a hip and the backrest, the flatscreen is still luminated as brightening day filters through the living room blinds.

Braindead fatigued ...heavy doubt in surviving, the weight of last evening keeps the body pushed down on the cushions, TRAPPED as though still out THERE! ...SPECK IN THE PACIFIC...

Then am startled by ringtone on the kitchen counter …cellphone inducing action to rise, FEAR still encumbering..! It rings.., rings.., rings…

1

Some fifty-seven years before ... Torrance, California.

In the detached garage, he's playing around. A little guy having some fun, thinks he'll head on into the house. In line with it but behind from the street, the garage's door for cars, which is closed, faces quarter-turn clockwise accommodating the driveway that runs alongside the house. A car must swing right after the house to enter in. Like the house's backdoor, the garage's side door faces it for direct access into the house. It's early afternoon, fair weather.

At a youthful pace he closes the one door behind him and crosses the uncovered partitioning walkway. Up a few back-porch steps due to the house's crawl space and into it. Barely in, yet to close the door behind, there's straight sight through the narrow mudroom with washer and dryer to the kitchen. Immediately to the left is a curving staircase with a few steps downward into the sunken den, sizeable view revealing it.

From ahead Mickey's sight is instantly drawn that direction to Mom and Dad; "What's happening..? ...what am I seeing..?! ...he is hurting her..?!!" mindfully. Some years before Mommy had become Mom, Daddy ...Dad, NOT now!

He spins around as fast as he can, out the backdoor ...slam! Into the garage slamming its door behind and circles the one of two cars that's parked inside seeking to hide! Crouches down between it and the big workbench! Doesn't know what to think?!! ...is afraid!!! Eyes whelping up trying to understand..?!! Turned five a month ago, has yet to start kindergarten.

For the longest time he sits back against the workbench, knees drawn up to the chest and arms grasping them tightly with frequent dipping of his head. Silence... ...alone.

Eventually the tiny form subtly cracks open the backdoor, his head slowly piercing the threshold peeking left towards the den.

Linda is resting on the lengthy sofa that's adjacent the far wall and is alone sitting upright equally amid the armrests. With the brim of her dress draped over the knees and her hands clasped on the lap she is looking at him trying to reconcile his weary gaze; "Did we... recklessly allow him to catch us in the act?"

Seemingly his dad Bill nowhere in sight, he rapidly enters the rest of the way closing as before the door behind.

Descends the short stairway and right up to her! Arms hanging limp aside him and their eyes adjoined, his are beginning to redden and glaze; "You okay Mommy? Did Daddy hurt you?!"

Reaching forth taking ahold of his hands, Linda narrows their four between them as she surrenders a maternal smile answering in soft resonance, "No sweetie, he didn't." Then in comforting pitch she asks; "Are you okay..?"

Mickey returns, "I was scared Mommy; what did Daddy do to you?!"

Linda's caught to the quick, fumbling to order her words while lengthening silence she can tell is promoting his anxiety. Finally tension enough; "Mickey.., honey? What you saw was something that you were not supposed to see then ...or to know of right now, I'm sorry. There are some things that happen with older people, they do together, like your dad and me. Later on.., when it is thought to be a good time to tell you about what you saw ...and why, your dad will tell you all about it. But sweetie, just know for now that it was okay..." She concludes; "Why don't you go out back and play with Tina while I fix your dad's meal? He's showering getting ready for work."

The Farrens are in their third house in Mickey's brief years. Bill, a Longshoreman going on nine years, earns a decent wage. Linda stays home to care for Mickey. But they have hardly settled into a residence before a 'For Sale' sign was staked in the ground and onto the next.

Bill ...nearly a pack a day smoker, is six-foot tall, heavy set and brutish in stature. Nil a smile shown, is willful and quick tempered ...cursive; loves to play the ponies. Linda is 5'7", slender but shapely with fair complexion. Pretty and timid, loves to sew and paint flower arrangements. She's 37, he's 41.

There is a half-brother of Mickey's, ten and a half years older on their mom's side from her first of three marriages. James two years ago, about to start his final year of Junior High, wasn't getting along well with his stepdad Bill …and thus, was put on a bus to Colorado to be with his grandparents on his biological dad's side, a preacher who was serving time for cattle rustling. Of the three caught, was the scapegoat taking the greatest fall; multiple counts, stiff prison sentence …few years remaining in his fifteen-year incarceration.

James barely a year old when that happened would soon after find himself with his first of two stepdads, Pete, a Naval Aviator temporarily assigned in Colorado. Shortly after Linda began dating him, he got transfer orders to Long Beach, California but they hit it off …so, divorcement filed against James' dad and to the West Coast they went with Pete. Two years later she was again a single mom without enough income to adequately care for her three-year-old, would pound the pavement looking for work.

Finally out of dire need to provide for James, she begged for a job at a downtown Long Beach department store and got it as a Window Dresser. Linda was talented at that …and going it alone, raised her son there for the next six-plus years. Then in June of 1950 …like prior summers, James, two months beyond nine and a half was during school break off enjoying country life in Colorado with the grandparents.

Linda the youngest of five siblings has three sisters and a brother, they all except for one living in or around Brownsville, Texas; the one, a sister and eldest sibling, not far away in Anaheim just a stone's throw from Disneyland on the other side of the Santa Ana Freeway.

Up until then she like Linda had one child but hers was grown and had recently married. Up until then all of Linda's siblings had been enjoying singular stable marriages. The contrast caused seldom communications with the Texas ones but not such an indifference with her nearby sister. Notwithstanding, a waywardness by virtue of the marital breaches had become her. Parents were alive residing in Brownsville.

Then came Bill, shortly after James had departed for Colorado.

A weeknight, bit after 10 p.m., Linda had just gotten off work putting in extra hours to get the store windows displayed in mid-summer attire. There's a little café near Terminal Island where Pete, she and James use to frequent but that was long ago and Pete had moved on. She still from time to time on weekends took James out for dinner there; great meals! …usual chow down spot for the variety of dockworkers during their mid-shift hour breaks, noon for day workers, 10 p.m. for swing-shift. She and James' timing though, certainly missed those rushes.

But tired, hungry, and not anxious to head right home to emptiness, Linda that night found along a wall in the café a small table to sit at. Few minutes later in strolled Bill with a couple of his co-Longshoremen. They were working swing-shift at a Terminal Island pier. All found counter seats to buddy up to. As with them, the entire place was loud being packed full of dockworkers.

Some minutes drifted by and just before receiving their plates, Bill with coffee cup in hand turned a bit to scope out the place. Linda sitting alone slowly eating caught his eye! Setting the cup down, he said to the fellow worker next to him, "Save my seat," as he slid out of it. Circling the path between center and wall tables to mosey on up to her, reached his destination while she was looking down at her plate but aware he had approached.

She kept looking at the plate ...then; "How's it goin' tonight?" he asked suavely, so he thought!

Not looking up to a grinning Bill, "Not interested," she blandly replied.

His ego beginning to tank; "What, I'm not good enough for you?" rhetorically matching her demeanor.

"Not interested," she repeated anyway.

He gazed down at her for another half-dozen seconds then made an about-face, she not looking up.

By the time he reseated himself the pastrami sandwich in front of him had lost most of its heat but not him. Linda got up, paid her tab and left. Why would she want to return there alone a later date at the same time..? ...the seven-year itch coming on since Pete..? ...plenty of guys to choose from..?

But two months later, just before James was to return from Colorado, there stood she and Bill in front of a Preacher to wed ...in Tijuana. What..? ...why then and there?! It would be fifty-nine years into the future before Mickey sets his sight on a Mexican Marriage Certificate. Unable to piece anything together as to why that location, balancing it with a Birth Certificate, would leave him wondering if he was conceived out of wedlock or otherwise a two-month preemie? Never would be told of either ...not by his dad, mom or half-brother. Maybe James wasn't savvy to their marriage date. Many decades down the road Mickey's mom would only tell him about his health condition when he was born. Still puzzling; "Why a south-of-the-border wedding?"

James not yet ten years old, soon arrived home to meet his third dad having not known his own; introduced to a new place to live due to Linda of course moving in with Bill ...and, she pregnant with either a new brother or sister. A third wedded last name for Mom, his hadn't changed from the first and never would; and soon, the only one of four in the household not similar. All of that surrounded by stress filled Southern Cal compared to where he just left from. Within three months they were in a bit of a larger house in Wilmington, amazing...

Four and a half months later Mickey William Farrens entered the world underweight, sickly, and needing an IV in a foot for feeding. Eventually went home. James had to endure the inordinate amount of attention given his new half-brother by Mom and especially, by the stepdad.

A couple months after Mickey's arrival, James was again bussed to Colorado for another summer. Didn't want to see California evermore. Loved being with his grandparents; the indelible calmness in things done together with Grandpa working the farm. But Linda had final say with Bill a way of mixing certain words in!

Returning, James would stay for the next three years, he and Bill never bonding, tension abounding. He turned to gang association to act out his resentment, but he and his buddies refrained from unlawful mischief, mainly congregating between pickup games voicing mutual contempt of their home lives. One evening after his stepdad left for work, Linda enlisted him for future care of Mickey when they'd be alone. Took him hands-on through the feeding, bathing and diaper changing routines.

Then the moment occurred for reasons unknown, the start of her going out the door early evenings after Bill drove away for work; the first few, brief visits next door before making dinner leaving an eleven-year-old overseeing a six-month-old. Early on Mickey would just be in his crib, but in advancing weeks not so much as their time together grew with Mom now also taking off in the car.

At times following her departures, James' pals showed up for some streetball resulting in the diaper of his brother hastily being safety-pinned to the crib mattress, upsetting him for not being able to crawl around or standup holding onto the railing; or maybe try to climb out?!

An hour later and pooped, James strolled in and to his surprise was Mickey upright in his birthday suit joyfully testing the railing. Puzzled by a collapsed diaper where he had left his brother and between on the sheet a smeared brown blob; "What?!" Grasping the diaper, "Still pinned!" Pooped and hungry; big brother had to cleanup poop..?!

Over the next six months, time spent together was allowed within the fenced-in backyard. Linda demanded of James to keep her intervals away a secret.

Mostly on weekends Bill would let loose brief rants of cussing with Linda virtually the target even though at times James being the object of his irritability. Other times there'd be shouts to quiet down if the boys happened to be playing indoors when he was trying to get horse racing results over the radio.

Two years into that house then again, up for sale. Two months later were moving into a Torrance one. Within a cul-de-sac, it rested atop a leveled lot about a dozen feet above the street, the front yard and driveway sloping near thirty degrees.

James was angry for having to leave his buddies behind and transfer to a new school a month in. When not withdrawn at home, he countered that loss by taking it out on the football field. Allowed to tryout late, was soon a starter as a bruising Junior High Freshman ...and likewise the following season, fortunately at the same school as the Farrens had again uprooted to another Torrance house after just a year.

But finally enough was enough between James and his stepdad. The end of summer of '54, three months shy of turning fourteen, Greyhound once more showed James the sights along the highway to his grandparents for an indeterminate time away; Mom now left without a babysitter for his brother.

The evening before leaving out, the boys were sitting on the floor in Mickey's room playing with some of his matchbox cars, his eyes intently on the one he was motoring around, James' eyes on his brother with mixed emotions; happy that soon he'll again be with his grandparents, sad at leaving Mickey behind. Nil a moment raising his voice out of anger to his little brother all the months he cared for him.

"Move your car around, let's race!" Mickey exhorted, then to his car again subtly humming the sound of its motor as his big brother had yet to resonate.

James gazed down at him with an ambivalent smile, heart was hurting …and then; "Little brother?"

"What big brother?" from Mickey.

"I'm going to be leaving tomorrow morning for Colorado," slowly James said.

Gently from his little brother; "Why?"

"It's been a while since I've spent time with some family there," James answered.

"My family, too?!" from Mickey.

"Well, sort of..," from James, not wanting to alienate.

Mickey; "Where's Mommy and Daddy gonna be?"

James, "Here."

Mickey; "Can I go with you?"

James, "Wish you could, little brother," as his eyes began to redden.

Mickey looking down at his car slowly moving it back and forth; "Why not?"

James, "You got to keep your mom and dad company."

Mickey looked up to him, eyes reddening …watering, "Don't go..!"

James went silent staring at him and fighting back tears, reached to pull Mickey into a hug. With their heads touching aside, "Just for some time.., then I'll come back," big brother offered looking straight ahead. Lesser than little brother's, he blinked tears.

To Mickey, from then on Mommy started becoming Mom, Daddy ...Dad, except for the future moment of witness!

Two years gone by, a month beyond five years old and yet to start kindergarten, he's heading out the backdoor after what had been observed and told to go out and play with Tina awhile; he still much rattled!

Down the back porch, goes right onto the partitioning walkway ending at the garage's corner, the backyard opening from there. Equal to the twenty-four-foot remaining span of the house's width, it runs adjacent the garage's backside where at its far corner a chicken-wire fence with gate crosses to the side property-line. Beyond the fence the lot extends a hundred feet but some thirty feet from it begins a row of a half-dozen empty walk-in pigeon coups that run to forty feet short of the back property-line where a small wooden storage barn sits. The previous owners raised the birds. At this end of the coups sits a large wooden doghouse.

As he is closing the gate behind, Tina's running out from it and practically nose-crashes into his shins, her hind end a waggin', the tail a whippin' more! He runs aside a few paces diving headlong in the grass rolling around teasing her to lick his face, but to no avail in preventing as she tongues him over and over finding its mark between blocking forearms! Giggling..! ...he sits up, the front of her perched on his lap still going for the face! Allows Tina to lick a few times more as he jostles her hanging hound dog ears! Weighing in at about twenty-five pounds, she's a standard Dachshund with reddish-brown coat.

Her entrance into the family was bit of an anomaly …no, miracle! It only took the day after waving goodbye to James two years ago that Mom noticed her youngest moping around the house. A cure for that came through the front door the next afternoon, Bill walking in carrying a somewhat small cardboard box with holes punched in. Sat it down in front of Mickey telling him to open the flaps. The look on his face as the contents appeared in concert with, "Mom, Dad..!" and then reaching into grasp the five-week-old light-brown Cocker Spaniel.

Two weeks later the three of them and Charlie the pup were outside enjoying a sunny afternoon, Bill sitting on the raised front porch ten feet or so from the driveway aside the house, a glass of iced tea in hand. Mickey and Mom are in the yard a third of the way closer to the street and a couple of feet nearer the driveway. She is sitting cross-legged while Charlie still running a bit clumsy is plopping in and out of her lap, Mickey close by to corral the pup when going out of Mom's reach.

He looked to Dad and loudly asked; "Can I get my bike out of the garage?!"

"Go ahead," Bill answered.

Mickey aided by training wheels had been told to go it slow for a while on his new Schwinn. Way back from the street he brought it out through the garage's open door where one of the two cars was parked. Positioning just in front of its tail end, hopped on and off he went alongside the house but not very fast.

Clearing the front corner of it he was coasting waiting to apply the footbrakes just before reaching the street-end of the driveway. About ten feet before passing Mom and

Charlie, the pup plopped off her lap and headed for the bike. She briskly rose to go after him…

Mickey an inexperienced three-year-old not envisioning the fun of Charlie coming close turning into tragedy, did within a split second see him crumple beneath the back wheel! …hear the pup let out a sharp yelp tumbling out the other side as he quickly slowed to a stop momentarily looking forward, then back seeing Mom rush behind to his squirming pet!! …Bill on his way there!! It happened so fast, and Mickey trying to grasp the scene of Charlie being gently picked up …wanted to undo it all..!!!

"Here, give him to me!" Bill said to Linda. She rushed into the house swiftly returning with a folded bath towel!

He placed the pup in it saying, "Put him in the car, I'll head for the Vet!"

Tears had already begun rolling down Mickey's cheeks! With one leg still straddling the Schwinn, he hopped it out of the way of the car backing to the street, Mom at a slower pace behind.

As she neared the house's front corner, the vehicle fading, he let the bike fall from beneath and for the house he ran! Eyes filling with tears wanting to absorb her little one's pain as he stormed up the porch steps slinging the screen door open, she turned toward the bike after he disappeared. Gradually up righting and slowly rolling it over to lean against the porch, she then circled to the steps and up …subtly opening the screen door, disappeared also. An hour later the scene was repeated by Bill, without Charlie.

Uncertainty surrounded buying another pup; when if so? But one thing was for sure, Mickey was crushed emotionally. Maybe three days out …four, a week …two, or a month from the accident might have worked; no rejection of a new one? When was best? …wait for vibes from him? Didn't matter.., for it seemed that a higher power had bit of a different remedy.

Two days after his trauma, Mickey went out to the garage to find something to do. Did not want to see his bike in there, would be a long time before he got on it again. It was after dinner with Bill already at work. Like before, only one car was parked inside leaving the same empty space adjacent the side door to mosey about.

Closing it behind, he spotted the bike off to the right leaning near the back corner. Just a couple paces in he drifted into walking round 'n round in a small circle dipping his head each time the bike came into view.

Passing it the fourth time, head still lowered, something caught his eye that was peeking out from behind the back wheel of the car …a brown snout, big eyes, and flappy ears!

Funny; they stared at each other for the longest time.., then he squatted to his knees and before could utter a word, flappy ears and all, a wienie dog, moved so ingratiatingly toward him with tail a waggin' …gently nosing up as he began to pet.

Then he jumped up …out the one door and through the other, "Mom! …come quick, there's a dog in the garage!"

"What?!" as she approached from the kitchen.

Mickey, "Dog! …come see!"

She went ahead and slowly opened the door not knowing what kind it might be? And there it was right about where Mickey had left out …looking up at her, its tail a waggin'. "Oh..?!" as she bent down and began petting, "You're so cute..!"

Mickey looking over her shoulder, "I told you, Mom..!"

"How did it get in here, you let it in..?!" she asked.

"No..!" he answered.

Looking around, she noticed nearby the side door that a metal-wire venting-screen framed by a foundation-cinderblock was pushed in. Seemingly the only way to have gotten in, "Likely came through there, must've been a tight squeeze," pointing to it.

"What kind of dog is it?" he asked.

"A Dachshund," she answered pausing to look beneath …then added, "and she appears well cared for except for some good amount of dirt on her front paws;" as she continued to pet, "No collar; wonder who the owner is..? …haven't seen her before in the neighborhood?" Lastly to Mickey, "Tell you what.., stay here until I get back with some food and water."

Mickey, "Okay, Mom..!"

Returning, a good size plate of cutup leftover pot-roast, mashed potatoes all covered in gravy and a bowl of water were laid …and, "Wow.., Mom, look at her go!" from Mickey stooped beside the chowing hound.

Mom, "Yes.., I see!"

"Sure is hungry!" from him.

"Sure is," from her. As they watched, she said to him, "You know we can't keep her."

Mickey; "We can't," slowly stroking the dog's back, "why not..? …you see she needed us to feed her."

"Yes, but nonetheless someone might be looking for her right now," she replied.

Mickey rose to stand next to Mom and when the dog had finished, looked up to them waggin' her tail. "What now, Mom?" from him.

"I want you to hold the end of the screen up as high as you can, careful not to get scratched, and I'll slowly nudge her back out through it. We also need to be careful that she doesn't get scratched," Mom answered.

Gingerly it was accomplished, Linda straightening the screen back down as she loudly voiced repeatedly, "Go home..!"

Mickey bravely joined in!

Linda remarked, "Let's circle around the back of the car.., quietly out of sight for a few minutes giving her time to turn to where she came from."

Eventually the side door was eased open and they peeked out, the dog was gone.

Quietly they entered the house, Mickey ahead of Mom. He went for the sofa to sit and try to resolve yet another loss, the third in that many weeks. Linda sat down beside him leaning forward some with her hands clasped resting on her knees like his and offered, "Mickey, I hope you know we did the right thing."

His head dipped a little and eyes a bit more, "I guess so..," he replied lowly.

As if was asked, probably couldn't come up with the notion why again he would step into the garage the next morning an hour short of noon. Opening the side door, he spun around and shoved the house backdoor open yelling, "Mom! ...come quick, there're two dogs here!"

Bill had just gotten out of bed after a night's Longshoring and heard Mickey's commotion.

This time Mickey led out and Mom's eyes widened in amazement at the sight of two pooches huddling around them, tails a waggin'!

Then Bill stepped in; "What's this?!"

Linda squatting explained to him the event of the evening before, pointing to the again bent-in screen.

"Mom, I think this one is the same," Mickey purported!

"It looks like her," she replied adding, "and that one, a female also, looks somewhat older; maybe her mom?"

"Now can we keep her?! ...both?! She came back and brought her mom, must want to live with us!" Mickey declared.

"Well.., they're probably hungry;" Linda suggested. "I'll fetch some vittles and drinks."

A minute went by from her departure and Mickey still petting; "Dad, what do you think?! ...can we keep them?!"

Bill took a slow deep inhale then puffed out and, "Don't know for the moment, gonna take some thought."

Mom returned with a double portion more than last evening, a plate each of sliced franks and segmented pieces of bread instead.

"Wow ...look at them go!" from Mickey.

After returning once more with a couple bowls of water, Linda looked to Bill, slowly squinted. Looking at her, he took the same breath as minutes before. Squinting in unison with it, "Might as well keep them until we find out where they came from?"

It only took to the next afternoon that a couple sat down with Bill and Linda, Mickey told to go out and play in the front yard. Then the Dachshunds were brought in from the garage. About a half-hour later a collar and leash were fetched from a car parked curbside. Not long thereafter, Linda pushed the screen door halfway open saying, "Mickey, come in."

He entered the living room where all seated turned to welcome him. The Dachshunds were being held still by each of the visiting couple but only one had on the collar with leash attached, the older of the two sitting in front of the man.

"Come sit next to me," Mom said to Mickey.

Bill then said; "Mickey? ...this is Harold and Sandra Townsend, owners of the dogs."

"Hi," from Mickey.

"Pleased to meet you, Mickey," returned from both the Townsends smiling.

Mr. Townsend continued, "Mickey; during the recent three days, Sandy and I were away from home for two of them, the first and last, and believed that our beloved pets were left safe in the backyard with sufficient nutrition to last them. Even with that, they managed to stray away and we're so happy they were found by you ...and cared for, thank you..."

Mickey just nodded a couple of times in agreement.

Then Mrs. Townsend said, "Mickey, that's Lady Gretchen," gesturing to the older Dachshund then back, "and this is Lady Christina, her daughter."

Mickey again nodded.

Mr. Townsend weighed back in, "And young fellow, it is out of grateful hearts that we want her to stay with you; if that is alright with you?"

Mickey's eyes broadening; "Really?! ...for how long?!"

Mrs. Townsend, "She is yours to keep."

"Christina!" he shouted as Mrs. Townsend let go, Christina going right to him!

He of course was kept out of the particulars for keeping Lady Christina, soon just to be called Tina. About a month later the Townsends conveyed ownership providing Pedigree Certification and a big 'ol Ancestry Chart; all the Sir's and Lady's, Champion' this... Champion' that! A short time thereafter, Mickey was told by Mom that a hole, must have been by Tina, was dug beneath the Townsend's backyard fence to get out and is why there was so much dirt on her paws.

Tina was a year old then. Some six months later she was taken away by the Townsends for a couple of days and returned apparently not any different; man, did that change. She started getting fat fast, so it seemed to Mickey! Soon, he was told the nitty gritty; gonna have babies and how to take care of her for the next couple of months.

A cold misty Saturday morning and as usual, he called out to Tina as the gate closed behind. But not as usual, she wasn't stepping out from the doghouse ...so, looking roundabout he kept on calling.

Then he caught sight of her slowly exiting it but only halfway, surprised by her appearance! ...so skinny ...drawn ...and kind of mellow eyed.

He stooped down next to her not comprehending what she had gone through overnight; maybe is hurt? As he peered down her length his attention went into the dim house and was suddenly startled by the sight of a bunch of wee puppies all huddled together! ...squirming movements, chirp-like sounds..! A month shy of four, it might've been the fastest he ever ran, the quickest ever opening the backdoor! "Mom! ...come quick, Tina had puppies!"

They with Tina were brought in the house to stay until weaned off her. "Mickey, we're gonna care for them just for a little while, so we shouldn't become attached family-like," Linda instructed.

He asked; "Why?"

She answered, "They belong to the Townsends. That was part of the deal to keep her. The first time she had pups, they were to be given to them." As fate would have it, would be her only litter.

Two years gone by, approaching age six and nearing the end of kindergarten. On a fair-weather Saturday, mid-afternoon, Mickey is heading for the fence-gate.

Closing it behind, Tina's running out from her doghouse and practically nose-crashes into his shins, her hind end a waggin', the tail a whippin' more! He runs aside a few paces diving headlong in the grass rolling around teasing her to lick his face, but to no avail in preventing as she tongues him over and over finding its mark between blocking forearms! Giggling..! ...he sits up, the front of her perched on his lap still going for the face! Allows Tina to lick a few times more as he jostles her hanging hound dog ears!

...13 years to Johnston.

2

A year later, in the same house.

It appears that things have settled, no hankering to uproot living here the longest. But the tradeoff to that is intruding nervousness, confusion and doubt. Looking back, I really didn't know those words as defining how I felt, do now. The home was Dad's empire, Mom and I his subjects. She far more took the brunt of his outbursts though never seeing him strike her ...or hear such when they were in another room, just all the loud cussing!

The words of choice always colored something that occurred to his displeasure but not overall directed at her or me personally, though at times when I had inadvertently crossed his ballistic line and she not intervening, was colored ...physically!

Am hightailing it to stay ahead of the strap! A frantic dash to my room and flying onto the bed trying to squeeze down between it and the wall, "Please Dad don't, I'm sorry ...don't, I'm sorry!" jostling trying to dodge his attack, WHAP to the legs! "Don't, I'm sorry!!" ...WHAP, WHAP!!! A reddish branding that matches his feverish hisses; on his face the fierce expression while whipped repeatedly by a wide belt, is being stored up in my memory bank.

Turning his back going for the door, am at age six left wondering with the burning; "When before the first time, was it a loss to him that love begets love, hate ...hate? Who am I to judge? ...but I don't remember when James was with us years ago that we were corrected in that fashion?"

His moments of fury are quick, one needed virtually every day. The calmness that follows each feels so great! ...not afraid or worried, especially when he's off to work.

Tina is brought in the house shortly after he leaves. So sweet at night when turning in, she jumps onto the bed crawling her way beneath the covers to the base of my feet and falling asleep with me. Funny; how she doesn't suffocate is beyond me? ...but I feel safe with the lump of her down there touching.

In the First Grade and just like the year before getting up early in the morning while Dad's still sound asleep, I take her back out. It's a nifty routine; only on schooldays when he has worked the night before, do I get Tina out the backdoor soon enough to miss a knock at the front. If that happens, in a protecting run right up to it, she'll bark him awake! For sure on his days off she stays out back.

Time has gone by that way. Holidays are kind of neat, Mom cookin' up big meals ...taste really good! Cookies, cakes, pies, and ice cream too!! It's okay to hand Tina pieces of food off my plate. She really loves it, sitting straight up with her front legs drawn and paws hanging over! At times I tell her to speak and she barks!! Dad hardly says an angry word during those days celebrating but only the three of us celebrate them ...and Tina. Aunt June and Uncle Roy near Disneyland did stop by momentarily to say, "Hi."

I have only one friend, Eric, who lives five houses down. He used to spend as much time here as I did over at his house, but then he began not so much. Told me one day that on a recent weekend day when he was coming up to our front door, heard my dad mad yelling very loud, saying bad words! ...so, he turned around.

I told him that Dad has to be at work on our schooldays by 5:00 p.m. and gone all night. Now on some of those days my friend spends a little more time over after dinner but has to get back home soon enough to do homework just like me. Most of our time together on weekends is spent at his house.

I've been having a dream but not every night. Don't know if it's good or bad but something about it makes me glad; don't want to tell Mom or Dad. It's about my teacher. She's pretty and very nice to us.

In the dream she's at the front of the classroom next to her desk and has no clothes on, is sitting up in a large steel tub-bucket filled with soapy water. Can't see all of her but most that's out of the water. We're all washing her gently with washcloths. She's not smiling but not angry looking also, just sitting still and quiet ...water running down all around her shiny body from her shoulders. I don't cause my dream to happen, it just does and goes until stopping.

Turned seven five months ago, will be starting Second Grade soon. Walking into my bedroom with Mom, we're carrying sacks and boxes full of new clothes and shoes, also school supplies. It's neat seeing all the new stuff!

Maybe I'll do better this year. Dad was mad at me nearly all of last for the two report cards; a 'B', two 'C's, a 'D' and an 'F' on the first, the second about the same. A whole lot of raised voice with some threats of the strap! Was grounded a bunch and given grass cutting chores using the two-wheel push-mower. Don't know why I can't do better, think I'm kind of stupid.

There was a girl in my class last year that was really pretty, tried not to stare at her too much. Good thing she sat some to the side and in front of me. I didn't know where she lived but must have been way down on our street. Would beat her home after school and many times see her walk by with some other girls. At times, went out to the front yard acting like I was doing something and they just happened upon me! Looked like she had a little bit of glitter in her hair strolling by, sure was pretty! The courage wasn't in me to say, "Hi," when they were nearly in front of me, just sneaked a peek at her when passing most of the way hearing them giggle. Over the summer I hadn't seen her, must have moved; hope not, really like Trisha!

It's been a long time since James went away and Mom is going out again, not for very long but leaving me alone. Now this one night, Dad, Mom and I are at a restaurant having dinner and he has brought a small transistor radio along to listen to the horse races, setting it facing him on the table between me and him. Keeps its sound down low while almost all the time leaning his head close to it. Maybe other people sitting around can't hear it but are looking at us a lot.

Then I do wrong; "Hey, Mom..?"

"Quiet ...awe {redact}! I missed the finish!" Dad raising his voice, people staring at us!

"Come on ...Mickey, let's go out to the car," Mom quickly says but not too loud. We sit quietly in it, me in the back right behind her waiting for him to come out, not being long after. We hadn't finished eating but I'm not hungry anymore, just scared of getting whipped at home!

He starts the car and Mom begins to say something but, "Shut up," erupts loudly from him!

She abruptly responds, "I will not!"

"Yes you will," he shouts at her!

This is the beginning of what will be many arguments between them in the car, he cussing her down! After this one, what will also be the many times when the car comes to a stop that she'll open the door and quickly get out slamming it behind walking away..!! ...and I every time frightfully wondering if she'll be seen again..?! I'm confused and fearful as Dad yells at the door, "Get back here; where're you goin'..?!!" Early on Mom got back in, now she's stopped doing that but shows up later at home. I can't sit up in the back without her up front as he drives just the two of us there ...so, I lay down peering at the floorboard trying not to cry too loud!

Any fun times are not alone with Dad. Eric is a buddy and of course Tina my best friend! Playing in my room with the trainset that I won with Mom's help on the Engineer Bill Show is the most fun when by myself. She got two tickets to that in Hollywood, leaving for there while Dad's still asleep.

Before filming begins we are picked out of the audience to go up on stage for a contest with one other boy, his mom and two girls with theirs!

Before starting it we must put on over our clothes Engineer Bill overalls inside-out with our moms latching the straps on top of the shoulders. Then the train whistle blows! Moms unlatching, we take off the overalls as fast as we can and hand them back so to be turned outside-out as fast as they can! After that, are rapidly passed back to again be put on as fast as we can, moms latching the straps a final time!! Once more the whistle blows because me and Mom finished first!!!

Her time away is lengthening when Dad's at work, leaving me home alone except for Tina. Mom tells me to do my homework while she's at the store. I drift around the house doing just about anything but. Get into the frig looking for a snack for me and Tina. Then I wander into their bedroom to explore what they have in the closet and dresser drawers. Close the bedroom door to keep Tina out. Seven years old and searching for some identity..?

Slowly sliding the top right-side dresser drawer open there is a small brown-paper-covered booklet resting on top of everything else. Sketched on it is the side of a woman sitting with her legs together and feet pulled to nearly touching her bottom! She's leaning back a little supported by one arm and is twisted some from the hips up! Her head is turned the rest of the way facing me smiling with the other extended up and bent over on top of her head! The smile, the shape …especially her chest, is tugging at me..! …is wanting me to peek under its cover..!!

Subtly lifting it out of the drawer, I venture on! The first page; what am I seeing..?! …an image like something I might have seen before but blurred buried, and not remembered all this revealing! Don't know what to think but there's a sense of excitement in what I'm spying!! Can't seem to want to stop looking through it over 'n over but finally put it back in the drawer sliding it closed. Decide that maybe I ought to try to do some homework. While so, it's really hard to forget those images. There'll be a couple more times when Mom's away, Dad's at work, that it's scoped!

A month passes by, then one night after I've finished homework going on 8:30, Mom tells me that we're going for a ride.

I ask; "Where to?"

"Some place. I'll tell you about it when we get there," she answers.

I climb into the front seat of her big Buick. Over the next half-hour we weave our way out of Torrance and into Gardena cruising along on Normandie Avenue. Not much out of the ordinary to look at, stretches of houses, some businesses then more houses but the lights at night going by are kind of neat.

We turn right on Rosecrans Avenue and soon are slowing to turn left into a parking lot going under a big sign that has, "Normandie Club," lit on it. There's the side of a large fancy lookin' building in front of us, moving closer to it. We turn down a path between two rows of parked cars and finally into a slot facing the front of the building, parking right next to a post-light.

"What is this place?" asking her.

"Mickey, I'm going to be in there for only a short time. I'll tell you about it later," she answers.

"Can I go in with you?" I ask.

"No, you have to be a bit older. It's about your bedtime …so, I want you to crawl into the back and try to get some sleep," from her.

I slide over the backrest of the bench seat as she gets out, turning around to peek back in as I'm sitting up and tells me to lay down, she won't be gone long.

Watching her walk towards the entrance, I also see other people heading that way. Looking around for a while see no more …so, I do what she asked, stretching out on the long backseat. Gazing out through as much window space is available, the post-light isn't directly seeable but the shine from it sets a glow the quiet mist surrounding; stare at that for… I don't know how long, relaxing.., relaxing…

Then I hear a door lightly shut.., still wanting to sleep. Hear the motor starting.., still wanting to sleep. Open my eyes a wee bit seeing the back of Mom's head, then close them. Mellow vibrations and stop 'n go momentums are all I sense…

What's next happening …is Mom waking me to try to slide out of the seat as she's holding on, "Come on sweetie, we're home..!" supporting me upright to the front porch. I just want to keep sleeping. Even though on my feet, it feels nearly like I'm being carried through the house.

Finally, I'm lying back on the bed. "Sweetie stay awake a little longer," feeling my shoes being removed. Am in 'n out of peaceful comforting rest feeling body parts being rag-dolled by her pulling clothes off …then pajamas going on.

"Goodnight …sweetie," might've heard with the blanket being eased atop me. Waking in the morning, I don't really feel like caring about what happened last night, just get dressed for school.

The next week another trip to the same place happens but there is a difference on the way home, the smell of doctor-room-like medicine mixed with maple syrup filling the interior; doesn't completely wake me though. Mom again helping me out of the backseat, the odor is super strong coming from her mouth! I'm coaxed to wake more so to better walk with her weaker supporting. Those trips happen many more times over the next two months.

Suddenly! …in bed …after a trip …in the middle of the night, I'm jolted awake hearing Dad yelling, "You {redact} …you {redact}," coming from their bedroom! Haven't heard those words before, don't know what they mean but must be cusswords! Again, "You {redact} …you {redact}!"

Then I hear Mom barely say, "Don't…"

He loudly asks; "How much did you lose..?!"

"Not much..," hear her barely answer. I think about how she at times after some trips would tip my piggybank over trying to slip out dollars.

A dreary silence comes from there.., then he yells those words again!!

She repeats, "Don't…"

What's been heard is slowing, can't tell how much time has passed; fifteen minutes, more..?! Seemed forever..!! From last hearing Mom say, "Don't..," fear's been growing for her..!! Maybe she's hurt, or worse …also has attached a horrible sensing; I'm all alone..?!!

Don't know what to do?! I wait for the longest time not able to go back to sleep …then can't hold back; "Mom..?" lowly call. Again 'n again, getting louder each time..! Finally there she is!!

Looking back to then, I don't remember ever seeing them hold hands, ever hug, kiss or smile at one another …or say, "I love you," to each other.

The third week of October '59, nearly a month beyond eight and a half years old, two months into Third Grade, and am being told that James is coming to visit! Maybe stay for a long while! He's been going to a religious school in Oklahoma called a Seminary but wants to take a break. Because Mom has become very sad and it's quiet a lot between her and Dad, don't know how it's going to be between him and Dad. How neat it will be to see my big brother again after five and a half years! But his stay would last only a month.

Three weeks into his arrival home it's been for the last only the two of us in the evenings. Just like before when Dad had left for work after dinner, Mom is again heading for the casino; their big fight long ago in the middle of the night having changed nothing.

Sitting with my brother on the sofa in the sunken den, he turns to me and asks; "Do you know Jesus as your Lord and Savior?"

"No," answer.

"Would you like to?" louder he asks.

"I guess so," return.

Then James grasps one of my hands and with the other of his, rests it on my head and begins to loudly pray fast over me! I don't know what to think..?! ...am a bit scared and as he goes on, feel pressure to react ...so I callout, "Jesus!"

A moment later he asks; "Now do you know him as your Lord and Savior?!"

Reply, "Yes!"

He responds, "Thank you Lord for saving my little brother, Mickey! Amen."

Can't grasp all together why that exchange brought me to tears ...but it did.

A week goes by, seems peaceful. Mom cooks up a Thanksgiving meal but she and Dad are hardly saying words to each other, and James the same to them; so far it's been okay between me and them. Then the next afternoon, Dad storms out the front door into his car and speeds away! She tells us two to quickly go out and get into hers!! Me in the back, James upfront, we watch for her to come out!!! She does holding his suitcase and another smaller one, setting them down and locking the door, then quickly down the porch passing our side of the car opening the truck and, Slam! Jumps in behind the wheel..! ...backs out and off we go; whereto, I don't know?!

Don't know what to think..?! It's real quiet as Mom appears to know where she's going. Moments later we're on the Artesia Freeway going east and not but a half-hour later are pulling into Aunt June and Uncle Roy's driveway.

She tells us to stay in the car, will be right back! Goes into their house. James isn't saying anything, I'm quiet. About five minutes later she's back out opening the trunk, and with smaller suitcase in hand opens my door. Passing by brother, his head is lowered.

In the house without him Mom tells me that I'm going to stay with Aunt and Uncle overnight and she'll be back in the morning, "Don't ask why …sweetie, I'll tell you then; everything will be alright. I love you!" with a kiss on the cheek. Out the door..! All of this is a blur, confusing. That tomorrow morning won't happen.

It's been a couple of hours since Aunt June made dinner, couldn't eat but a bite or two. Numb, trying to understand everything.

Suddenly! …pounding on the front door! Dad's shouting, "Open the door! Give me Mickey or I'll kick it in!! Open the door now {Redact redact} it, I'm going to break in and kill you if you don't give me him NOW!!!

Aunt and Uncle look horrified.., he grabbing me and quickly to the door opening it, "Here he is!!" shoving me out, the door slamming!!!

I feel Dad's hand at the base of the back of my neck, "Come on," rapidly he says! Opens the passenger-side car door, "Get in," fast from him! He gets in 'n starts the motor, into reverse we jerk back out of the driveway! The same into drive likewise starting down the road! "Son, you're going to have a good life with me! Going to buy you anything you'll want!"

I'm petrified by what just happened! Silent, hanging onto the ride!! Don't know whose I am?!!

We get to the house but nobody else is here. The empty, soundless grip. What's happening?! Where's Mom?! ...James?!

"We're home..!" Dad says.

I ask; "Where's Tina?!"

"Outback," he answers.

Thinking; "Wonder if she's okay..?!!"

...10 $^1/_2$ years to Johnston.

3

"Can I bring her in?" ask him.

A week goes by and haven't seen Mom or big brother; "Wonder where they are? Are they okay?" Each night falling asleep I'd almost begun to cry but didn't, maybe because Tina was allowed in bed with me.

I'm afraid to ask Dad about Mom and James. He hasn't said a word about them but many times told me to go out back 'n play, and during a lot of those, Tina with me, I peeked through a window seeing him on the telephone wondering if he was talking about them.

I've been kept out of school since what happened, Dad not going to work also. He has seldom cooked meals, we going out to restaurants a bunch.

All the days' long hardly a word is said between us. A lot of television or playing outside, mostly backyard but at times allowed up front when he sat out on the porch, kept to each self as he gazed around often not looking happy or sad.

Today's Friday and like many recent ones he's gotten up early. "Mickey? I'm going to take you over to Rusty's to stay for most of the day while I take care of some business," am told. Rusty's one of Dad's gang Longshoremen and they don't have to work Friday or Saturday nights.

His house is in Signal Hill, on a short neighborhood street where its backside overlooks a large reservoir. No fence separates the backyard from a bluff that has a hundred-foot dirt slope not too steep but enough to slide down pretty fast in a cardboard box.

It bottoms out to stop and about fifteen feet from there begins a dense stand of tall, slim, bamboo-like reeds that circle much the reservoir. At the slope's bottom, view of it is blocked. There're some zigzagging paths made by trampled down reeds but the closer you get through to the water, about fifty feet in, the soggier the ground gets under them, quicksand-like.

Rusty doesn't have a wife but has a son, Dillon, fourteen years old. In his bedroom are two twin bunkbeds where he and their neighbor's son, eleven, and daughter almost thirteen, sleepover weeknights because their unmarried mom works late-shift until 2 a.m. Two nights later,

Sunday, I would start staying over taking up a second bunkbed, then the fourth one through Thursday night. From the second day on, back in school, Dad'll pick me up when it lets out, including Friday his night off. Except for Friday after school, we head right for Rusty's only stopping at a restaurant on the way. Soon after getting to his house, he and Dad leave out for work taking their own cars.

The neighbor's son and daughter get up early enough to go home next door for breakfast and get ready for school. Dad picks me up at 5:30 a.m. and again we stop off at a restaurant on the way to our house for breakfast. Enough time is leftover to see Tina and get ready for school, he driving me there.

I'm supposed to finish homework at Rusty's but it usually doesn't happen. Dillon's rowdy and can care less about school, his dad seemingly not concerned. We four often play outback before it gets too dark, sliding down the bluff and throwing rocks off as far as we can trying to reach the water over the reeds.

One evening I headed down the slope in a well-used flimsy box lying squatted on my side. Excited to get going, started out too far right forgetting that at the bottom was that old fallen tree trunk with a remaining limb about two feet straight pointing back up the hill.

Positioned well inside and not able to see anything but the inner wall a few inches from my nose, down I slid bumpety…bump, a hollerin' and laughin'! Moment later, BAMM abrupt stop! Startled! The tip of the limb nearly touching a knee had punctured the box's bottom darting right up alongside one of my shins!! Oh.., did God show mercy that evening sparing my b' hole!! ...probably my life!!! Being like the others ignorant of redemption by a higher power, just laughed it off with them! But the experience caused some smarts...

About two weeks later and less than one 'til Christmas, going on 6:00 p.m., am moseying to our bedroom after fumbling through some homework at the kitchen table and the door is closed locked. I knock with no response and hearing nothing the other side. Try again, the same. Is weird but maybe they're ignoring me as a prank ...so, decide to go out to the buff to throw rocks although already dark and won't see how far they'll reach. Stuart, neighbor's son, is already out there heaving away and; "Where's Dillon and Janet..?" by me, Janet his sister.

"In the bedroom," he answers.

"The door's locked," by me.

"Yeah I know," by him.

Ten minutes later, "I'm going in to watch some television," by me. As I'm stepping in closing the backdoor, Dillon and Janet are coming out of the bedroom with somewhat subdued smiles as if to be a bit embarrassed shying sight away passing to the door. Shortly thereafter, the three of them are entering robustly laughing staring straight quickly passing to the bedroom, the door closed almost all the way. Of course I feel somewhat ganged up on, put off alienated, but there's nothing I can do about it. They just keep on carrying on, laughing and chasing her about the house and out the backdoor as if I'm not here.

Not many evenings later, Christmas Eve, we're down at the bottom of the bluff weaving our way through the reed-paths just goofin' off. A couple of other neighborhood guys between mine and Dillon's age have joined in.

Then comes a moment when Dillon tells the rest of us that he and Janet are going off to explore for some time, wanting only the two of them. We hang back sitting in a camp-like clearing starting to tell jokes as they slip out of sight. Ten minutes goes by …maybe a bit more, then one of the other guys that joined in says, "Let's look for Dillon and Janet!"

"I'll stay here," her brother Stuart says.

Rising with the other two I pause looking back down at him picking up a reed-twig and tossing it like a spear as quiet as can be. "You guys go ahead, think I'll hang back here with Stuart," say to them. They takeoff down the same path that Dillon and Janet took quickly disappearing.

Might be about ten minutes later that they're darting out from it yelping laughter rushing right by us two! Dumbfounded; "What's that about..? …should we look for Dillon and your sister?!"

"Yeah… okay," from him but seemingly not all that worried. Just then Dillon casually appears with a drab disposition quietly parking himself, a moment later is Janet likewise.

I ask; "What happened..?! …why did those two guys go zooming out of here laughing?"

Dillon, "Don't know other than we were caught kissing."

"Oh..," by me even though it being new to me that they are boyfriend and girlfriend.

Stuart's just sitting quiet flicking reed-twigs.

"It's getting too dark and cold for me; can we go..?" she asks.

For the rest of the night I can't shake how overly excited those two neighborhood guys acted, a bit too bizarre causing me to wonder what else could have happened? What I'm beginning to think might've leaves me feeling uncomfortable, making me want to stayover no longer. Should I mention it to Dad? Can't keep it hidden inside. Anyway, I don't like Dillon enough to.

The next morning riding in the car not as early as usual but before reaching a restaurant found open; "Dad..?" from me.

"What?" from him.

"I don't want to stay there anymore," tell him.

He; "Where?"

Me, "Rusty's."

"Why?" he asks.

"I miss taking care of Tina," reply.

"What? ...is that all..?! Don't you like the fun you're having there?" he questions.

"No," answer.

He asks; "Why not?"

"Ohh... awe, Dillon and Janet are doing something together I think," return.

"What are they doing that has you so troubled?" asks me.

"Something, you know..," reply.

He gets quiet as we turn into a restaurant parking lot. Pulling up to the building and shutting the motor off, he twists to me; "Mickey?" sounding firm and, "You are to say no more about what you think is going on; do you hear me?" just as firm.

I respond, "Yes."

His voice the same, "To no one; do you understand..?!"

"Yes..," again.

"Good, better not;" staring at me like he's been doing - -then back to facing the windshield, "{Redact}!" lastly from him.

Looking back to then slowly shaking my head, I now realize the dilemma he anxiously saw approaching. "Hey.., Dad couldn't leave me home alone while at work; could he having recently started divorce proceedings..?"

Later that evening at Rusty's there's a strange aura, a deadening silence occupying in the absence of Stuart and Janet with their mom. Having been told that they were to join us four guys for a Christmas dinner, turns out they won't be showing. The eerie quiet leading up to the meal, Dillon much the part of it hanging out in the bedroom with the door closed as I head out to the bluff to throw rocks. Like aged photos, I can hardly recall anything from the few months that followed until the event of stark composite renderings, providing no saving grace lookback to then or even it.

Cannot say exactly when it happened but seems like shortly before my nineth birthday. I'm in a big authority building in Long Beach, sitting in a large hallway on a shiny wooden bench next to two large shiny wooden doors that swing into it. Quietly going through them are people dressed business-like. I'm not sitting alone. Next to me is a woman also dressed business-like who just minutes before along with a man in a suit, Dad introduced to me.

Said that they are lawyers for him in the separation from Mom.

For the longest time he has said that such a thing would happen and when asked by anyone; "Who do you want to live with?" to answer, "Dad." The moment of questioning ever closing in on me with increasing pressure to answer that way! Overbearing fear instilled; "That if not him, then who else?!"

Haven't seen Mom or James since the day he threatened to kill Aunt June and Uncle Roy! Haven't seen them either!! What have I done to cause all this?! Where's Mom?! How long ago did Dad go through those doors with the man lawyer?!!

Maybe a half-hour later a man dressed like a policeman comes out the doors and tells the woman that we're to go to the nearby corner and proceed down the hallway to the Judge's chamber. Such a lonely stroll even though she's leading; seems nice but doesn't talk. Out there quiet in the hallway and now likewise sitting in a big fancy office surrounded by packed bookshelves, life looks to have come to a stop.

Much more time passes; so what? Then from another door than the one we came through, in walks a much older man than the woman, he wearing a long black robe; Dad's other lawyer right behind him.

Resting himself in a big comfy lookin' chair on the other side of a giant desk, he says, "Hi.., Mickey," and tells me who he is. Suggests also that I know the other two in there, the man standing back some to one side of me while the woman remains seated on the other. I nod to him thinking; "What next is going to happen to me?!"

Slowly but steadily he asks questions, in a caring sort of way. But two times after the first he circles back to ask; "Who do you want to live with, your mother or… father?"

Just like I'd been trained.., again both times it rolls off my tongue, "Dad," amiss answering, "Father."

For several seconds he stares at the other two, then tells the woman to remain here with me until called for; the man lawyer following him back out the door they came through. Might be twenty minutes have gone by, then the same policeman as before comes through that door and says, "It's okay to proceed into the Courtroom."

Following behind her and he behind me, we enter a big soundless, empty appearing room. Coming into view is Dad with the man lawyer, both standing on the other side of a large wooden table shaking hands --THEN, there's Mom..!!! …from opposite direction is somberly turning away left from them, going through a small gate!!! Head drooped; she's dabbing her eyes with Kleenex not seeing me!!!

I don't know what to do?!! …walking on silently not closing distance between, the woman lawyer partially blocking!! …onward to Dad as I watch Mom beyond get closer to two exit doors --then disappear..! …startling, incomprehensible sequence pushed deep in me..!

Dad has the look of joy! I feel none.., for I hadn't seen Mom for months and don't know when I'll see her again?! To me, they all seemed not to notice that I saw her!

The four of us.., I, Dad and the lawyers end up at a restaurant table across the street from the Courthouse. As the waitress hands us menus, Dad sitting next to me says, "I can eat a horse; how about you, son?!"

I can't say a thing.., just stare across the table through the gap separating the man and woman; the image of Mom.., how sad she looked.., filling the slim space between.

The lawyers.., seasoned counselors.., experienced actors in the drama of kids forced to choose between parents.., sensitively mitigate Dad's robustness in contrast to my trauma; how they at times subtly squint his way while mixing in soothing words to me trying to slow the growing burn in my eyes.., the burn to nearly that of when he smokes in the car cussin' away ...and the smog of the L.A. freeways adding.

Dad catching on, "Mickey ...try to eat a bit, it'll help you see things clearer."

Not yet nine years old, not yet an hour ago, had to be in an unfamiliar place surrounded by three grownup strangers; and to hear the one of them determining my fate ask me which parent do I want to leave out with..?! Now, am at this table feeling again like I'm surrounded by three grownup strangers; one for sure that way having threatened to kill family members is telling me to eat a bit..?!

In Southern California ...1960, that was how such a thing went down, breakup of the home finally completed, legally; with clearer days ahead..? ...couldn't understand..! ...no reasoning..! ...was lost..! ...had forgotten my brother's prayer..!

...10 years to Johnston.

4

On the way back to our house..,

"Son? You're not staying over at Rusty's anymore. I want you to be at home indoors all the time that I'm at work, keep the doors and windows shut and locked," not taking his eyes off the road.

I ask; "Can Eric come over?"

"No," he answers.

From me; "Can Tina stay inside with me?!"

"Yes, but not before I start out for work," he replies. Goes on, "For a little longer, I'll be taking you to school and picking you up. A number where you can reach me while I'm at work will be left next to the phone each time I leave out. It'll be the Dock Foreman's office at the pier

I'll be working. I won't be in the office but on a ship. If you call, and only for emergencies, it'll probably take me at least a half-hour to return the call. Do not call unless an emergency; is that clear?!"

"Yes," from me.

"Good. I'll call you anyway when I go on lunchbreak between 10 and 10:30, so you got to stay awake until then. Do some homework or watch television, or something else but stay indoors. If the dog wants out, let it out the back. Don't answer the door for anybody," he concludes with a quick look at me then back front --and suddenly, his road-rage flares up..! ...a common occurrence going berserk cussing at other drivers! "{Redact} you..!!" over 'n over so loud echoing throughout the interior, windows all rolled up!!! And what he shouts with it to women..?! ...their startled lookbacks?!! ...I want to scrunch down out of sight!!! The constancy of it, ingraining, ringing in my ears long after getting home!

Back then, "Kids at risk" or "Latchkey kids," were not coined plights. Earlier I was taken to a Courthouse, and now back to what'll be a prison. Won't make it in, "The Big House," without Tina. Somehow my schoolwork doesn't get any easier but Dad's not going to call me out on it.

Few days later a 'For Sale' sign is seeable when passing by the house. There are knocks at the front door but I don't respond, sitting quiet although Tina is all over it barking her head off! All the curtains are drawn and hopefully whoever's out there can't see through catching sight of the television on back in the den. Either they leave or Tina wears herself out turning to stroll back to me. I wonder who was at the door; "Mom..?! ...James..?! What if so..?!" ...becoming sad.

This is the beginning of a loneliness that'll stalk me for the rest of my life. An evening afterschool, after Dad's left for work, I'm venturing into what now is only his bedroom looking for remainders of Mom. Would find none.

The closet is a third full of his clothes and most of the dresser drawers are cleared. But there's still the one.., top-right with that little booklet in it coming into view ...and a gun!!! Next to that is a tan cardboard box with, "Fifty Rounds," written on it!! As slowly as was opened, the drawer is slid closed! Made fresh is the threat that Dad yelled to kill Aunt June and Uncle Roy, as if it were yesterday ...slowly leaving the room never to reenter. The cover-sketch of a naked woman with an unforeseen gun pointed at her, more disturbance added to his loneliness, is for Mickey sinking deep into the abyss of no self-esteem.

Just after schoolyear ending, the house that last had family in it is being emptied. Though it was Dad, me and Tina, it hadn't felt like home for the longest time. An old, little white stucco, two-bedroom house on the gentle slopes of San Pedro Canyon is where we dwelled through my Fourth and Fifth Grades. I cannot remember the school's name but Cabrillo Avenue Elementary rings true.

This period in my life was quite dim, being the initial place lived without Mom or James. I recall only the look of that house, the view of the harbor and ocean off in the distance ...and, taking one of a pair of metal roller skates, separating front wheels from the back, then nailing them to a piece of wood making a skateboard. Don't remember having any friends or even playing with Tina, just a whole lot of fast skateboarding down sloped neighborhood streets by myself, always by myself.

Next from the underlayers of obscurity, the tiny horseshoe shaped, motel fashioned, one-bedroom flats in West Carson; squatter abodes with no front yards but small back ones. Off 40mph Vermont Ave., no neighborhoods are around us, only dirt fields.

Recall as if in the moment we hardly have any furniture with Dad sleeping on the sofa, how often he eats onion and liverwurst sandwiches, the drive-thru dairy little ways down the highway where guys come up to both sides of our car handing milk, ice cream, etc. through one window …and cheese, eggs, etc. through the other. Existing not far from 223rd St. Elementary, I'll be bussed starting the Sixth Grade.

Almost all the time when not at school am having to stay indoors with Tina mostly watching television and getting fat. When it's time for her to do her business, we often cross Vermont as fast as we can between traffic to the field on the other side. Trotting close beside me, no leash is on her.

Approaching the edge of it where if not clear to cross, like right now, we pause together. Tina's always done that with me but as I'm slowing.., this time she's darting ahead! I yell for her to stop, "Here Tina, here!!!" Again a higher power must have been at work, she stops!!! "Come back!!" and she does!

But a day that soon follows, we're out for the same and a stray Doberman-type dog which shows up a lot, real friendly though gangly looking, unknowingly trails us crossing back from the field and is ran over! ...hit and run, just twenty feet behind!! The sound of body mangling, quickly turning about seeing it tumble to a stop near our side of the road..!!! ...the horrible twitching and murmurs of life ending!!! I've seen something like this before, Charlie...

Rattled, I run Tina to our front door and rapidly enter locking it behind, the curtains kept closed, Dad at work! Sickened with sadness, sit quietly on the sofa petting her sitting alongside my knee. Before going to bed I write Dad a note about what happened, leaving it on the sofa. It'll be the last time I take Tina across the highway.

The next morning, the whole time from getting up to opening the front door leaving for school, the image of a lifeless dog lying near to where the bus stops haunts me. Closing it behind, going to want somehow shy sight away from the ugly reality, but as I turn to face the road, "Oh thankfully, it's gone!" Later back from school nothing's said by Dad.

For the next half-year at that place no one my age is going to live close enough to make a friend, and at school am not wanting to because of where I live. But there are Abbott and Costello, Red Skelton, Ed Sullivan and Looney Tunes to watch, and of course I got Tina.

School-midterm and we're on the move again. Halt at an upstairs two-bedroom apartment located also between Carson and Torrance off W. 225th Street across from Normandale Park. Three straight-line two-story buildings paralleling, two of them bridged at the rear making a horseshoe with six apartments top and bottom facing inward on its lengths, three top and bottom at its rear. The third length to their west with an alleyway separating the backsides is ours, fourth apartment upstairs from the street. The living room and a bedroom's window lookout over a large dirt field. Will now be walking to the same school instead of bussed.

The Park is a bit of a life changer. I'm allowed while Dad is at work to be out over there, but only there. It will be an added distraction accommodating, "Out of sight...out of mind," not having seen Mom or James going on three years. Looking back; how could that have happened?! No visitation rights..? ...no redress to parental alienation? ...no family other than Dad, and Tina? Just a kid roaming through fate.

On Park grounds is the recreational center with ping-pong and pool tables inside as well as an office for checking out basketballs, volleyballs, baseballs and bats. Half of the large open recreational room in it has rows of folding chairs to seat about a hundred and are facing a wall-width stage at its end.

The Park has been for a time advertising that a dog talent show is to be held, open community signup. Of course I enter Tina. The evening of the competition, a Friday but Dad staying home, the place is packed full of people and dogs, lots of barking!

Announced, "Up next is Tina and her owner Mickey!" To all the clapping, she just follows me right up onto the stage. I brought a light-green tennis ball to entice her to do all the tricks she knows. "Stay..," and she does as I take several steps back facing her! "Sit..," and she does! "Speak..," and she barks! What a trooper..! ...and it keeps gettin' better!

"Catch..," and yes not droppin' the ball, like a fly snatched out of the air! "Bring..," right on! "Sit up..," and like a lamppost her front legs are drawn with paws hanging over! One more time while she's sitting up, "Speak..," …what ending to the perfect performance!!

I hand the ball back as she drops down, jostling her flappy ears while the hind end's a waggin', tail's a whippin' more! Starting to walk off, "Alright Tina and Mickey..!" from the Announcer.

Wow.., so much clapping! There're three Judges. Leaving out from the center …happiness, pride, happiness… staring at the Blue Ribbon with Tina trotting right along. Closing the living room door behind; "Look what we won?!" to Dad.

"Hey, that's great!" by him.

At this edge of the Park across from the apartments are two basketball courts where becoming quite active in pickup games I'm honing hoop skills and losing the fat. Not unlike the afterschool ones just outside its fence, there're rowdy fights almost as frequent in the Park, most by those in Junior and Senior High, and typically off in the distance.

But on one occasion between two grown men it got quite bloody. They moved about with all others keeping distance, but the ongoing sight of it was hard to avoid! The one hardly touched kept trying to give way to end it but the other getting busted up kept closing only to get more of the same!

It's a midweek evening about a month to summer break and Dad is a half-hour gone to work. I'm over at the courts waiting to get in a game when suddenly it's shouted, "Girl fight..!" It too is off in the distance seeing many rush that way, a crowd growing around. Jumping on the bandwagon, for it I go! …running past the office that had closed also about a half-hour ago!

At first can't get a good glimpse. All the shouting of excitement, more so when one apparently gets an upper hand over the other, draws me closer piercing gaps!

Then, full view! One of the two fighting is a neighbor, high school age, with a more feminine body than her counterpart who is outmatching her at every move, and she trying to give ground is kept fenced in by onlookers forcing her to defend rather than escape!

And here I am uncomfortably a part of them, most older but no adults, and she being a neighbor feel like I'm getting beat up too. Want to do something to stop it but the ruckus all about cowards me, reaching a climax when she is thrown to the ground with the other straddling on top cross-pinning her wrists above her head with one hand and slapping her face repeatedly with the other, just hard enough to make passive with her eyes shut.

A chant without me begins for her to be stripped and she gestures her head, "No," just to have one side of her chin tapped to still it. I see droplets forming at the tips of her petrified squint as the chant becomes unison, bolder!

Lying there motionless with her wrists held down, the top button of her blouse is being unfastened. She cannot be heard over the feverish encouraging's but is visibly voicing, "Don't," only to be tapped again a little harder causing a slight twitch of her shoes. Then, the next button down is unfastened.

There's a new awkwardness battling up in me, the appeal of seeing a girl that's older being unclothed but not by this way, not by force or other means coerced. And to see this to a neighbor?! Looking back; what if it was the neighbor being the aggressor? Would my next move have been different?

Turning around, I pushout through the masses and back for the basketball courts drawn line of sight through them to the apartments across the street, distancing the frenzy heard behind. Maybe her mom whom I believe is single, not ever seeing a dad, is at home to tell her about her daughter …my strut purposed to stop what's happening! Knocks to their upstairs door and moments later she's rapidly descending the steps! …the expression on her face!! Lagging behind, the gap between us grows as she closes fast on the frenzy!! Then I stop halfway from the courts seeing her bust through the crowd!!! As the spectators all go quiet and quickly disburse, the other girl is seen leaving with her friends, and left there alone is the mom swiftly redressing her near-fully exposed daughter!! She's quite shaken as they pass by, head lowered and loudly sobbing with her mom supporting. Am turning to watch them move off --THEN, out of nowhere is this bigger guy in my face landing a sharp blow to my stomach! I'm doubling over grabbing it crumpling to the ground!! The PAIN, rolling side to side in fetal position feeling like I'm going to throw up.., MOANING!!!

Can't say how long it takes to gather my wits but am alone by the time my vision clears!!! Having never experienced this, fear envelopes me and am staggeringly on the run for home!! Inside, I'm getting on the phone to

Dad! Like he had said, it takes the longest time for him to ring me back, believing all the while that guy is going to show up to call me out for a fight!

Putting the receiver to my ear; "Hello..?!"

"It's me; what's wrong?!" Dad asks.

"A big guy punched me in the stomach at the Park!" answering him.

He asks; "Why?"

Reply, "I don't know?!"

He responds; "What do you want me to do about it?"

"I think he's going to want to come over here and fight me; can you come home?!" asking him.

The phone goes quiet for the longest time; "Dad..?"

Then, "Alright.., I'll see what I can do to get off," by him.

Answer, "Okay..!"

After a bit more silence, "Now it'll take some time to leave here but you need to calm down, see you when I get there," he says.

"Okay," from me.

He sounded quite perturbed with me. When he got home, I told him all about it only to hear bluntly, "Mic', don't be a stool pigeon!"

That puzzled me and more so …saddened, for thought I had done something good, help save my neighbor …and, was the first time to hear me as, "Mic'."

I want to ask him if he'll take me to school tomorrow but can tell that would perturb him more …so, I don't. I'll gut it out zig-zagging a couple blocks out of the way on guard that the guy might at any moment jump out from a blind spot. Later, on the move from school, am taking the same route back. Silly, paranoia; he knows that I go to that school..? ...but now by the way that guy appeared, a certain weed of bias has taken root.

Before leaving for work, Dad asks if I'm going over to the Park. I heehaw around arriving to, "I might."

He probably saw through that saying, "Have fun..."

"I'll try," reply.

Calling me later on his lunchbreak, he asks if I had gone over there. "No, Dad..," answer.

"Why not?" from him.

"Just didn't feel like it," by me.

"Oh.., see you tomorrow," he returns.

"Sure, Dad..," is mine.

"Click," is heard.

For the remaining month of Sixth Grade, I stay indoors on his worknights. Friday's and Saturday's afterschool, his off nights, I'm all over the hoops ...and more so early summer. But after a few weeks into it, he asks if I would like to go to work with him. With a bit of hesitation, "Alright..," answer. I feed Tina and take her out to run around, do her business; leave a bowl of water behind. Wanted to take her along but he wouldn't have it.

We stop off on the way at a Bob's Big Boy for double-decker burgers and drinks. It isn't long thereafter that we pass by a sign that reads, "Port of Long Beach," entering an area of piers with rows of big 'ol metal storage buildings and supersize ships docked alongside. We stop at a small house-like building where Dad must check in with the Dock Foreman, then continue on making some turns. Eventually pass between two rows of three storage buildings with segments of ships showing through gaps between their ends. It's all humongous!

We make a right at the second gap towards a ship and quickly swing left to park among a few cars and a pickup that are adjacent a building's end. Painted high above on it are the pier and warehouse numbers.

Before getting out of the car Dad turns to me saying, "Mic', besides Rusty who you know, there're two other guys in my gang that I'll introduce you to. I'm their boss also. Those three have been with me for many years and we're all good friends.

Not yet turning the corner of the warehouse to walk down the pier, much of the front of the massive freighter docked is protruding and, "Wow, it is tall and becoming long!" mindfully, following him around the corner. We don't have to walk far to the backside of a small flatbed trolley with a makeshift wooden hut built on to sit in next to where pallets of cargo lowered from the ship land.

Passing by its side to the opening, Rusty and another guy are standing right in front, and one is sitting. After brief; "How do's..?" by Dad, he introduces me to the two I don't know. The one standing with Rusty is White and seemingly a bit older than Dad, he's Lee. The other that's sitting is a short, really old, mellow lookin' Italian with a big 'ol bushy mustache and is wearing a medium size sombrero, he's Nicolo.

Right away I'm made to feel like one of the gang. Dad to me, "For the time being, you'll be hangin' out here with Lee and Nico'. I'll look to get you aboard ship later."

"Okay," I reply.

He adds, "Now you need to listen to these two, do what they say."

I nod a couple times. Taking a seat next to Nico', we three watch Rusty and him walk off, then turn heading up an inclined walkway onto the ship. It isn't but about fifteen minutes later that a wooden pallet with boxes stacked on comes drifting over from its topside guided by a steel cable maneuvering up, down, and sideways through a pulley mounted at the tip of a huge steel beam hanging out at an angle over the dock; the pallet lowering about six feet from where we sit, stopping short of final landing by about a foot until exactly positioned by Lee and Nico'.

Looking up, I see Rusty standing ship's topside-edge watching the pallet's progress and motioning with a hand, signals am told, to Dad who is controlling the cable's movement. It's a smooth operation. Shortly after one is carried away by a forklift through the doorway of a nearby warehouse, comes lowered another pallet. Teamwork is neat; the smiling, jokes and laughter as they work.

Seldom are there moments to sit for a couple of minutes or three between, but when one happens sittin' next to Nico' ...he says, "I see a flea in your hair," reaching and rustling slowly through as to be tracking the critter. Then feeling like it is pulled away near an ear, I hear a tiny click as if it's popped dead between a couple of his fingernails but didn't see it before being quickly brushed off.

"Thanks!" I say to him.

"You are welcome, il mio ometto," he replies with a gentle smile, Lee standing there with a grin.

I ask; "What does il... mio... oget..." --then he repeats, "Il mio ometto."

"Yeah; what does that mean?" asking him.

He answers, "My little man," keeping his smile. I just stare ahead feeling all prideful!

And their whistling.., singing. Nico' asks; "Dad sing you the hobo song?"

"No…not yet," answer.

He asks; "Want to hear?"

I nod yes. He tells Lee to sing it, guess because of his Italian accent.

As if on a stage Lee begins, "Down by the western water tower… on a cold November day.., beside an open boxcar… a dying hobo lay…" "Beside him sat his partner… with a sad and droopy head.., listening to the last words the dying hobo said…" "I'm goin' to a better land… where everything is fine.., where cigarettes grow on bushes… you stay out all the time…" "You needn't even worry… nor even change your socks.., for a little drop of alcohol comes drippin' down the rocks…" "So tell my gal in Denver… no more my face she'll see..? …for I'm goin' to a better land.., I'm goin' C.O.D.…!"

Smiling …I think; "How cool was that?!" rhetorically. Repeat times with the guys, I'll come to memorize the hobo song.

About two hours later Dad joins Rusty at ship's topside-edge, then with a slightly raised voice facing down says, "Come on up! I'll meet you at the top of the boarding ramp."

I'm thinkin', "Neato..!" heading for it.

"We're on a short break. I'll take you on a brief tour," he says.

Still thinkin', "Neato..!"

We go up to the bridge where the freighter is commanded but cannot go in without Captain's permission, though are able to peer inside through the windows; can see the Captain's chair among others, and all the instrument panels with gages.

Next, we walk around to just in front of it looking out at the deck's expanse, the two large square holes with the one right below covered and the other beyond open, and from here are only able to see halfway into it, thus the hand signals.

Dad points out how the second of two beams for that one is angled a bit seaside to permit center-maneuvering of the cargo in and out, and the metal chair right below us where he sits controlling the cable. The chair is perched high enough so to look directly into the hole right below without needing signals, except for dockside edge.

He and Rusty take turns in the chair every two hours, is Rusty's now. Break nearing an end, we head back down standing next to the open cargo hole looking in. Four guys are in there who have begun again to stack boxes onto a couple of pallets.

We then go over to the deck's edge looking down at Lee and Nico'. Dad tells me to watch his signals to Rusty so I can eventually give them. The next worknight is when I begin to, with him of course standing behind. Looking back to then; wonder if all the while he was also giving signals? Awe ...really doesn't matter, was fun and I felt important. Funny though that first night at lunchbreak going to a restaurant, Dad clued me in that Nico's flea tracking was just a gag to ingratiate himself, clicking his fingernails as if he popped the flea dead; was told to go with it.

Cruising the pier on the way back to the jobsite, a fine cooling mist is blanketing the harbor. Roundabout, all the port lights are brightly silhouetted by that, especially those aboard the docked ship as we near; the gleaming lights a contrast to the inherent silence of night. Seeing the quiet movements of cargo ahead, hearing the subtle splashes of ocean against the dock, peacefully blend it all. Pulling into our original parking spot; "Mic'..? You ought to try to get some sleep," Dad says. As he rounds the corner, I slide down flat on my back in the backseat inclining my head on the door's armrest and peer out at the bow of the towering ship seemingly only arm's reach away.

There are mixed emotions; one of confidence from the emboldened surroundings, but one also of doubt falling asleep in the car ...for again it is more out of necessity than by choice; ring of familiarity despite a different backseat ...different setting.

Arriving back at our apartment somewhere around three in the morning, Tina hasn't fared well. Bumbling up the stairs and likewise along the walkway to the front door, I can hear her barking. Entering behind Dad, "{Redact}..!" he shouts. There's a turd pile right in the center of the living room and nearby a puddle stain where she peed. Also not lookin' too good is our only small sofa pillow that she tore into. Dad gets off on her yelling and swatting before she can get away causing her hind end to stumble aside and letting out a sharp, "ARP!!" "Don't Dad," I shout!!!

"Quiet and get the {redact} picked up, throw it in the toilet!" he abruptly voices. I wonder how many neighbors we woke up..?!

Passing by my bedroom to the bathroom, I see Tina squatted beneath the bed shivering. Back out to the living room, he's on his knees trying to dowse up the pee grumbling, "{Redact redact} mutt.., gonna kill it someday."

Hearing that, "Guess I ought to stay here instead of going to work with you."

He responds, "No, we'll take her with us," as he's beginning to calm down.., "but she'll be your responsibility to walk from time to time; don't want {redact} in the car or it torn up."

On those occasions to the end of summer, I grow more so into a Longshoreman than is taken away when a near latchkey. But with the start of Junior High, the latter would once more enunciate lonely miscues in social acceptance, except, there's something afoot again that this time will avail peer attachments.

Five weeks into being bussed a short distance south to Fleming Jr. High in Lomita with a 'C' average left behind at 223rd St. Elementary, "Mic', a week from now we're moving to a new place," Dad tells me.

It'll be the fourth in less than as many years. But man, he's right on; New! A townhouse neighborhood in its early stage of development called Scottsdale, off S. Avalon Blvd. just north of E. Sepulveda Blvd. is nestled between the cities of Carson and Wilmington.

Surrounded by brick walling, it's a rectangular community, to be, with sixty six-unit lanes spoking around its middle and four long lanes running the length of that, interrupted by a Community Center and Park. Each long lane will contain fifty units. All townhouses in the lanes are connected. Inside the Community Center Sales Office, the legend on a large development model reads a total of six hundred two-story dwellings.

The lanes are mirror designed so that dwelling fronts face their neighbors across lawns separated by a center running sidewalk. The backside garages are mirrored likewise facing the neighbors separated by an alleyway.

Dad has bought in early with a lane and a half completed, we to move into our townhouse which is the fourth in from S. Avalon on the half-lane entering side of the subdivision's entrance/exit drive. The drive's duel directions are separated by a center running flowerbed up to a gated guard shack. As are the two half-lanes that straddle it, so is the half-lane behind ours ready for occupancy but its mirror half-lane must be finished before move-ins as a safety precaution due to close construction activity. The Community Center and Park are ready for use.

Virtually the rest of the massive community is a bunch of staked out dirt plots resembling future lanes, but the building process is fast, continuing from the mirror side of the one behind ours. For now the big 'ol Community Center packed full of recreational items, the Park with two tennis courts, one baseball and football field ...and the colossal swimming pool belong to a few. A year out is projected to complete Scottsdale.

Facing the entrance drive, our front door mirrors the neighbor's to our right; abutting kitchens with windows create distance between the doors. The hinged side of ours is adjacent the living room's front wall running towards Avalon.

Entering through it, only the living room is noticeable except for door wide accesses to other areas, but at the far right corner beyond the front windows are wall hidden stairs. At the far left corner is access to a hallway running leftward between the kitchen's backwall and half of the attached garage's, ending at a half-bathroom abutting the neighbor's. Immediately to the left is into the kitchen with another access about eight feet down next to the one into the hall.

Upstairs, the hallway runs the width of the dwelling and parallels the one running half the width below. As is below, another bathroom ends the hallway but is full size. To the upstairs frontside are two bedrooms, and to the back is one; all are the same size. Carpeting throughout is light-brown lowcut shag with the curtains close in color.

Of the two front bedrooms, Dad's chosen for him the one on the right. The one next to it will be furnished some as a study for me. The back one with rectangular port windows that look directly over a short length of half of the garage shingling, and neighbors' mirrored backsides showing above that, will be mine. The windows are so high up that it'll take standing on a chair or the bed to see out. Am told that early on Tina can sleep in my room. Maybe it's because of her that lately Dad hasn't been saying goodnight, only see you tomorrow.

The weekend of October 26th, 1963; two months settled at Fleming Jr. High and into the rhythm of class periods, the teachers and other students.., he and I are out 'n about buying new furniture for the old to be tossed out when we move, and to fill in gaps where none are.

During the years that's just been he and I, times like this have hardly been shared; shopping sprees. He's acting like we've now begun a new life, really happy and ringing up cash registers as though a big sack of money fell from the sky! All the new stuff in a new place is going to be kind of neat! But then ...on the way back to the apartment, "Mic', you're transferring to another school this Friday. We'll be out of where we're at by Wednesday and you'll miss school Thursday to settle into our new," am told.

"Why? Both are about the same distance to Fleming, just from different directions," quickly I respond.

"Scottsdale's out of its School District, no bus runs there whereas one does to Wilmington Jr. High half the distance to travel," he replies.

"But I'm doing good with homework and liking the teachers where I'm at," whisper.., wanting to shout it but feel drawn down instead.

"Don't fret it ...you'll do the same, I know you will," by him.

Two months in ...and just like it was with James.

...7 years to Johnston.

5

Coming of age …at Scottsdale.

Friday morning; am crossing to the other side of Avalon for the bus heading to Wilmington Jr. High as there aren't yet enough students living in Scottsdale for it to turn into, just me. I'm thinking about the breakfast I had fifteen minutes ago while Dad was asleep, another bowl of corn flakes. Do miss how often we stopped off for bacon, eggs, hash browns and toast on the way back from Rusty's.

Although I boxed up the few things of mine, Dad made the move the day before yesterday without me after I left for my final day at Fleming. He picked me up when it let out …then on the fly for takeout burgers, fries and sodas from McDonald's to Scottsdale cause of being tired from the move having slept only a few hours after work, early rising; and not wanting so soon to unbox kitchen stuff to whip up a meal also needing enough time to gradually chow down before leaving out to work.

Beginning with Fleming, bowls 'n bowls of cereal schooldays before the bus, but there were some late Saturday and Sunday mornings before our move that we went out for bacon and eggs breakfasts. The rest, he didn't want me smelling up the apartment trying to cook causing him to wake before he liked. Been given fifteen dollars a week to buy lunches at school. Yesterday I slept in 'til the last of the new furniture arrived, spending the rest arranging and unboxing; was bought a bed when we moved into the apartment.

Entering the new school, I check in with the Counselor and get my classes lined out. Missing the first, she escorts me to my second period class which is considered homeroom. If it's like Fleming, school news will either be told to us there by the teacher or piped over the P.A. system.

Can't believe I'm having to do this all over again two months in even though being hooked up with the same level of subjects. For most of them it appears I'm a bit ahead in knowledge but not so for two and of course, those are English and Math.

There's an indoor cafeteria but also an outdoor food stand for short ordering.., cold cut sandwiches, hotdogs, chips, etc. Man, there are four order taking windows with about twenty other students lined up at each, seems like the period's going to end by the time I get up to one.

Cool.., do end up with twenty minutes to chow down at a large pavilion with rows of park-like bench tables. Many have brought lunch pails. It's a hopping place, especially the minorities who end up not being so. Each race groups together.

Wilmington Jr. High is profiled inner-city, already seeing guys choosing off for afterschool fights. During the two twenty-minute recess periods outside, I get into half-court basketball games at one of three side-by-side full courts. Will try to stay out of trouble that way and have already become a rather good player although still bit pudgy, I guess. Wish recess wouldn't end!

On the way home on the bus am overhearing two guys sitting behind chatting, "When are you coming over?" one to the other.

"The same time after I finish my paper route," from the other.

I begin to imagine what it would be like to deliver newspapers in Scottsdale, being sort of bored; no friends there to play with. It's Dad's night off, think I'll say something.

Closing the front door behind, he's sittin' back on the sofa and asks; "How was the first day at Wilmington?!"

"Not as good as Fleming but okay," answer.

He remarks, "Give it some time, you'll like it;" then says, "Hey, I'm hungry. I know a good place nearby called Domenick's!"

Having not ate that much at lunch reply, "Yeah, I'm hungry too. Think we passed by it on the bus to school," adding.

Only takes three minutes to the Italian restaurant, turning left out of Scottsdale going south a mile on Avalon crossing E. Sepulveda, then short of railroad tracks pull into a slot off to the right just in front of the place. "It's all good here..!" Dad says.

I order spaghetti and meatballs, he their lasagna. Also orders up two dinner salads saying, "You got to try it;" having already ordered..?

Man, he's right though ...it's all good! The salad has really green lettuce coated with a mellow oil dressing. Getting halfway through all, "No one can beat their subs," he says.

Agreeing, "Don't think anyone can beat any of this!"

Pushing away from the booth table to let it digest, finishing a tall glass of Pepsi to help; "Dad, I wonder how it would be to have a paper route in Scottsdale?"

"Alright I would think. Instead of streets to head up and down, there're compact lanes," he answers.

"Yeah.., can easily memorize my customers," I remark.

He asks; "What made you think of delivering papers?"

"Heard a guy on the bus not living in Scottsdale who's doing it," reply.

"You know, maybe you can get in on it early enough to have all of Scottsdale to yourself, lots of deliveries, good bit of income," he comments.

Respond, "Wow.., could be up to six hundred deliveries someday!"

"Well.., if you get one-fourth of that, plenty of work;" and adds, "I like that you're thinking about a job but schoolwork comes first."

"I know," nodding.

"Okay, so long as you know," by him.

Nod again.

He continues, "Tomorrow's Saturday but we can try calling a couple of papers to get the ball rolling. Let's see..? ...there is the Herald Examiner which commands a lot of readers.., so does the Press Telegram I believe. We'll try those first; how's that sound?" he asks.

"Good," answer.

"Even with the money you'd earn from that, fifteen dollars a week will still be given you for lunches," he concludes.

Smiling, I nod once more. Just then, an old chubby Italian fellow with a big handlebar mustache wearing a long white apron stained with tomato sauce comes up to our window-table that looks out to Avalon. Smiling he asks; "How was..za your..aa meal?!" with the neato ancient.

Enthusiastically Dad responds, "Excellent ...Domenick, it all..!" I with some amazement bringing a smile am noticing that the chubby guy looks just like the one sketched on the menu's book-like cover.

"Goodaa.., datta makes..za me happy! Have..aa goodaa night," with his smile and slowly turning away for other patrons. Since getting here, now going on 5:30, the place has quickly filled and names are being taken up front. "Well, ready to go..?" by Dad.

"Yep," by me.

The next morning at ten, he's on the phone to the first newspaper mentioned ...then the second; and within two hours, that one has a Route Supervisor sitting down with us. He enlists me for Scottsdale saying, "It will be all yours and there are prizes for achieving levels of new subscriptions, and for the lowest complaints in a month." Gives me a newspaper carrying satchel for either over-the-shoulder or drape bike handlebars.

He instructs me on proper delivery placement and how to fill out the order form for new subscribers, will leave behind twenty papers to be delivered free to the lanes completed. That'll be done for a week before I begin soliciting subscribers. Am told that any new call-in orders for Scottsdale will be credited to me. At about noontime Monday through Friday, bundled papers will be left at our doorstep for early evening deliveries, and, left at about three in the morning Saturday and Sunday for their early morning's. Leaves his phone number and wishes me the best! Going to earn eighty-five cents per month for each subscription!

After he left, Dad helped me rollup and rubber-band the twenty papers. I put the satchel over my shoulders and plop them in somewhat neatly, plenty of room for more and not even heavy! Off I go after he tells me that when I get back, we'll head out to buy a bike!

Man, is it fun strolling and thinking as I deliver, "Have a business of my own, that is, all of Scottsdale! ...and will have ended up by day's end with a new Schwinn Stingray!! Wheelies all over the place, and there's still Tina to fetch the ball with over at the Park!!!" As the community grows, so will the route at about one-in-five residents subscribing.

Dad makes it easier on me afterschool by having the weekday papers rolled, banded and stuffed into the satchel for my first trips; the same size Saturday's and big 'ol

Sunday ones also by the time I wake, he getting up an hour before. On rainy days..? ...he stuffs each in a plastic sack that's supplied. Cannot recall ever thanking him for the help or, he asking for such. Wish I had it in me then to have.

Tossing them, it doesn't become so much place memorization but more of timing and pattern; the peddling pace and amount of return stops to refill with a particular number of papers to complete a particular number of lanes each trip.

On his Monday through Thursday work nights, moments are hardly spared to see him. Off the bus at around 3:45, just a half-hour sit-down for a bite to eat with him, then start out so that papers will be lying at the doorsteps of all customers by 5:00. He's off to work ten minutes after clearing the table. Just thirty minutes to cram in a day's worth of conversation between bites, but mostly hearing what he has anyway. Four days' long a near latchkey, no family atmosphere but am fast growing into a keen player of the hand dealt me.

"A keen player of the hand dealt me;" so I think..? For there's something beginning to churn within and maybe because of it, am more 'n more grasping certain sights that had been oblivious to me; some of them by way of the eye-catching headlines on the papers, but more so by the growth in Scottsdale's residency. Something beginning to churn...

In a sort of way, this walled-in community has become a growing extended family, the guards so close at the entrance hut a daily drop by to chat with. Living the vision of wholeness with a sense of belonging ever converging

…but, between Thanksgiving and Christmas not far off, that fantasy will be snapped back to reality!

All past world events have been an abstract, each hurled against the backdrop of naught, thrown by the arm of forced soul-searching having the reach of inconsequential sentiments. The stark moments in recent years when by teachers it was yelled, "DROP..!" …only to see it as a game of the fastest under the desk seat.

Year ago it came close to being the last time hearing that "WORD" or any others; the Soviets building missile and bomber bases in Cuba, the U.S. challenging; perpetuating nuclear bomb tests by them and us, mostly in the Pacific. Threats of, "The Commies are coming," touted nonstop and bomb shelters all around; Berlin Wall, Space Race and the beginnings of involvement in Vietnam.

But seemingly at the forefront of public arousal is the Civil Rights movement. Negros demonstrating in Birmingham, Alabama six months back has led to retaliatory bombings and riots, a reverend named Martin Luther King, Jr. becoming highly regarded for a counter led massive peace march in Washington D.C. the past month …only to render up four little girls killed in the bombing of a Negro Church in Birmingham two weeks ago. On 'n on… nuclear radiation, outer space, Cambodia, Laos …Vietnam; demonstrations, riots and bombings …on 'n on..!

Though those things might have colored my yesterdays' …and likely tomorrows', today I'm all about playing a lot, making friends entertained by, maybe touched …in good ways. Dad and I have never hugged, not remembering if so before his hand went on the back of my neck leaving out from Aunt June, Uncle Roy's. Never an "I love you" by the both of us. Yes.., got my paper route, playing, future friends and of course, Tina! Oh yeah, got homework.

Three weeks to the day at school, Friday the 22nd; am sitting outdoors eating during the extended period's first of two split-lunches when a woman teacher standing nearby activity monitoring is quickly approached by another woman teacher dabbing with tissues tears from her eyes …saying, "President Kennedy's dead..!" The other teacher begins to tear and is further informed, "Following lunch period, there'll be a public announcement."

Kind of weird how the atmosphere settling into my next class is as the second split-lunch starts for the other half of school. Virtually all that have entered seem oblivious to what I'd observed, carrying on as usual and our man teacher though looking kind of serene, not repeating what I overheard. Am feeling somewhat abandoned, insecure; "Did I really hear what I heard?"

Actually in a mixed emotional way, am relieved when what happened to the President is finally communicated over the P.A. beginning my next class. Am not crazy but as this teacher gets into discussing the tragedy, my sentiments haven't changed since first hearing of. A bit later over the P.A. comes that the Vice President has been sworn in as President.

Wow; how the world seems to have stopped spinning.., for sure the U.S. appears to be at a standstill. So many people are bummed out, a whole lot loved the President, the grownups. A bunch of conspiracy theories are being tossed about as to his assassination but it's all so clear to Dad, "Those Commy {redact}s..!" In times gone by he most likely would've said that with a cigarette nuzzled in a corner of his mouth, but now is smoking much less indoors since we moved here even though there's a large square clear-glass ashtray in easy reach on the coffee table; am a bit baffled by that, oh well.

The second day in December; Thanksgiving was so-so, just Dad and I again but he cooked up a fairly good turkey dinner. Three full lanes behind us are completed and already have eleven subscriptions, but still tossing extras to get more. Midway in on the near side of the farthest lane finished lives this girl maybe three years older, spotted her a few times on my route going in 'n out of the same front door but doesn't ride the bus.

Is she out of sight..?! Long sandy-blond hair, pretty face and ...what a body..! Glad I have two throws down that lane. Her place isn't a subscriber, hope that changes, going to help it out for a while with freebie papers. Although some might call it puppy love, she's my first and there're no better lookin'..! It'll be a spell before hearing her name said.

The Park is seeing more residents using it but nobody yet my age; adults with preschool kids or Dads from time to time tossing ball with sons much younger than me. The pool will be closed until April.

Often as I'm about to do after tossing the last paper, going to stop by the entrance hut to visit Gilford our guard. In the future with the guys I'll be hanging out with living in here, he'll first be nicknamed, "Gil the guard," then later just, "Gilguard." But none of them will ever become as good a friend to him as me, not caring for what he'll be called by them though will bear the sound wanting to stay in the gang.

He told me that his friends do call him, "Gil," and it was okay for me to. In return I said he could call me, "Mic'," the first one outright said that to, feels good. Looking out the hut's window to Avalon he doesn't see me riding up from behind --then, "Hey, Gil..!" from me grinning.

Turning around, "Hey, Mic'; how ya doin'..?!" by him bringing a big 'ol smile.

"Okay; how about you..?!" ask.

"Super, man.., like Superman!" he answers.

I think he's thirty or so and wants to become a policeman but hasn't been able. Always has some sort of law enforcement magazine by his side, "Detectives Undercover," or "Cops In Action!" ...etc. But Gil's one easygoing guy, the off the wall things he says but not dirty. Has a quick goofy laugh that makes me also laugh about things, and he shows a subtle sincerity at right-on times, "Yeah.., that Kennedy thing ...a big downer, Mic', but we got to pull ourselves up and carryon," encouragingly shares. We have three guards rotating shifts, his is weekday's evening 4:30 on, and I've gotten to know him much better than the others.

The middle of December, am on Holiday break from school. All the Christmas lights wrapped around the Community Center and strewn down lanes are rad, making me feel belonged! On a few good weather afternoons Dad and I toss baseball at the Park, me having a year-old glove, he going barehanded. Tina fetches the pass balls tearing out as fast as she can, at times snatching them up on the roll then trotting back with tail a waggin'! It feels sort of neat.

On a Saturday walking back home after one occasion; "Son? If and when there're enough to field a league team, I'll look to be the coach," he offers.

I reply, "Neat, Dad."

That night, not so neat. Am sound asleep --suddenly I'm awaken hearing him downstairs yelling, "Go on, get out of here!"

Then I hear coming from outside a faint, fragile, woman's voice saying, "I want to see Mickey..."

He shouts back, "I said leave, Now..! ...you don't deserve to..!! ...he doesn't want to see you anyway..!!!"

"I want to see my son," the fragile voice repeats.

"No," very loud from him and a jarring slam of the door!!!

Its Mom out there..! Nothing more is heard!! It was all so fast!!!

Silence, my head stilled; the left side on the pillow staring at the wall across the room for I can't shut my eyes. Will there be a knock at the front door?! More silence, then bend my sight to the clock-radio a foot away on the nightstand ...fifteen minutes to midnight.

Silence, rollover onto my right, the lump at my feet shifting. Stare at the wall a couple feet away becoming sad. Roll back onto my left, the lump again adjusting. Staring straight, my eyes are blurring up with water, but then for some reason just as quickly cease, only a drop blinked from each. I can't separate out from my mind the swirling feelings of happiness, sadness or angriness, nor within able to coordinate them peacefully balanced leaving me wondering why it seems like I'm hated? ...nodding out...

The next thing happening is I'm being awaken gently by a song coming from the clock-radio set for 6:00, the same time every morning, weekdays for school and weekends for early deliveries. In place of the silence after last night's petrifying blowout, is the low volume rhythm of, "It's all in the game," pacing in mind the replay of every word heard in the dark of night.., staring across at the far side wall. Unable to get rid of last night, feel more hated than loved.

But I need to get going to get the Sunday papers at the front doors by 7:00. Throw the covers partly open and slide out, Tina revealing herself from that remaining over her. She hops down onto the floor, got to get her outside to dump. I quickly dress and we leave out left from my room, and distancing from Dad's partly opened door am hearing snoring coming from there.

Bringing Tina back in from doing her business, not enough time is left after feeding her to have breakfast; will be really hungry coming off the route! When I was outside with her, all I could think about was Mom, putting together the sound of her voice last night with how she looked that day leaving the Courtroom. Throwing papers will clear most of that from my mind, not all.

Dad like always had the papers ready to go. A bowl of cereal after the route, and when he came down to start his day he just carried on as usual. I don't see him the same way as when we walked back from the Park, now more like an object.

Christmas blows by spending some of that day at Lee's. He and his wife Emily are tenants in a single story two-bedroom apartment building facing much closer the shoreline in San Pedro than where we lived. She looks old enough to be his mom, got to be pushin' seventy but is real energetic, kind, and he appears very happy to be with her. Their place is cheerfully decorated old style, lots of different colors, pictures all over and packed full of knickknacks. They have no children between them.

While I'm comfortably sitting on the sofa ...she says, "Got to get a picture of you, Mickey!" Flash and within a second comes sliding out from the Polaroid a still-shot of the slightly freckled kid sporting a flattop.

New Years comes and goes. Scottsdale is making its first corner turn in outside lanes and one of the four long center lanes is near completion, moving vans a frequent scene. Sometimes on weekends two or more of them are parked along the already paved avenue circling between center and outer lanes. Reserved for use by construction crews is an alley access to Avalon at that first turn which prevents conflicts in movement between them and us residents.

It's right about then at the Park that my path crosses a guy my age who recently moved in at that turn, says his name is Archie Rollins. He has red hair and face full of freckles, also running up the forearms to beneath his tee shirt. We'll become longtime buddies but he won't bring himself to associate with those I'll also hang with months down the road. He has a seven-year-old sister.

On the bus to school after the Holidays, am finding myself peeking more at the girls riding. Some that are

Mexicans aren't too bad lookin', also one that's Negro …but a couple of White ones got me eyeing them often. They almost excite me as much as my love a few lanes down. There's an urge to get to know them but don't feel adequate, got a big pimple growing at one edge of my mouth.

Two weeks later, on a Monday evening after deliveries and the pimple 'bout gone, I'm soliciting for subscriptions down the first of two southern long lanes completed. Near fourth of the way from beginning it, a fairly wowing lady appearing three times my age answers my knocking, "Hi; can I help you?!" with a charming voice, smiling.

"Ohh..aa, yes! I have a paper route (dah), I mean I deliver the Press Telegram in Scottsdale," fumbling out the words.

She responds, "Oh yes, we've been receiving some free; wait a minute?!" turning away.

Short moment later a fellow about her age, average build and studious looking, comes up to the door and says; "Lookin' for new business..? …you got it!"

"Thanks..!" return.

After signing them up, Gerald and Pauline Gibbons, he asks; "Are you a hobbyist?"

"Awe…no," answer.

He; "Well.., do you have a few minutes to spare, and what's your name..?!"

Reply, "Mickey; yes …I got some to spare, Mr. Gibbons."

He responds, "Great, come on in and call me Gerry!" beginning to follow him through to the garage.

"Yes sir," I respond.

"No sirs …just Gerry," correcting me as we approach the chest high workbench along one wall.

"Wow, those are--" I'm searching…

"--slot cars!" he completes. With a desk lamp spotlighting, looks like he's in the process of creating another one.

"You built these?!" scoping out two other cars sitting nearby.

"Yep …and race them," he answers. Melting with the hot tip of a soldering iron …solder that's flowing into the joint of two slim brass tubes, he continues fabricating the new car's chassis and asks; "What do you think..? …see yourself doing this?"

Answer him, "Yeah …I can; if it doesn't cost a lot?"

"Not terribly, but I can help you get started; if you want?" he offers.

Not really using any smarts as to what I'd be getting into as far as expense, "Okay;" respond thinkin' I'm now up to twenty-eight subscriptions adding, "My last two paydays haven't been all that good but the next one should, and I'll pay you back."

"No sweat, when you can," Gerry concludes.

To my left, just off to the side of the workbench, is a short stack of magazines sittin' on a wooden stool. From time to time my eyes drift down to the top one's cover which shows an action shot of a giant slot car track in a sizeable room with several guys surrounding and all excited holding plunger-type handles staring at their cars racing! The Gibbons apparently have not yet any children.

Just then his wife is heard; "Gerry, can you come here and help me for a minute..?!"

"I'll be right back," he tells me turning away.

Few seconds gone by, I reach for the magazine to flip through waiting for his return and lifting it from the stack reveals a Playboy Magazine beneath!

Woe..! Without jostling it, I gently lift a chunk of pages hoping not to get caught! Let a few at a time slowly fall closed, stop and peer.., stop and peer.., again another -- then, stop to split the Centerfold wide open, Miss January!! Oh man.., she's awesome!! ...her breasts!!! The rest though, the most private part, is hidden by fabulously proportioned legs crossed!! Burning the sight of her in my brain, am also becoming enamored by the look of lovely feminine feet!

Better stop and put the car magazine back on top before gettin' caught! Doing so I also bend my sight a bit down and aside noticing that the rest of the stack of about a dozen under are Playboy's too!! Don't know what to think about Gerry or his wife..? ...but in a way, don't care; think I'll like coming over here to build my slot car!

He returns and I say, "Well.., probably ought to be going, get back to trying for more subscriptions."

"Stop back in a couple of days, we'll begin making your car," he offers. Walks me to the front door passing Mrs. Gibbons, "It was nice meeting you Mickey, bye..!" she exhorts.

"You too, bye..!" I respond, the image of the Centerfold burned in my brain heading out and gawking at the lane directly across the road where my first love lives. Wowing Pauline, the Centerfold, my first love, Pauline as the Centerfold.., liking how the day has shaped up ...but got to concentrate on more soliciting! Finished working that long lane with no more success.

The next day is a bummer. Wanting to see if the two girls on the bus are attracted to me competing to sit close to them, but they pay me no mind. Then later just before arriving home comes the rain.

Dad's already got half the papers stuffed in sacks. As I'm finishing up the rest skipping dinner with him, he heads out for work saying, "There's a sub sittin' in the oven for you."

"Thanks, Dad!" I respond. Opening the oven door there it is ...golden, a Domenick's sub! Can't wait 'til after the route to get into it but gonna try not to cram down half of it only, the remainder when the satchel is slipped off!

The papers stay dry as the downpour increases, making sure they get right up to the front doors; but man.., am I getting drenched from the knees down wearing a raincoat with a hood and peddling standing up! The satchel is dripping wet too.

Finally done, gonna have to change out of the soaked jeans, socks and tennis shoes before downing the rest of the sub, and probably get Tina out to unload even though the rain's still coming down. On the front lawn is where she's snooping about to her liking. She's so funny twist-shaking the dowsin' from her head every few seconds, ears a whip-flappin'..smackin'! Wastes no time finding the right spot and lets it go..!! A couple of quick back-scrapes with her hind legs and indoors we head. Just inside, I towel dry her off also making sure to clean up the wet grass tracked in by both of us --then, go ahead with a can of dogfood and some water for her …and yes, the second half of the sub for me!!!

Going on 9 p.m., am finishing up homework. Into the shower, then clean unders and pj's. Slide into bed holding the covers open for Tina jumping up and snuggling on down. I reach for the clock-radio turning on the alarm and its radio station to automatically shut off in an hour, then back on in the morning.

The volume low, it's soothing hearing, "The lion sleeps tonight," followed by, "Venus," and then, "It's now or never," going under looking forward to stopping by Gerry and Pauline's tomorrow.

I don't know what time it is or what else is happening in my dream except she's about to quickly open her front door --when, there's a rapid heightening of exhilaration in my crotch and just as soon felt is an easy release of gushin' wetness filling my unders; a real pleasing experience of never before..! …but not completely pulled out of the dream, quickly slipping back deep and there's Pauline opening the door revealing herself in a pink silk nightgown accentuating her soft white skin…

6 a.m., am slowly awakened by a song on the clock-radio wiping dry-crusty tears from my eyes and beginning to wonder if I dreamt some new unreal relationship during the night? Thinking possibly so, I slide upright at the edge of the bed and unsnap the crotch area of my pj's to check if there's something on the front of my unders and there is, a sizeable yellowish-tan blotch that's stained dry rigid. I don't know what to make of it but it's not pee..? …too thick.

Then Tina hops down from the bed and low tone but firm I tell her to stay, not wanting to even come close to waking Dad; but do I tell him what happened when he does? Really don't want to because I'm kind of embarrassed ...and it felt rather good, actually really good!

Do I shower again? What about my unders? Not enough time to shower and don't want it to wake him anyway. Won't worry if I ought to wash down there, just change out and stash them way back in the closet until later.

After school and throwing papers, taking care of Tina, I make the final decision to try while Dad's at work to wash the stain out in the upstairs bathroom sink, then hang them far back in my closet to dry. It takes about fifteen minutes to do, and after, head on over to the Gibbons' going on 6 p.m.

Mrs. Gibbons again opens the door, "Hi, Mickey; how are you?!"

"Good, thank you!" answer. Good seeing her..!

Then quickly she says, "Gerry's in the garage."

I nod smilin' subtly entering and passin' her for it. "Hi, Gerry!" entering the garage closing the hallway door behind.

"Hey, Mickey; how you doin'?" he asks.

"Good, thanks; how about you?" returning.

"Also good; ready to get started on your car?!"

Respond, "Sure am!" noticing that the stack of Playboy's are gone.

How cool it was building my car's chassis with all four wheels put on, Gerry a great instructor! Later when am in bed with the clock-radio on low, "She's real fine, my 409," is a soundin' while staring with pride at the beginnings of an awesome slot car sittin' at the closest corner on the nightstand, the lamp a stage light. Staring.., all seems right with Tina also undercovers at my feet; am drifting out…

6 a.m., I'm being awaken by a song on the clock-radio, "Where the boys are..," and already lying on my left side, listen to a couple more, "There's a rose in Spanish Harlem..," and, "I'm a travelin' man..," while admiring once more the workmanship only a few inches away.

All the clothes needed to dress are both on top of the dresser and in its drawers. I get Tina taken care of and gobble down a bowl of cereal trying to fully wake, am running a bit late.

Having rushed to catchup, I begin to slow and mosey to the front door to leave out for the Community Center where the bus now stops. Opening the door --the thought hits me, "The underwear left hung up in my closet, Dad might come across it!" I run back upstairs trying not to excite Tina and reaching for it think, "In the dirty clothes hamper downstairs in the garage, fast!! Gonna miss the bus if I don't hurry..!!!"

Clearing the bottom of the stairs passing the drawn living room curtains, I hear screeching brakes from the bus outside as it's coming to a stop at the guard gate!! Mad dash and split mid-height the dirty clothes pile in the hamper stashing the unders, then back through the living room nearly tripping over Tina and out the door trying not to slam it!

Closing on the bus that's still stopped am seeing through a window halfway someone new taking a seat looking like Archie. Yes! …as I top the steps huffin' 'n puffin' turning into the aisle passing the two girls giggling at me, plopping down next to him as he makes room!

"Ridin' the bus?!" from me.

"Yeah, for about a week. Mom's down sick, but I'm getting a new bike to start pedalin' to school," he answers.

I remark, "Hey! …maybe we can do it together!"

Subtly, he cool-smirk nods a couple of times.

I add, "Get a Stingray! They're sort of expensive, fifty bucks but easy to ride, wheelies for a mile!" as he continues cool-smirk nodding that he might.

Tipping my head a bit to him I whisper; "See those two girls up five rows..?"

"Yeah …so?" from Archie.

"The one on the left has a crush on me!" I brag.

"Oh yeah..? …sure..," he snubs.

Right back to him, "For sure..!! She tried to kiss me but I got a girlfriend!" grinning.

"Yeah right; who..?" asks me.

"Well, don't know her name yet and, she doesn't know mine or that I'm her boyfriend …yet," answer him.

He busts into puffing laughter and remarks, "Right on.., I have one of those..!" as I join in laughin' and we swapping hand slaps!

For the next two and a half years to graduating Wilmington, we'll race virtually daily to and from trying to be the first on the way to plop a bike down and dart inside the little Ma 'n Pa grocery store across from Domenick's for a packaged Hostess blueberry pie! If the only one left on the rack of that fruit, then settling for second place strawberry isn't much a loss. Heading back home, would try to be the first to beat the bus there.

Surprising that neither of us will ever take a spill or get runover. Will stop for red lights at two intersections but then run them when a gap in traffic shows. Never a cop chasing; a higher power looking down on us? Bookin', we'll always beat the bus to and from school! Now though maybe a week more to ride it pulling up to the Community Center to get off, Thursday 3:45.

At the onset of chowing down with Dad before deliveries, he asks about the slot car chassis noticed on the nightstand. "Oh..aa, yeah; there's a new subscription that I signed up a few days ago, husband and wife with no children. He's been building and racing slot cars for a long time and has begun helping me to get started," I answer.

Peering at the center of the table resting an elbow on it and subtly rubbing his chin, "Oh..," responds raising his head to face me seemingly to no end.

I don't quite know what to make of it but am feeling that it must be my turn again ...so, "I'll pay him back for the cost from the money I earn."

He squints while oh so slowly nodding a couple times --then, "I'll take care of the cost, just ask at those times you need me to," he remarks.

"Well..aa, okay ...thanks," I reply.

Upon Reflection; didn't realize up until then that I had been deviating from him, much less recognize the beginnings of such, but along with the rising awareness remains the gist to not dismiss the apathy for him without Mom if not the Gibbons. Surely he has surmised the futility in forestalling what has ought to arrive.., the eroded partiality for a divorcing parent by his son.

Actually, the elements for that wasting had four years prior abruptly stuck to Mickey's will-wall which in any foreseeable future, Bill won't be able to sandblast off with any ingratiating force.

It isn't only the Gibbons, a wedded influence for replacing that which far back had been between Mickey's mom and dad, but also Archie and his apparent tightknit family, Gil's friendship, the paper route and school, slot cars and a first love; people and experiences.., the which in mind's eye are constantly pushing his dad aside to facilitate a more holistic illumination of self.

But how did a soon to be thirteen-year-old who for the first time ejaculated the night before cultivate such a wherewithal to relegate his dad to be at best a cohabitant? Earmark it as a seized traumatic stress disorder by virtue of unimaginable separating from a mom, brother and others of family, the bitter criterion for a kid to be condemnatory.

Bill four years ago left himself a bought son bond, Mickey since… a dad buying perspective that will for the most part lie dormant while he's earning money.

And his dad lied that night two months back about him not wanting to see his mom, detouring him around any envisioning's of warmth at home upon returning to their front door. Bill's never-ending vengeance for Linda keeps him from reconciling that Mickey too felt the blows used as a weapon; the irate blasts weren't heard by his son?! Yeah …right.

So confounding; for a few years thence he won't yell at his son or direct a cussword his way, but always headin' down the road with Bill behind the wheel, the dissolute perception of other drivers loudly reinforced …especially for women.

Why should Mickey feel tapered by that …or adhere to a stayed length outgoing from his dad? The supplanted ambience of just existing together will seem to work. Bill supplies the peer valued necessities as he's counter purposed away from giving advice, Mickey feeling free to seek any from the world. He'll alleviate vanity, lust and temptations by all the good that's in him. There was to be a talk by his dad, as his mom once said. No need to now, it'll all be worked out…

…6 $\frac{1}{2}$ years to Johnston.

6

Getting a handle on the future.

The meatloaf, rice and green beans cooked up by him taste about the same as before despite being told he's going to cover the cost of the slot car hobby. Finding that I'm a bit beyond halfway eating, "I got to get going on the route, sorry Dad. It's really good! Would like to finish when I get back."

He replies, "Leave it, it'll be in the oven covered with foil when you do."

I was looking forward at the sit-down to ask him if it would be okay to ride my bike to school but given the vibes that came across the table probably not the best time, will try tomorrow.

As I'm sliding back from the table; "Got homework tonight?" he asks.

Wanting to say that there's not much even though probably not true, liking to stop by Archie's, I go ahead answering, "Yes," thinking it might be for the best anyway to stay here after the route giving my all studying for an English quiz tomorrow since I recently got a 'D' for the first Semester.

If he was bent when he saw it, didn't show. Possibly because I got 'C's in Social Studies and Math, 'B's in Beginning Wind/Trombone and P.E./Health, and an 'A' in Industrial Drawing but only 'C' in Gardening; can't figure why? It was mellowing, kind of dug it.

In Health, human reproduction was taught but not in a promisingly descript way, it hung down. But things past seen countered the lack of expectation.

The next day following school, off for Dad, we head to Domenick's after my route. A meatball sub this time, he insisting I also try a small antipasto salad instead of the regular dinner one. Somewhere around three hundred pounds, he's quite knowledgeable about food. And okay.., the antipasto salad! There will be times when a large one with lots of grated parmesan cheese piled on, and some garlic bread, make the meal.

Hangin' out with him for dinner, calmly making our way through, I bring up that Archie's going to be riding his bike to school in about a week. "Is it alright for me to ride mine there with him?" ask low tone.

"I don't know, there's a lot of traffic along Avalon," he answers likened tone.

"I'll be careful. His dad's letting him," remark challenging.

He's just sitting there grinning at me as I stare back, then; "Well..?" from me.

He returns, "If you two give yourselves plenty of time and watch out for cars.., okay."

"We will ...I promise," back to him with a quick nod.

Later that night turning in, Tina's real hesitant to leap onto the bed, sizing it up with near attempts but doesn't takeoff. So helping her up, I keep her above the covers which she seems at ease with. Telling her to stay, I then head to the top of the stairs to call for Dad.

Joining me already back in the room, he asks; "What's up?"

"Had to help Tina up onto the bed, she hesitates but not leaping. Last night I noticed her making two tries before she did," explain.

He tweaks her stubby front legs, more at the ankles and at one, she reflexes it back.

"Feels to be sprained," he says.

"What do we do..?" I ask.

He answers, "Well; you can keep on helping her up and see how it pans out, but we also ought to be recognizing that she's gettin' along in age. Your bed might not be the best place for her to sleep any longer; wouldn't you agree?"

Begin to answer him, "Well..," --then he interjects, "She can have her own up here but sooner or later in the garage is where it'll end up. Remember, she was originally outdoors for the longest time."

I reluctantly, lengthily, nod a couple times surrendering. He really doesn't like her that much so it seems. Hardly refers to her by name ...just, "That dog or the dog."

"In the morning try not to eat much if anything before your route. When I get up we'll head out for brunch, then afterwards shop for a dog's bed," he instructs.

As before, I nod.

The next night, on the floor beside the foot-corner of my bed, Tina seems to take simply fine to her new one. "Well …he was right," think. But the following Monday afterschool, "Dad, I don't feel any more like gobblin' down dinner before the route but slowly after;" resting my ring-binder and textbooks on the coffee table, "Because of how many throws there are now, I need to get going sooner to finish by 5:00," isn't fully the reason.

He with a somewhat glaring face, "Makes sense.., I'll keep your portion of the tuna casserole in the pot in the oven; do you though have a few minutes to say how school went?"

"Okay.., like usual but not caring as much for the bus, Archie feeling the same," answer.

"Are lookin' forward to biking to Wilmington?" rhetorically by him.

"Yep …in three days," still give an answer.

Soon there'll be stretches of four days not allowing for many words between us, and from the beginning of the now second Semester, actually the day I met the Gibbons, Dad's lunchbreak calls halted. He opted for… when I believe there is an emergency, then call the Longshoremen's Hall to find him. It is what it is and I'm okay with it. Anyway, most evening hours when he's at work are spent with Gerry or over at Archie's, not on homework.

After the route that's how it'll go without Dad as Scottsdale's nearing half-completion; doing slot cars, Archie and I competing for the longest Stingray wheelies through the complex, ping-pong and shooting pool at the Community Center, and the pinball machine at the Rexall Pharmacy/Soda Shop a mile down on Avalon where it sits barely noticeable in a narrow back-exit hallway.

Frequent stop-offs there to play bookoo amounts of games for just a quarter, placing a tiny folded square of cardboard underneath each of its two front legs to keep the balls from rolling fast to the flippers. Doing so before dropping the coin fools the machine into not sensing a tilt; all the loud rapid mechanical popping at the end of a game, awarding more for surpassing certain score levels when it was played!

Quickly after the machinegunning stops, we remove the squares before an employee might show wondering about the rapid-fire racket. With ease ten games added are displayed and we compete fairly from then on alternating games.

One quarter is much better than eleven of them for that many games. Stealing..? Well, it's not like shoplifting! But to think that somebody has invested in the machine trying to make a living..? ...plus, I've been saving up money from the route, all the tips..? Of course I'm not bothered by that since a whole lot more people play it, and Archie seems to agree with me that it's just too much fun!!

Gerry and I have begun traveling to business run slot car tracks throughout the county, Archie comin' along once borrowing one of our cars to race. He's not into it as a hobby but man, I sure am! Bought a small soldering iron and some jeweler size tools, also a tackle box to tote those and my cars in as well as several replacement parts.

Dad's kept on with the money while Gerry and I the fun! But Dad hasn't on weekends just been sitting at home with Tina waiting for my returns. He's apparently, though I not knowing where, gone out for fun also, each time leaving Tina in the garage and a note on the coffee table suggesting when he'll be back. Then one early evening on a Saturday, after pulling into the garage, he cracked open the door between it and the hallway calling out for me!

Pushing it the rest of the way entering, I see him in the midst casually standing next to the passenger side with an arm resting on top of his new late model beige '64 Rambler station wagon and; "How do I look..?!" he asks sporting a big grin.

"Not bad..!" answer, then; "Just got it?"

He, "Yep, for trips or… go on double dates; what do ya think about that?!" back to his grin.

"Sure…Pop, sure..," reply with an insincere grin.

"Hop in, let's go for a ride!" he exuberantly proposes. With the windows down and our elbows resting on the sills, we're a cruisin' easy; and of course, a Domenick's stop-off.

A midweek night, thirteenth birthday week away; I'm getting out of the shower readyin' to turn in. Am towel drying the groin area and begin to feel something not felt before, the need to satisfy an itch but not a familiar one. Seems like some no-itch itchiness …no, some no-ache achiness …no, is like a longing…

Going on to dry my legs and feet --then straitening back up am nonchalantly sliding the wadded towel up along my scrotum and naturally by friction lift the still lifelessness some. Unexpectedly the upward rub beneath somewhat satisfies the longing but not diminishingly, increasingly…

Without reservation or forethought I'm sitting down on the edge of the bathtub seeking to copy the towel's movement. With every perpetuated slide grippin' tighter, "This feels acceptable," dismissing all consciousness to postpone any pending doom..!

OH My …rapid exhilarating spasm and there she blows, a forced oilrig like gusher..!! Seeing that with no recall of reproduction taught in Health Class, am wondering; "What have I just done..?!! …belly and hand drenched..!!! The out of this world release and mellowing after-twangs felt are like that of not too long ago in my sleep!! Better step back into the tub for a quick rewash, then get to bed..!"

Mickey resting on his left side gazing across the room, Tina in her bed and the radio down low, things regressed in his memory are trying to catch up but are hindered by lingering sensations from moments ago. Past sketches, girl fight at the park, and the Playboy Centerfold might have formed his psyche invoking the self-indulgence; or was it just flat out a physical need..? Must have been for those bygone displays hadn't imparted an immodest storyline. Squinting… widening …back 'n forth, a new bit different scenario though is ushering fatigue towards final shuteye, "Someday soon, he and his love will be holding hands." From the moment wakening in the morning through entering the garage for his bike to head to school, wanted to keep last night's installment to himself.

The last Saturday evening in March, day before my birthday; Archie left a couple of hours ago after we played with my new miniature slot car track, really cuttin' up, destruction derby with the tiny cars that came with it flying off the circuit bouncin' off the walls..! Earlier had gone over to his place, then he and I returned but Pop was out having left another note.

When we arrived, I first whipped up a couple of baloney and cheese sandwiches for us and enjoyed glasses of really cold milk. Gave Tina a couple baloney slices. Archie remarked, "Wish our milk at home was this cold!"

Upstairs in the study after he left, Tina nearby curled up asleep, am working on the initial stage of a new car reaching for the fired up soldering iron when I barely hear Pop down below talking to someone apparently just gotten home. Then; "Mic'..?!" a light shout from him at the bottom of the stairs.

"Yeah, Pop..?!" likewise shout back.

"Come on down for a few minutes," same resonance.

Bottoming the stairs, "Mic', I want you to meet Carol," he says.

She's a nice-looking lady with short bright reddish-brown hair. "Hi," I say to her.

"Hi, Mickey …nice to meet you!" she replies.

I nod agreeing.

She continues, "I understand it is your birthday tomorrow and I have something for you," extending it.

The box not giftwrapped, there's a neat lookin' black soldering gun pictured. "Thank you..!" taking it.

"You're welcome," she responds.

Looking to Pop, "I have my soldering iron plugged in; if it's okay, I'd like to give this a try?"

"Go ahead," he consents.

"I hope to see you again," she says to me.

"Okay," I return, then turn for the stairs.

Within an hour the aroma of chili had made its way up to the study ...then; "Mic', you hungry..?! Got dinner ready!" from Pop at the bottom of the stairs.

"Be there soon..!" answer unplugging the gun. Hadn't heard Carol's voice for maybe a half-hour.

Sitting down at the table, a bowl of chili 'n beans, buttered bread and a glass of Pepsi is in front of me, and as he slides on in ...asks; "What do ya think of Carol?"

"She's okay..." I reply.

He continues, "Well ...Mic', I've been seeing her off 'n on for quite a while, on weekends when I've gone out and we've become quite close.., maybe get married; how about that..?"

Sharply I respond, "No!" plopping the bread down rapidly sliding back, stand and bark, "And I don't want the soldering gun..!" turning away...

Entering the study, I circle up its cable and put it all back in the box; plug in the iron. Calling to mind that moment, not then the wiser, I had concluded, "What I've become to them, more so to Pop, is God's revenge for the breakup of our home! Revenge against him for Mom and James' loss of me!! The Higher Power's wrath by way of me!!!" ...or; was it just the first wiles of free will? Not knowing the final triggering of Mom and Pop's split, none of those edicts had veracity ...but I didn't care, Carol wasn't Mom ...nor by me, was there gonna be another!

Haven't known since how they bade each other farewell, only that I saw Carol the one time. Pop didn't say another word about her or even bring another woman in; never any reference to that night or crossword suggesting disappointment in me. In fact, it brought about an unspoken resolve between us. Was the last woman to see him with, and would never again hear his sustained spurning of them as depraved; how could he after showing such regard for Carol? On my part, remembrance of Mom would be likened to a fallen leaf floating off downstream; James..? ...further ways down.

April brings the swimming pool's opening, So. Cal's climate affording a hastened one for all the clamoring residents. Scottsdale's three-quarter's finished. But it wouldn't be until later in the month that --There she is..! ...my, "She doesn't know I'm her boyfriend," girlfriend!

Wow ...she looks hot in her swimsuit! And it just happens as she's passing by ...I'm stealthily flexing my muscles... that she stops, being called by another girl, and passes back!! Kaylee's her name!!! Ought to again throw some freebie papers her way...

It is also there that I join up with three other guys for water football using a small Whiffle Ball, taking up about a fourth of the gigantic pool without intruding on others. Good that its touch football but still manage some yummy gulps of chlorinated liquid.

After the game we four gather poolside carrying on laughing, acting all macho! "Hey, what's your name?" the seemingly oldest of us asks me.

"Mickey," answer.

He continues, "I'm Stan, seen you around school but you don't take the bus."

"I used to but bike now, seen you there also and..," replying as I start to turn to another.

"Kyle ...seen you too," the one I turned to interjects.

Stan gestures toward the third saying, "He's Allen.., is finishing out the year at Fleming Jr. High. His dad passes by it to and from work, rides with him." Then he asks; "Alright to call you Mic'..?"

"Yeah..sure," answer with a nod, then glance over to Kaylee opposite poolside with other girls.

Stan, taller by a half foot and turning fifteen in two months will be graduating Wilmington at the end of the Semester. Bit slim, he has dark-brown, nearly black, hair and tannish skin, brown eyes. In years to come he'll be looked upon as our gang's girl bait, grooming porkchop burns. He's also taken up slot car building, racing. Has a sister that's a couple years younger than me, I not paying that much attention ...but oh, the next three years that'll become her, rosy eyes an instant blink for her! But it won't go beyond ...because of Kaylee.

Kyle's a few months younger than me and a bit shorter, fat with blond hair and fair skin; will pitch his weight bullishly never giving ground, it'll seem to me. But also won't push his way in when showing up, holding his own joking about and laughing right along.

Allen's a year older and a year ahead in Grade, 'bout as average lookin' as they come except will hardly be seen without a smile; mellow natured saying the least among us but right there with laughter though barely appreciable.

Won't seem to be into much except studying and hangin' out.

None of those guys coming to hang out with, usually congregating in the alley at Stan's, are into sports as players, as is the same with Archie. There're others increasingly showing up at the Park to get into pickup basketball games with, and small team football, but it's Stan, Kyle and Allen that's evolving into buddies like Archie has, though differently. Ongoingly, am spending less time with him for more with them …wishing he'd join us!

The gang, Archie, Gerry and Pauline, Gil, the paper route and slot cars, pickup games and school, I've never been as alienated from Pop or for that matter Tina, and am not giving them much thought garnering a confident taking for granted her companionship, his custodianship. He's still going out leaving her in the garage. How excited she looks whenever I return! …how somber he does when seeing him return alone.

Summer's gonna bring some rebound between him and I. Eleven more move-ins about my age will be enough to qualify for an inner-city little league baseball team, he the Head Coach and a teammate's as Assistant. He'll hold Friday evening practices, the other Tuesdays' and both coaching Saturday games. Scottsdale's home field.

Win or lose, Pop will treat the team to aftergame pizzas and sodas at a nearby pizzeria; not surprising how well liked a coach he'll become. To him though, I won't amount to be, "All you can be," because of my casual stance at first base right before pitches with my glove bent-in perched on a hip suggesting that I think I'm too good to make an error…

Might be right …but, I'll keep on being the disgusting ball player not caring that much about it. Feeling at ease to frustrate him, an emotional hurdle for him to jump, also acquits any thought that I'm failing the team. What had I become or am becoming..? …more wet-dreams and unfettered sit-downs on the edge of the tub superseding any sense of guilt or morals in the enlightenment of wholesome self-expression?

My start of the summer isn't completely ill felt by Pop; is it? Though Social Studies went from 'C' to 'D', I raised English two grades 'D' to 'B' and Math from 'C' to 'B'! …but no 'A's. If only could've gotten that 'A' in Metal Shop like I did in Industrial Drawing? Made a decent looking iron hammer. Come on Pop …smile, hadn't flunked anything..!

He signs off on it with, "There's room for improvement." A few years down the road, grade point average staying the same, that'll be replaced by, "You're not going to amount to much..," remarked by one whom had said that he only went as far as Eighth Grade. But hey.., he's been working steady at the same job goin' on eighteen years and houses bought along the way.

Some things haven't changed with us. We still occasionally see picture shows at some of the drive-ins. At thirteen, I've outgrown the playgrounds below the giant screens, hightailing it back to the car when cartoons flash up before the features. Really love the taste of those drive-in tamales with mustard splashed on top! They haven't yet begun to do what some other foods have, especially sweets, cause near intolerable pain-flares in my jaw! Those fast passing episodes as well as rowdy itch-stings in my crack cause gurning facials!

Summer vacation's drawing to an end and Scottsdale's seeing its final touches. Ninety-eight papers are being thrown, a whole lot of work but am saving up a bunch of money. Also been receiving lots of Certificates of Acknowledgments and plenty of prizes, mostly 45 rpm records.., mostly of The Beatles. First choice was, "I Want To Hold Your Hand," way back after first spotting Kaylee!

Our baseball team won half of its games and I made the league's All-Star Team at first base; go figure..? There was though a lot of grumbling from other players, the consensus being it was due to Pop as Coach, maybe so. It really doesn't matter to me, not into baseball nearly as much as basketball or football.

A year passing, middle of June '65; am walking out of Eighth Grade with two 'B's and four 'C's. Finally no 'D's but lost the one 'A' of the prior Semester in Science, exactly same stinking grade point average for two years runnin' in Jr. High. Pop asserts, "It looks like something has got to give to improve," probably thinking it's gonna be slot cars or hangin' with the guys.., wrong! Stan has gotten a driver's license and his dad's letting him borrow the car once in a while.

"Pop..? I'm going to optout continuing my route," catching him off-guard by his expression, "but stay with baseball," practices starting up next week. I believe that ought to satisfy his remark figuring; "How can he keep on coaching without his All-Star son..?" But to make sure, go on to say, "Also I have nearly five hundred dollars saved, so you don't have to pay for my slot car hobby anymore!" and me exhibiting a prowess to do good next year in school. What could he do but give in..?

There went his behind the scenes bonding by helping me with the route, readying the papers, and supporting my slot car enthusiasm; things a dad wants to do for a son? But starting next school year there'll be more time to chat between my getting home from school and his leaving for work. It won't matter, greater silence will evolve between us. When not doing homework, I'll just want to head out and hang with my buds'. But that'll be profoundly curtailed by him two weeks before summer's end; a happening a short distance away causing...

August 11th ...Watts. Horrific rioting breaking out in that predominately Negro city due to an attempted arrest by Police. Pop's all riled up, buying a shotgun and leaning it next to the front door spouting, "Our home isn't gonna be firebombed! If you go for a ride with your friends, you stay clear of there and be back here by 8 p.m.; are you hearing me?!"

"Sure...Pop, I hear," respond thinkin' stink, there'll still be an hour of daylight left!

But admittedly by what's being shown on the tube that place looks like a warzone, just down the road! And to hear of White motorists in there being jerked from their vehicles and beaten ...well, it brings to harvest the homegrown intolerance that he has sustained all along. The developing fear of Negros comes with it cynicism, not respect, for they appear to be burning down their own town; for reportedly an isolated mishap? I just can't wrap my mind around all the frustration they're rampaging.

Compared to the somewhat peaceful antiwar demonstrations, their hostilities are too rad..! There must be a history that's unknown to me.

The riots lasting a week, and for one after, Stan couldn't borrow the car ...so, hanging out in his garage or at the Community Center and Park was our gang's action. Also during this time he and I lost interest in slot cars. About the only things left for me aside hangin' out were the last baseball game and showing off my near quarter-mile Stingray wheelies through Scottsdale, especially over the speedbumps! But, several other interests are on the horizon...

For Christmas, Stan's parents bought him his first car; a far-out slightly used '65 2-door Plymouth Belvedere with a 273 cubic-inch V8 and 3-speed manual trans! Weekends..? ...not gonna be around, we're cruising with the stereo a blastin'..!! ...up 'n down Crenshaw and Hawthorne Boulevards doing the Dairy Queen loop-thru at night, rappin' the engine circling with the caravan..!! ...and scoring when we can a sixpack or two..!! Like Stan, Kyle and Allen's parents, Pop's slowly but steadily resigning to let us be...

When suntan days afford, North Harbor Drive, Hermosa and Manhattan Avenues will see us scoping out the babes in bikinis along Redondo, Hermosa and Manhattan Beaches! Spectatin' drag racing at Lions Dragstrip will be a weekly must, slot cars passing into history ...and, Gerry for the most part. Even time spent with Archie will continue to give way but holding onto pedaling to school our last year, a good buddy but different things taking us in different directions. He probably should be setting good examples for his little sister.

Two weeks to turning fifteen, and what personality gap exists between Kyle and me appears to be widening. He's grown a bit huskier while keeping the fat. Seems to want to use his size to shut me out more 'n more. Am at school one day and in the middle of recess, I see him standing with some guys we both know in a near shoulder-to-shoulder circle.

Stepping up behind him and another, he when catching sight of me sidesteps closing off the gap between. Tapping him on the shoulder, he turns around and shoves me back. With another tap am again shoved back, the others watching. So, with both of my hands going equally to his upper back, I jolt-shove him forward! He spins around as I'm backing a bit and starts toward me!! ...BAMM, right to his snout!!! Head rebounding, he quickly reaches for his nose as I'm posturing for a repeat!! But all too swift, two teachers are here taking hold of us!

The whole way following him through the building's door and down the long hall to the office, as he is arm guided while keeping his head tilted back pressing Kleenex to the nose trying to stop the blood, Man.., am I heady with pride..!

It just so happens the next day and again at recess, entering the outdoors restroom, there he is already at a urinal. With all confidence I pullup next to him, a small partition separating, and suavely gazing at the wall coolly ask; "How's it goin', Kyle..?"

Hesitantly, "Okay," low voice he answers.

Grinning straight ahead I return, "Good…" As he leaves me there finishing up, my swelling grin ruptures into puffin' laughter..!

Unforeseen, from then on he and I will grow into rather good friends …but, there'll come a day when I witness an act by him that'll cause me to think back, "I surely caught him off-guard with that punch," though he'll never hear it from me.

Despite that, my strut will still possess a hue of cockiness distinguishing me as a winner. In the month and a half remaining 'til graduation from Wilmington, I'll come close to mastering the horizontal bar in P.E. as well as always ending up in the top five out of nearly a hundred finishing the quarter-mile run at the beginning of P.E., 'bout winded dead at the finish line.

Becoming the stud I am now didn't lock in a final grade 'B' for the year because of my laziness that preceded. Since the beginning Semester of Jr. High making a 'B', nothing but 'C's thereafter in P.E.; won't be that way in High School, not even close! I'll graduate here with only one other 'C' in Spanish 2, the rest 'B's in heavy duty subjects. Pop doesn't attend my graduation.

Summertime..? …no more baseball for me or he coaching; will be lots of pickup football and basketball games at the Park getting ready for the start of Carson High Athletics. I want to make the Freshman Football Team! Otherwise, gonna hangout 'bout all the time with the guys cruising more the beach scene and taking in Pro Drag Racing.

Archie? …too good a friend not to still spend time with. His dad has bought a Hodaka dirt bike for the family to get out in the country with and surprisingly, for one mid-summer weekend day I'm invited along. The place found has much more desert terrain than forest and looks to have been well visited. Throughout the day I've sat around watching first Mr. Rollins kicking up dirt on 'n off intersecting trail loops, jumping dunes and drifting in 'n out of sight; Archie and I chatting about starting Carson High.., then he takes over on it.

Taking three hours for boredom to settle in, a jealous mindset that I've been left out of the fun is causing me from time to time to walk away from the rest of Archie's family now gathered together watching his dusting feats. Even his mom and little sister eventually are taken on saddleback rides by his dad. Am kicking up my own dirt moseying off 'n back.

Well, wouldn't you know it? The picture of me moping about must have sparked them to think that I didn't come along just to spectate and eat some ham sandwiches, potato chips. Brief time more passes, I'm sitting when Mr. Rollins comes over parking himself beside me while his son's out cuttin' up --then tilts a bit to me and asks; "Want to give it a try..? ...ridden one before..?"

"No, but would like to try," answer. After being shown the shifting sequence and stalling out a couple of times, off I go but cautiously ...thinking, "Better not fall and break their Hodaka." Returning and shutting off its motor, "Was really neat, thanks..!" remark to him with Archie standing there.

"You're welcome!" by Mr. Rollins.

Evening time has us loading it up on a small flatbed pull-behind and for Scottsdale we head, Archie's sister sitting between him and me in the backseat. It's about a two-hour drive and sort of quiet, only a few low indiscernible words between their parents without turning to each other.

I'm peering out the side window when all of a sudden Mr. Rollins begins to sob and within a minute into an outright cry..! ...but not wailing, alternatingly wiping his eyes with the backs of his hands as he steers! Don't know what to make of it, Mrs. Rollins frequently turning her head to him but sayin' nothing while us three in the back remain quiet. Before now, I hadn't seen firsthand a grown man cry! It's perplexing but for whatever reason am feeling sorry for the guy. When we get back to their place I only say, "See ya," to Archie as he nods agreeing. It'll be the last time I go over there, and he mine because of Pop.

Won't see him on the bus to Carson High either, and too distant to bike, but our paths will cross there and sit from time to time at lunch refreshing our friendship. Three months older than me, he'll have a driver's learner's permit by summer's end but for a while catch a ride with his mom to school, and the same for his sister to hers. Although Stan's going to be driving to Carson, Pop's against me catching a ride, concerned about reliability.

Few days after the motorcycle outing with a little over a month to the start of school, and Freshman Football tryouts to begin next week, I'm at the Park in a pickup scrimmage going balls out to get in last minute shape; am looking forward to making first-string offensive tight-end.

After the play's been called, am running a crossing route for a pass but the ball's thrown a bit out of reach diving for it. Landing twisted some with my arms stretched, the right one slams hard to the ground. Although onto grass, the brunt of impact is taken just above the wrist! Am getting up with something feelin' shockingly ugly!! ...a numbing high-frequency vibration running up my arm from there and beginnin' to hurt!!!

Two hours later I'm leaving out from a small clinic with Pop and am wearing a plaster cast going up from the hand to just below my elbow. X-rays revealed a fracture of the radius bone, the larger of two in the forearm; the rift located two inches from the wrist. Doctor said that I was fortunate, no bone fragmentation with only a slight displacement --but {redact..!} when he went to set it?! "Easy, Man..?" holdin' all the words in but extreme grimacing makin' the point!! Gonna have to sport the cast for five weeks, then the arm wrapped for two more with no strenuous activity for the same after that. There goes Football.., a Sports Star.., and Carson High Idol..!

My arm beneath the plaster is real burdensome, always smelly and itchy among other things; and why all the weirded offerings sketched atop from Stan, Kyle and Allen..? ...plus, more pimples are breaking out on my face, shoulders, chest and back. Good thing I'm left-handed, sittin' on the edge of the tub affairs will go unfettered easing all the stress, years of bared female accounts now playing a role in the upliftin' reliefs...

To Carson I'm starting up again on the bus --but wow, all the girls..! ...especially the two from before, Yoo..!! ...an affirmation from below!!! Like in the past they pay me no attention, probably the cast I'm wearing and ...the pimples. "It's okay," mindfully, gazing out a side window. Wondering though; "What is there other than the usual to help me resist feeling like a romantic loser? Having no hotrod to drive, turn to academic excellence? Did apply for a College Prep/Science major near the end of Jr. High."

To seclude myself a bunch in the study putting time in the books..? …it'll hinder hanging with the gang, cruising, chasing down babes..! The isolated quizzing of my love life as if becoming a lost cause..?! …not gonna happen, I'll let the grade point average slip, but no lower than 'B' as required by the major. That too ought to keep Pop from layin' a brick.

It's kind of neat when getting off the bus making my way to the alley to go in through the back …because of Tina! She's usually taking in the sun's warmth lying in sight snoozing just outside the garage.

There she is again! I stop short to hide at the back corner of our townhouse row, barely peeking around. Lowly I call; "Tina..?" …nothing. Then again a bit louder; "Tina..?" …the anticipation!

She raises her head slowly looking about, the rest of her dead flat. With only my eyes and above noticeable, one more time; "Tina..?" She spots me, jumps up and comes a tearin' toward me, hearing the friction of claws against asphalt trying to gain traction burning toenails! She's so funny..! …nearly nose crashes jumping her front legs to my knees, tail a whippin'!! "How ya doin', girl?!"

Christmas comes 'n goes, the cast long gone but feeling all sucky even though Pop tried to make it festive. I went to work with him a few times during the Holiday break. Always good to see Rusty and Lee, but, Nico' had passed away a year ago, will never forget his flea tracking gag, will miss him…

Know I'm bummed because Archie's gotten a car; mint condition burgundy '64 Corvair 4-door. Am happy for him but more so self-pityin', only a bike to ride and back on the bus following the break. The last available day before it ended Pop took me to get a driver's learner's permit, good up until turning sixteen and getting a license or six months from obtaining the permit whichever comes first.

Heading out one Saturday morning with me behind the wheel.., it's his initial attempt to teach the do's and don'ts of safe motoring despite knowing that I'm taking Driver's Ed. this half-Semester of Second Semester P.E. This ought to be a real object lesson.

Just south of Scottsdale, we're turning left off of Avalon onto E. Sepulveda and am settling in pretty good passing by oil refineries and storage tanks on both sides of the road, cruising right along --then it gets my attention, not long to enter, a fog bank! …something not yet touched on in class!! No place to turn off, can't just stop in the road!!!

Pierce right on in.., can't see a thing beyond the nose of the Rambler, Pop yelling, "Slow down, gonna rear-end someone!!" then, "Not that slow, gonna get rear-ended!!"

In panic-mode mind, "{Redact}, I can't see the line on my side!!" reaching to switch on the headlights, wrong..!!! …whiteout!!!

He shouts, "Turn them off, {Redact redact} it!!! …trying to kill us?!!"

I sharply respond, "No, stop yelling..!!"

Louder yet right back at me, "{Redact} you, don't care if too loud, do what I say!!!"

Few seconds later the fog just as quickly clears and I see to the right a short turn-in after the oil tanks, enough to pull off although a chain linked gate shortens it!! Spinning in and jerkin' to a stop, I hop out! He remains in the car as I pace around not wanting to see the sight of him!

Eventually he gets out circling to the driver's side door and when reaching it says, "Lesson done for the day; ready to go..?" Dead silence heading back and, I'm torqued by what he shouted, "{Redact} you!!!" still ringing in my ears...

Few weeks go by just like it was in the car on the way back, but begins to lessen over the next few. End of February '67, am handing him the report card for this same first half-Semester of the second Semester; 'B's in English/Guidance and Math, 'C's in Biology and Spanish 3 ...and thinkin'; "Hey, look Pop..?! ...an 'A' in Social Studies as well as Driver's Ed..!" He just gawks at it sitting back rubbin' his chin, then subtly nodding, "Fairly decent," are his only words reaching for a pen.

Am thinking; "What? ...that's it..?! Oh wow, you moron..."

Silence as he stares up at me handing it back. All I can do is squint back for a few seconds then turn away to take Tina out back to the alley to fetch ball.

The next morning he's up first catching me as I finish dressing, and says, "Mic', let's go eat out." Waiting for our breakfast specials to be set before us, he unpredictably asks; "How are you and your buddies gettin' along?"

"Fine," I answer.

He comments, "Won't be long until you have a driver's license like the rest."

"Except for Kyle," I correct.

He's slowly nodding, then rhetorically, "Stan's a pretty good driver?"

Few seconds pausing with a couple of slow nods, "No tickets yet..," still giving a reply.

"How does his car run?" he asks.

"Really good ...keeps it tuned," return.

He nods like before. Nothing more is said.

Walking out of the restaurant he stops me short of opening the car door peering across the roof at me ...saying, "Let's go look for a car, I think we have time..."

"What..?" I react.

"Look for a car, for you; whata you think, got time?" back to me.

I respond, "Sure...do; but before the driver's license?!"

"So.., I'll have to ride along with you for a while; a problem..?" inquiring of me.

Bit hesitant, "I guess not..," letting him slide more for cussin' me out. I ask; "If we find one, how do we get it home with you driving yours..?"

He answers, "Don't worry about it."

Staring ahead through the windshield, there exists doubt as to why he's doing this; now..? But hey, a car..! Gonna keep my mouth shut...

It only takes one stop off at a large used car lot where the salesman after an hour of haggling is joyfully riding shotgun home with me in my dark-blue '65 Mustang 2-door hardtop with whitewalls! ...Pop following behind. Is no problem for the salesman, a check having been handed him for full amount. He's driven back to the lot while I sit behind the wheel of my 'Stang parked in the garage blaring speakers romanticizin' cruising the Boulevards for babes.., "Round round get around, I get around, yeah..," tuning up my fanatism!

Wow, what a mood changer.., for I hadn't gone out for Carson High Basketball after missing the football season due to the broken arm; and the bummer of being bussed to school and asking for rides home after basketball practices would've seemed like life's passing me by. When he got back from the lot, "Thanks, Pop …really neat!"

Looking back.., funny how ignorance was bliss, thinking the car was my own despite not penning my name to any documents, and Pop, not burstin' that bubble. But a month when turning sixteen I'd be made savvy at the DMV to who really owns it although putting my signature on the registration.

But back to the day of purchase am telephoning Stan, "I got a car..!"

He comes back; "Oh yeah? …what kind..?!"

Answer, "A clean looking low mileage '65 Mustang 2-door hardtop with whitewalls, dark blue..!"

"Join the club, Mic'!" he remarks, then; "What's in it?!"

"Just a 200 cubic-inch inline-6 with single-barrel carb," answer.

He remarks, "Hey, that's alright …can probably burn rubber; tried it?!"

Back to him, "Not yet, haven't had a chance but gonna..!"

"The tranny?" he asks.

"3-speed automatic," answer.

~ 116 ~

Stan says, "Drive it on over, let's go for a spin..!"

"Awe ...can't yet, got to keep it garaged until on Pop's insurance, possibly Monday but come on over now to see it if you want?!" respond back.

"Be over after dinner," he concludes.

Getting a driver's license in a month will be far-out, motoring to school in my 'Stang with two months 'til summer break; and hangin' with the guys..? ...out of sight! But for every action is a reaction. English will go from 'B' to 'C', change in Math/Algebra to Math/Geometry 'B' to 'C', the downward slide sustained in Spanish from 'C' to 'D' ...and 'A' to 'B' in P.E.

But what can I do to keep it from happening? Just a guy streamin' puberty! Every action a reaction, especially in English..! ...Amanda Kohl, teacher..!! From the get-go, "You're so fine...," it's gotten harder. Also has to be that way for the other guys observing her instruct. Maybe she's a dozen years older but one thing's for sure, a fox! About 5'6" with black hair that drapes the shoulders, dark-brown eyes that can start a wildfire, cheeks ...nose ...lips ...chin... and voice, oh man.., Miss Kohl's so fine..!!

The only thing she could wear that would make her look bad, a tent ...especially if I'm not in it with!!! Her winter outfits gave me the hots but now movin' into Spring..? ...too distracting among other things happening!! She's into these form fitting button burstin' fine linen blouses tucked into her just above the knees' skirts! Where ought not to be any fat, there isn't. Where to be other things, are..! Killer legs, not needing nylons..!! ...and, often wearing black semiformal half-height narrowing-heel slip-ons where the beginnin' crevices of her toes are a tease..!!!

It's one thing to have her back turned reaching high at the chalkboard liftin' the skirt a bit ...but help me.., another seeing her sitting back on her desk facing us with legs crossed danglin' the backs of the slip-ons off her bare heels..! Those lovely crevices, and so much bare thighs showing..!! I can't concentrate on all the adverbin', pronounin' and past-participlin'; but congregatin' with her..? ...seems a no-brainer..!!!

Arousal of worry too, thinkin'; "But please Miss Kohl, don't call me up to the chalkboard..?! ...my lacking-slacking evident as I come to you broadening your pretty eyes, and help me, brush by sidestepping to the end of your desk to block view of it from my under control classmates!! Keeps on replayin'; "Please don't call me up..?! ...don't call me up..?!!" Oh finally, the ongoing fear of embarrassment is taking over ...easing...

From now on not going to be sitting on the edge of the tub but instead, standing in the shower imagining while really scrubbin' the manhood ...in that; "So what if she sees my maturity coming at her?! ...those gorgeous eyes inflating with desire..?!! No one else being aware as it subsides at the chalkboard scribbling everything wrong, then as the class is dismissed she demands that I return after school for remedial training..!!!"

I'll serenade Amanda, "Wild... thing...," as I approach her, suggestive invite upon her perfect face letting the danglin' shoes fall from her feet and leaning forward for our lips to unite..!

All before times fanti-indulging in the bathroom I hadn't romanticized with Kaylee, and even just now my first love was kept untouched despite being no less alluring to me than Miss Kohl.   Though not consciously understanding why, Kaylee seems to make alright all the past inordinate affections, but now, the innocence that we have shared is being shuffled aside for a new …wild thing! Being so attracted to Amanda, only the 'C' pulled from her will be our true legacy.

Just over two and a half months ago Pop bought me the car maybe because of First Semester grades, improving upon Jr. High's, but the look of disgust now on his face squinting at the yearend ones..! …silence. He signs the report card and hands it back; silence…

…3 $^1/_4$ years to Johnston.

7

Feeling guilt; why? ...for how long?

Whoa.., backup the hormone fueled roadster! I did not ask to see Pop engaging Mom, the little brown booklet; for he to be abusive, she a gambler and drinker, or for the breakup of our home; to see the girl fight at Normandale Park, charming Pauline Gibbons with the Playboy Magazines ...and {redact} sure, all these zits..!

Kaylee..? She was to be my lifetime companion, my soulmate; wasn't she?! ...or was just a figment of my imagination though a real person..? ...my morality sustained until we were brought together by some event or higher power..? …all past unforeseen lude associations transformed into lifelong purity walking hand and hand..?

No..! She was my guilt catalyst, a mind messing charade. First time seeing her at the pool I didn't know that longing-liberalism was on the horizon, the quickening rise at the sight of that bodily glamor whilst never to invoke her erotica in the shower. The subliminal image of her in every other female unfairly buffets my yearning to embrace them. I greatly enjoyed interrelating with Amanda! No harm, no foul…

Do I feel guilty by my grades? …by the look of disgust on Pop? …or for letting myself down scholastically. Actually, looking back none of that was of significance, testosterone driven to touch Amanda with Kaylee yet untouchable was the volatile conflict begetting guilt. Will have to go on paying the price for shower rendezvouses to curb the pimples; what other therapy is there?!

Summer '67; Guidance and Social Studies relevant..? Two hours of daylight remaining I'm lying back bored on my bed a Friday evening with the door shut, Tina curled up in hers and Pop downstairs, that is predominately the prevailing wind. Resting on clutched hands on the pillow am staring up at the ceiling looking for some image, any image, sculpt out of stucco-curds plastered to it while, "Hello… darkness, my old friend," plays on the radio.

Staring; is there a face up there? …twisted one? …a clown's? …or maybe one of Amanda, "Good love, now gimme that good, good lovin'..," having taken over, fantasizing. Few minutes passing …then, "The eastern world it is explodin'…" I turn from my sweet teacher to pondering all the {redact} that's been going on…

Vietnam's a mess; six months ago the largest military offensive there, and since '61 some 6,700 U.S. soldier's dead. Soon after, three of our astronauts died in the capsule of their spacecraft during simulation of a launch, fire sweeping through killing them in 13 seconds. Conspiracy theories still swirling about JFK's assassination; recent U.S. bombing of Haiphong in North Vietnam messed up proposed peace talks; huge antiwar parades held in New York and San Francisco, New York's led by Martin Luther King, Jr. estimated at 300,000 marchers; riots that broke out in Negro ghettos of Cleveland continuing to other cities; Muhammad Ali having lost his boxing title over refusing to go into the military which now has nearly 400,000 U.S. troops fighting in Nam; on 'n on…

"We've gotta get out of this place…if it's the last thing we ever do…" comes on and again I'm picturing Amanda, next Semester with me. We are one day afterschool hoppin' into the 'Stang tearing out liberating ourselves permanently from mundane academic trappings! Gloriously blowin' down the road, windows' open; where we're heading? …who knows, who cares..?! The wind rustlin' through her hair as she repeatedly turns to me with expressions of thrill, pinning kisses on my jaw and loudly serenading, "He's a rebel..!" --then there's a knock on the bedroom door. "It's not locked..," respond.

Pop slips his head in and with a rhetorical delivery, "Nothing planned tomorrow, right..!"

I nod a couple times anyway …trying to preserve my daydream.

"Got some folks I want you to meet. We'll be leaving out early and gone most of the day. Dinner will be out of the oven in a half-hour," he concludes turning about, familiar aroma of meatloaf having followed him up, Amanda fading until again our opportunity to flee farther. Few songs later, "<u>Be true to your school...</u>" causes me to picture more of next Semester having tucked her away.

Carson High Colts; the school only four years old and already Varsity Football going undefeated last season. Cool times taking in the games with the gang! At one away though, against an inner-city team, we stood high up at the back of the Visitors' bleachers and by the end of the third quarter had been sporadically pummeled from behind with gravel thrown from the bed of a passing pickup from the street below, probably due to the unrelenting trouncing upon the opposing team. Missed the associated glory of Freshmen 'B' Team by the broken arm but want to try again next season for Varsity; it's gonna be tuff, got to get in shape!

I shutoff the radio and head down to the kitchen, Tina following; am thinking that after dinner might cruise on over to Stan's. If he and the others aren't there, I'll drive some around town. With Pop buying me the car also came an increase in allowance to $20 a week for petrol along with the school lunches. Having gas wars going on a gallon's only 28 cents for regular, but in keeping it filled I've been slowly but steadily dipping into my savings, little over a fifth gone.

At the table I ask; "Who are we going to be seeing tomorrow?"

Pop answers, "Only going to tell you that they're family and to keep an open mind 'til you meet them."

Nodding am thinking, "Well.., okay; but what does it matter? Been no family for the longest time; now there's gonna be..? Open minded enough? ...for I'm hankering that it's kind of weird, all my life not a speck said by him about having relatives!"

Anyway, my buddies are my extended family and a new one recently joining the gang. Marty, not a Scottsdale resident but goes to Carson and drives a boss dark-forest-green '56 Chevy Bel Air 2-door with blackouts on chrome 5-spokes; an aftermarket 283 cubic-inch Super Turbo-Fire V8 its muscle! Really sociable, he sees himself as a playboy, every girl's lover ...funny! Same age as me is about 5'10" and vascular with light-brown hair that flips back atop his ears, duck-tailing some around the back of the head lookin' kinda stylish.

Not ending up with much time after dinner to hook up with the gang, I decide rather to toss the ball in the alley with Tina then back up in the room for some TV, the set a birthday present a few months back. "Bewitched," and "Gomer Pyle, U.S.M.C.," then get ready to turn in for our early start.

Heading out the next morning Tina's left in the garage. On the Artesia Freeway going east and interchanging to others, we eventually along the San Bernardino Freeway take the Redlands offramp. Few turns later are pulling up in front of a Realtor's Office, "Bernbaum Real Estate." As we are entering, a fellow lookin' a dozen plus years younger than Pop is rapidly exiting an office behind a Secretary's desk, woman seated, and comes right up to

Pop, "Dori …oh Dori, how good it is to see you, Uncle..!'"
bear huggin' Pop!

"You also, Oren..!" by Pop.

Then, "Mickey..! …good to meet you, Cousin!" Oren
says extending a hand to shake --then quickly pullin' me
into a hug.

"You too..," reply thinking as we separate, "He called
Pop …Dori, a female soundin' name…"

Not long after that, we're following Oren to his house.
In the car; "Pop..? He called you Dori?"

"I'm Jewish;" he answers. Silent, I don't know what to
make of it before he adds, "Changed my name to a
Vaudeville stage name twenty years back."

I ask; "Is Farrens …Jewish?"

"No, Dori Nudel is my birth name," he replies.

For whatever reason, I don't care to seek out anything
more. Just along for the ride. He is who he is.., I who I
am.

Goodness; we pull into this circular driveway in front
of a boomerang shaped house …and, it is massive! At its
center-curve is the immaculate front door to his kingdom.
Just inside after Pop, I'm joyfully greeted by Oren's wife
Judy, their son Shay and daughter Marnina my second
cousins age fourteen and thirteen, and by this vivacious
Barbra Streisand lookin' woman my age, Roni! She flew
in from New York two days ago, her mom seeing her off
at the boarding gate and Judy greeting her upon arrival.

Instantly there're wow-vibes between us! Her exciting
widening brown eyes! …smile! …New York accent!
…and the hug she gives me..! Or is it because I'm the
long-lost cousin? Who cares..?! I'm taken by her..!! Why

did she have to be a second cousin also? Hey, we're far enough apart in the gene pool. I'm so messed up.., "Run away with me, Roni," fantasizin'!!! And just as quickly, a deeper intuiting tugs at me to halt. (Shoot, not the testosterone untouchable syndrome again!) I'm really attracted to Roni, but we're relatives...

Soon after, we're all sitting at a big 'ol dining room table for lunch, Oren bringing in from the patio a large platter of barbequed burgers, Judy providing salads, chips and drinks. To one side of me sitting is Pop, but on the other Roni! Insisting on being a gentleman for the first time in my life, I hold the platter and bowls of additions for her convenience to take from! "Thank you," by that lovely New York accent.

"You're welcome," by the suave Southern Cal's.

"We had to hire a private investigator to find you, Dori! It took a longtime," Oren says as we're eating.

Judy quickly adds, "We're so joyed you are well and here with Mickey!" Hearing the two am a wonderin'; "What's that all about?" But just as quickly it leaves me like water off a duck's back, "He is who he is, I ...me." Getting up from the table, "I got my buddies and, want to concentrate on Roni here," mindfully, followin' her retreating to the den.

She and I, Shay and Marnina, relax on the carpet as the older sit half-circling us. My back inclined up with legs stretched out crossed at the ankles beside one of Roni's knees sitting lotus style in my direction, she's looking away some conversing with the others and apparently doesn't realize that she's blossoming right here in front of me.., her legs angled up just enough and skirt not drooping..! ...seemingly all so casual to her...

Do any of the others notice that I'm sneaking peeks under it trying all I can to camouflage?! Oh Roni.., your inner thighs sucking me right in on the entrancing squeeze formed by them and the curvatures of your bottom, my mindbender ESP turning your pretty face eye to eye beseeching, "The purpose of a man is to love a woman ...and the purpose of a woman is to love a man; so come on baby let's start today, come on baby let's play ...The game of love, love, la la la la la love. It started long ago in the Garden of Eden, when Adam said to Eve ...Baby, you're --Shriek... my cousin?!" she still looking away.

"Mickey, do you like bowling?" Judy asks, turning my head to her as Roni does to me.

"Awe...yeah, I do," answer turning back to Roni's large smile ...intoxicating.

Judy asks Pop if there's enough time to bowl before leaving for home? He acknowledges that there is; staying behind with Oren as she chaperones. Roni's such a lure, her girly laugh as she's plopping down right against me on the back bench-seat after throwing two gutter balls! Oh man.., got to keep cool, be a rock, don't even nip at the bait but not turn her off..! It was nice being with her.., Shay and Marnina too.

As we're leaving out to head home, standing just inside the front door, "Love you, cousin, see you soon," Roni smiling says ...placing a kiss on my cheek.

Caught to the quick, more puzzled than startled, "Okay.., love you too, cousin," return smiling.

Taking out from their driveway …Pop asks; "How do you like your family?"

I answer, "There're neat," though still trying to put it all together.

"That Roni.., she's a spitfire," he adds.

Reply, "She's okay; but what did she mean by see you soon?"

"In a couple of weeks we're gonna fly to New York to see my older sister and oldest brother, your Aunt Etta and Uncle Louis, Roni again and more of the family as well," he answers.

Speedin' along on the freeway I'm thinking about Roni. As sensual as she is, the fact that she's a relative is taking me one step forward, two back, subduing my sexual yearnings. On 'n off thoughts of appropriateness is giving me bit of a headache. I ask; "What's Roni's last name?"

"Nudel also, from your Uncle Louis to his son Max who is her father, he being your cousin along with Oren, though he by way of Etta's marriage to Herman Bernbaum;" he answers adding, "Don't cook your brain over all the names and relations, will come together as we're with them."

A Friday, early morning departure; Tina was put in a kennel last evening. I haven't flown before; is surreal cruising above the clouds from LAX to JFK. Was nearly five and a half hours by jet, and three more lost heading east. We crossed over New York City, out to sea a bit then turned around to head back in for landing; as cool as could be, all quiet 'til touchdown.

Only Uncle Louis is supposed to meet us at the gate. "Dori..!!!" --"Loui'..!!!" as they embrace, kisses back 'n forth alternating cheeks and, all the tears by the two!!

They can't seem to stop! Then, "Mickey..!!! ...my Nephew Mickey..!!" embracing me with a kiss on each cheek!

Wow, okay..? "Hi, Uncle Louis!" by me.

"Uncle Loui' to you," he returns.

He has our suitcases delivered curbside right in front of the terminal's door where a limousine's waiting; "How neat is this..?!" thinking. All the reacquainting talk between them as I stare out the window speeding along on a freeway; nothing but neighborhoods, apartments and skyscrapers for as far as can be seen! "Queens is where we live, Mickey," Uncle Loui' says.

Moments later we are pulling up in front of a high-rise with a Porter opening the car door, "Will bring up the luggage, Mr. Nudel," he remarks.

"Family's all upstairs waiting!" Uncle Loui' exhorts as we stroll through the enormous fancy lobby stopping at an elevator to go up to the 15th floor.

"I'm anxious to see Roni again..!" is my thought as its door slowly opens...

Stopping at that floor, it opens to an elevator wide foyer elegantly decorated, and with a couple taps on the only door before us, "Dori..!!!" --"Etta..!!!" as a woman Pop's age rushes up to him, I behind stepping aside clearing the door for Uncle to close.

Five in addition to her and Loui' gradually approach and among, there she is, Roni..! ...with her charming smile but looking intently upon Pop like the rest. Then from Uncle Loui', "And here's Mickey!!!"

Amazing.., all the cheerfulness, all the hugs and kisses.., Roni respectfully waiting her turn. Finally, "How great it is to see you again," solemnly from her with a lite hug.

"Whoa …is this the same Roni?" wonder emotionally slowing and, "You too," like fashion smiling back.

"Please everyone to the den to relax," Aunt Pearl, Uncle Loui's wife, encourages! There's an inviting aroma filling the immaculate interior, the overwhelming appearance of wealth. "The table will be ready soon," she adds retreating to what evidently is the kitchen, Roni and her mom Anna, my cousin by marriage to Max, following.

Aunt Etta with husband Uncle Herman, the parents of Oren in Redlands, and the rest of us guys kick back. Taking it all in sitting quiet, I soon realize there're millionaires in the family! Loui's been with a major New York Publisher going on thirty years; Herman in real estate, he and Etta own a twelve-story office building along with some residential rentals; Max not far behind as an Accountant/Financial Advisor with a renowned Firm.

Then there is Pop, not saying much of anything likened to them. Is he embarrassed or not wanting me to know some things about his past..? Despite the contrast being obvious, not even soundin' close, it doesn't really matter to me. Still though, the ebb 'n flow dis in lifestyle makes me feel more than not out of place.

And Roni? Risqué away from home but chaste here..? It's okay, am still fond of her. For the first time two weeks ago it felt like there was a girl who cared about me.., a girlfriend. For a female cousin, she's perfect. Although foxy lookin', she's bringing the hormone tug-of-war between Kaylee and Amanda to a stalemate. Now, they in their place, if I can just stop thinking dissolute about her..?

Just like before at Oren's, Pop's sitting one side of me at the dinner table, Roni the other. A toast with sweet wine, told Kosher, introduces the meal; even she and I sip a little. Then a bowl of soup, told Matzoh Ball, is brought out; really good! Is soon joined by a chicken dish called Schnitzel; just as good!

Talk is mellow with laughter covering a variety of things but eventually turns to the race riots and recent march here. Max is a real card wanting to spin it comically to keep the ambiance festive. Things said fifteen floors up played well staying clear of malignant connotations. However, the takeaway was that I had assumed a narrow posture of receptiveness to the plight of Negros when reaching street level. But there'll come a day, a teacher, that'll change that.

The next day, our only full one here; Max, Anna and Roni are gonna show Pop and I some of the sights starting early afternoon. Due to staying up late and jetlag, it's about 10 a.m. rising out of bed in a guest room. Although a Saturday, Loui' and Herman have to spend much of the day at their offices but will with Pearl and Etta meet us five later for dinner at a midtown Manhattan restaurant along the East River.

Pop wants to see the fairly new home of his favorite baseball team, Mets' Shea Stadium, built a few years ago. How is it all the early years' been a New Yorker and he's lost the accent? ...last night talking a bunch about the good 'ol days here. But there was a gap in his reminiscing, seemingly ten years before going off to war. There wasn't any filling in by the others so I didn't care to cook my brain over it, let pass…

Mid-afternoon, Max is driving; I, Roni and her mom in the backseat, Pop upfront, we're pulling up in front of the Ballpark in Flushing right off from a bay; the Mets out of town. Pop getting his fill, we then travel west on Northern Blvd. eventually connecting with Queens Blvd. and cross the East River into mid-Manhattan to take in a bit of Central Park, see Times Square and the Empire State Building. Man.., the passing walls of skyscrapers looking out the window! The crowded sidewalks although a weekend, and yellow taxi cabs all over the place!

Going on 6 p.m., we five are sitting down with the Aunts and Uncles in this swanky restaurant ordering up large steaks, bake potatoes, salads …the works! Looks like $350 worth or more! There's gayety supported by a definite sense of wellbeing!

Then it happens.., an hour and a half later Pop starts bickering with Uncle Loui' wanting to pick up the check. "Dori, I got it!" from Loui'.

Pop snatching it from him and louder, "No, it's mine!!" The prideful stubbornness between them back 'n forth..!!!

Nowhere graciously Pop gives in. In the foyer before leaving out we say our farewell's to Max, Anna and Roni, "Let's write often," she endears.

"Sure," replying.

"Love you, cousin Mickey," stepping back from me after a hug.

"Love you too, cousin Roni," subtly nodding.

Pop and I ride home with Loui' and Pearl, those two guys upfront carrying on again about the restaurant bill!

Herman and Etta will meetup with us shortly. Back at the high-rise the elevator door slowly opens.., Pop and Loui' still at it as we enter --then, I dart back out as the door closing separates us …thinking, "I can't take all of this! …all too new!! …and too fast!!! Those two at each other..!!!" with tears beginning to flow drifting over to lean back against the opposite marble wall.

Few minutes gone by, Pop and Loui' are exiting the elevator toward me with worry on their faces. Coming across puzzled Pop asks; "What's wrong?!"

"Why are you two arguing so much..?!" I ask.

"We were not arguing, Mickey!" Loui' answers.

"Sure, were playing," Pop remarks adding, "that's how we New Yorker's do it, no big deal!" Just then Etta and Herman walkup. We enter the elevator, Loui's arm lightly draped around my shoulders. A couple of hours later we're saying goodbye to Aunt Etta and Uncle Herman.

Sunday morning; Pop wanting to get back to work tonight, goodbye to Pearl 'n Loui' and into the sky blue yonder to So. Cal; but man.., the last three days..? I think of Roni some but about a third to LAX my buddies begin entering my thoughts and she as well to fade never to see again; write a few times diminishing.

Between the first and second one's to her, Fall football practices are a week along and as I'm bottoming the stairs in my uniform carrying my helmet, starting to pass Pop sitting back on the sofa, he asks; "You gonna do any good in school this year?"

Stopping with the coffee table between us, "Made the team, Junior Varsity for starters. I'll have to work hard to make Varsity losing out last year," reply staring at him.

"I mean as far as bookwork?" he continues eye to eye.

"I guess so; why?" back to him.

"Awe.., can tell that nothing good is gonna show," sarcastically he remarks.

Mirroring his bearing, "Well …at least I made it to Eleventh Grade, not an ignoramus like some…"

He's darting towards the coffee table reachin' for that large glass ashtray that's laid dormant as an ornament! …the look of irate anger seizing his face!! Reflex turning away, I rush left and can see his hand laying hold of it!!! Second step into a dodging run, "I..EE..OUCH," sharply yelling!!! …the jarring impact ricocheting off my skull behind the right ear causing me to stumble forward across the hallway to the door accessing the garage..!!! …my hand rising to where it struck and keep checkin' for blood getting the door open..!!! …he not followin'..!!! I raise the garage door, jump into the 'Stang, back out and get the {redact} out of here..!!! …the horrendous hot throbbing pain..!! …water flowing from my eyes because of its intensity..!

From there to pulling up next to the High School gym and parking, a humongous knot has sized.., grown out to near touching the back top edge of the ear. The pain trying to slide on the football helmet.., constant pressure against! I go into the restroom/shower area for a look-see in the mirror. Helmet slid back off …{redact}, the size of it!! …the purplish-red color but thankfully no open wound!

Wondering; "How am I gonna make it through practice?" Walking out to the ballfield realize won't …so, I turnaround and head for the car; don't know what to do? I crawl into the back and lay down, head turned away from the injury …thinkin', "A couple bottles of brew or some Johnnie Walker would do right …right about now. Will never again feel guilty about grades." An hour passes dreading to head home, "That guy's dangerous..! …but I'm forced to depend on him for a roof and food."

It's really quiet between us from then on, he cooking up some meals but a lot of fast foods the rest when getting home from school having begun Eleventh Grade, but either way, we don't sit at the table together.

Stan has started Junior College primarily to avoid being drafted, I moving along primarily trying to make Varsity but being bounced back 'n forth between Junior Varsity and the practice squad for Varsity; getting lots of playing time in the Thursday JV games with virtually no spectators.

Academics mean little to nothing to me. Ironic, funny; my best class a month in is English but goodness, teacher is no Amanda Kohl..!

Mr. Lipkin.., the gentlest little pudgy Negro about mid-fortyish with a Bambie ore; a bit clumsy but there's this good thing between us, not queer but I really like him. I feel for Mr. Lipkin because most other students see him as such a weakling, a geek …dufus. But I admire him for his Profession, rising from minority origin, probably been bullied all his life. Amazingly he seems to go out of his way to make me feel special even though I'm grading middle of the road. There came a time when some prankster flattened his tires; how that happened without being seen is beyond me? …but if I could only find that punk? …the air taken out of him over and over..!

The end of October, there's a parent visitation day at school, meet the teachers. "Mr. Farrens, you must be quite proud having such a son. Mickey's very respectful, considerate and attentive. I'm fortunate to have him in my class!" robustly Mr. Lipkin says to Pop.

The expression on his face, must be thinkin', "At this moment Mic's wishin' Mr. Lipkin is his dad." If he is, "Yep despite color difference, am adopted, and at this moment is a turnabout well underway in my bias. Beginning to be cognizant of Negros referring to themselves as African-Americans, their opposition to the war on moral grounds, and the disproportionate number of casualties within troop totals."

The big picture is that there's nearly a half million now in Nam, over fifteen thousand killed and about one hundred ten thousand wounded since we joined in; forty thousand a month being drafted. But to me, those numbers are as distant in concern as is Southeast Asia.., am kinda diggin' all the campus protests at various Colleges.

When Pop's off to work, I knockdown about an hour's worth of homework, not based on subject intensity but time I allot, enough to get some sort of grades above 'D'. I take Tina out and feed her, then on over to Stan's to congregate and blowoff the bull{redact}.

All five of us, if that many show, hop into either his or Marty's wheels to cruise the Boulevards' night scene; jackrabbit burnouts from traffic signals and sneaking swigs from a fifth of Walker, then Beam, passed around that Stan's older cousin scored for us! Tunes, tunes, tunes.., Wolfman Jack the radio Dj..!! Southern Cal's happenin'..!!!

~ 137 ~

Never get pulled over; everybody's doing it, out of control..! And the wheels' pack full of babes cruising..?!! ...pulling up alongside them hangin' out the window loudly serenading, "Searchin', searchin' for my baby..!!" Their kisses they blow back, their rowdy giggles, out of sight..!!! Funny how then they're able to shake us off by accelerating at the last moment through a turning red light ...or hit the brakes. Not as intense as Friday or Saturday nights but the chicks are out, it's great!

I get home by nine, shower and flop turning tunes on down low. "I will follow him..," keeps me thinkin' about girls. One that's coming more 'n more to mind is Stan's sister, Denise; how she's becoming easy on the eyes, but she's his sister. Then, "Up on the roof..," sets me to thinkin' about New York's high-rises, Roni and me atop one taking in the skyline. But now she's just another sensual keepsake glued to the collage hanging on the backwall of my mind. "Baby, the rain must fall," is beginning to nicely transform my restlessness into a mellow self-assuring drift forward...

Two weeks later at JV practice I'm called over to Varsity practice on the main ballfield thinking, "Yes..! ...the hard work has finally paid off although I've been playing fullback instead of tight-end ...but, no more back 'n forth." Didn't suspect that I'd be a punching dummy for Varsity first-string defense, but here I am...

Knowing the play, I'm busting off right-guard through the line ahead of the tailback to block an oncoming middle-linebacker slightly to the left. Oh of course the defense had head's up on the play and clearing the line slanting left, but before I could catch sight of him,

SLAM!!! ...by another linebacker nearly head-on, a big Samoan, knocking me back onto my tailbone! Wobbling upright, my spine has a bit of an electrical buzz that's diminishing, so not giving it much thought. The play is called once more and {REDACT}!!! ...landing on my tailbone again!! This time the buzz is more pronounced traveling from mid-spine down the back of the left leg to my knee! Really gimpy; "Coach? ...think I ought to sit out for a while," say to him.

"Go ahead, take all the time you need," he replies grinning. It'll be my last football play ...and, is the beginning of accelerated periodic episodes of spinal misery that'll dog my future.

I'll go it easy for the remainder of the day waking up the next morning feeling fairly sound.., but it doesn't take long after sitting in the hardwood desk-seat in first-period class that a horrendously sharp pain starts radiatin' from the top of my left rump down through the leg into the calf! I try shifting the angle of sitting but doesn't bring relief! Ten minutes into second period; "Teacher..? I need to go see the Nurse, my left leg is hurting a lot!!"

"Go ahead," am told. Within a half-hour Pop shows up at the Nurse's office and is soon taking me to see an Orthopedist suggested by her, she securing an immediate appointment being made aware of the happening yesterday at practice.

I'm diagnosed with a low-back disc-bulge but not herniation. Am advised that my football days are over unless wanting to become crippled. Given a shot in the rump, prescribed meds and will undergo three weeks of physical therapy, all paid for by the school. Accordingly, am transferred from Football Athletics to General P.E. With uncertainty I do heal up from the pain but there went that Stardom..!

Friday, January 26th of '68 am passing by Pop, the coffee table separating us and the ashtray's long gone. I slowup just passed, turnabout and plop it down on the table --then continue. "Where 'you goin'..?" he asks.

"For a drive," answer, opening the hallway door to the garage. On the report card ending the first Semester he'll see a 'C' in Mr. Lipkin's English Class as well as in Drafting, 'D's in Chemistry and Geometry 2 …but, maybe the 'A' in P.E. will impress him given my low-back injury; not gonna wait around to see if.., heading for the beaches.

Along the way taking Pacific Coast Highway for the most part towards Palos Verdes, "I dig rock 'n roll music," sets the mood. "There's somethin' happenin' here but what it is ain't exactly clear..," gets me thinkin' about the civil unrest, then, "Time has come today," takes up a whole lot of drive time; am a shoutin' "Time..!" in concert with the song. Slowly descending along the coast off of Palos Verdes Canyon, "I can see for miles and miles..," is descript of the panorama to the left, the ocean to horizon.

Heading east back to Scottsdale there's a small hamburger café about three miles from Redondo Beach that I'm stopping off at. They make the best tastin' quarter-pound cheeseburger layered with a couple leaf's of lettuce, large slices of tomato and onion, pickles, mayonnaise and mustard! …and the best chocolate malt to go with! All for a buck seventy-five. Sometimes I down two of each.

Pulling into the garage Pop's car is gone. Passing by the coffee table the report card is lying there backside up and has been signed. Gonna need to change my major from College Prep. Science to General.

Allen now pulls up in the alley behind Stan's garage in his new '68 Pontiac Firebird 400, solar red with black vinyl top and chrome 5-spokes, 3-speed automatic on the floor and nearly 4 to 1 rear-end gear ratio; flat out hauls! Apparently his patience and good grades have paid off. And Kyle not to be left out.., has seat cheeks hangin' off both sides of his awesome 2-tone white/sky-blue '66 Harley-Davidson Electra Glide 74 cubic-inch Shovelhead with whitewalls. My 'Stang as nice as it is, pales to the rest. Soon will find myself wanting to walk rather than drive over to Stan's to meetup.

April 4th, Martin Luther King, Jr. is assassinated at the age of 39 and there goes more rioting in a hundred cities. On May 5th Senator Robert F. Kennedy the younger brother of JFK and campaigning for President is assassinated at age 42. It's an ugly time for the Country but man.., we fellows keep on a partyin', everyway and everywhere we can! Booze …booze …booze, girls …girls …girls although I haven't even kissed one yet; and street racin'..?! …but not with my car.

Can't put a finger on as to why but somehow the thought that I ought to do better in school has been weighing on me since the report card, but not out of guilt. What the saying is..? …"Work hard, party hard!" Maybe it's because I'm partyin' too hard and hardly studyin'.

Friday the 14th of June am leaving out of Eleventh Grade with an 'A' in Mr. Lipkin's second Semester

Journalism class …and in P.E., 'B's in U.S. History and Algebra 3, 'C's in Bookkeeping and Auto Shop. Dig it, a 'B' average! Funny, Pop has the look on his face; "Is this Mic's report card..?" peering at it for the longest time. He doesn't say anything though, only nods as it's handed back after signing.

First week in July and Stan has a new medium-green-metallic '68 Belvedere 2-door coupe with a high performance 383, four-barrel carb. He went with auto-trans on the column and front bench-seat so his dates can sit right next to him. It's a given that when we're cruising the cars of choice are either his, Allen's or Marty's but I'm always helping out with gas.

I tag along on Wednesday evenings for open-public drag racing at Lions Dragstrip, those three of us competing. Maybe it's due to my grades, don't know, but Pop's been quite observant. Like to think that I haven't been pouty not having a muscle car although there's been some talk between us about theirs.

Start my Senior year at Carson, then early November Pop and I are in the showroom of a Plymouth dealership scoping out the '69 model cars and two hours later have spec'd out a factory order for a new GTX to be delivered mid-next month..! "Son, that'll be your Christmas and birthday present," he remarks.

What a present, "Thanks…Pop, really neat..!" I reply. It'll be one long month and a half…

But it arrives.., trading in the 'Stang. A 2-door coupe, bronze fire color with a black vinyl-hardtop and black running board trim, chrome 5-spokes wearing optional Michelin radials and it keeps gettin' better; 375hp 440 cubic-inch wedge with Carter four-barrel, 4-speed Hurst tranny on the floor and 4 to 1 rear-end. Simulated side-facing hood scoops and black vinyl-leather interior with front bench-seat completes the factory ordered beast!

Of course I'm one prideful dude behind the wheel and Gil affirms the mindset when passing under the gate he's risen, "Lookin' good Mic'!"

All these years ...good 'ol Gil, especially with the dilapidated car he drives. Five years guards have come 'n gone but for him, five years that shack has been his home away from home. Looks like the time for becoming a cop has passed him by.., now sporting a beatnik look. But he's so well liked by the residents and has been shown by all the gifts, lots of batches of cookies. And he's married going on three years with a two-year-old daughter! All these years chattin' about life, all these years peering out the study's window overlooking Scottsdale's entrance and seeing him there at night as steady as all get out ...in the lit shack. What a friend he's been.

The '69 GTX? It's gonna be short lived and a part of the bag of stark emotions. Trippin' at Lions on weekends is rad; all the rails, funny cars and pro stock! The loud staging action, raps and burnouts spitting out header flames lighting up the starting line; the eardrums rattling at burnouts but when that starting tree hits the green lights they're a lost cause needing to press the canals closed! And to purchase a Pit-pass to check out the engines being torn down and put back together within an hour of a competitor's next race. But it pales to being part of the competition on Wednesday nights. Time-trials set the handicap starts.

One night I make it to the final matchup, all my buddies and friends from other car gangs lining the fence at the starting line cheering me on! Catch the green just right.., leaving the line a second ahead of my competitor, speed shifting without the clutch …jamming into second and third gears. But I botch, miss fourth some hundred and fifty feet from the finish and see myself passed a split-second later; $500 missed out that quickly …but hey, got a twelve-pack case of motor oil quarts, not bad for second!

Although I and the gang don't compete, there's a large gathering that takes place every Friday midnight at a South L.A. shopping mall; hundreds of street racers filling the parking lot! It's an underground happening run by the International Brotherhood of Street Racers formed and led by "Big Willie" Robinson, a six and a half-foot tall African-American who stands in the bed of a pickup holding a blow-horn surrounded by all gathered to hear the whereabouts of the night's illegal races. Because it's so well organized and otherwise peacefully involving all ethnic groups, the cops stay back. Big Willie's quite a sight stirring us up for the night's pairings! The races typically take place at one of several industrial areas containing a straight 1/4-mile road.

Moving with the masses from the mall to the race spot is a spectacle.., the convoy traffic jams, the rappin' off of engines! But once there, it's all out finding a place to park and hightailing to the races …so, I and the guys have passed after the first one but still enjoy taking in the mall gatherings, lots of honeys with Stan our babe-bait and obnoxious Marty somewhat.

At school, most times find a spot curbside to park where when walking between classes I can look over at the badass GTX all prideful. Then afterschool hightail it so can cruise some laps showing off rappin', such a stud I am!

Allen having graduated last year there's only Kyle and I left to hang at the outside terrace during lunch, except there's Archie, who I prefer to sit with. We're still good friends catching each other time to time mainly at the Park but relatively seldom to me hanging with the gang, wish he would join. But another has, Luke, originally approaching us parked at McDonald's on W. Carson St. just west of Normandie Ave. before entering Torrance. It has slow but steadily become our favorite meetup spot, parking our wheels backed in alongside each other leaning against any of the front grills with bags of burgers and fries perched on the hoods.

Luke drives a torqued out black '67 Ford Fairlane GT 2-door with optional 4-speed and 390 cubic-inch V8. Welcome to the gang..! Otherwise average looking, he's fit, outgoing and enjoys razzing Kyle. It's so funny seeing Kyle left with nothing to say except quickly, "{Redact} you!" back at Luke as we're all laughing..!

Times are still unpredictable as far as the war, racial tension and now ecology. The public outrage for the recent blowout on Union Oil's offshore platform spewing some hundred thousand barrels of crude oil into the channel and onto the beaches of Santa Barbara County killing over three thousand seabirds as well as dolphins, elephant seals and sea lions! Nixon was sworn-in as President a week earlier having ran on the promise to end the war; winning percentage 43.4, not too believable a promise.

There are Hippies and Yippies, Marijuana and LSD, the two I haven't touched; but the tunes..?! ...so much counterculture vibes! Diggin' it! And with it.., the guys and I a bit more spirits bingeing. And again, with every action is a reaction; first Semester Senior, 'A' in Journalism 2, 'C's in U.S. Gov't and Typing but 'D's in Physics and Algebra 4 ...and of all things, 'B' in P.E.! ...and now a month into second Semester not looking good. The {redact} will hit the fan unless a miracle's on the way. What? ...the draft, Nam..?!

Going to be turning eighteen in three weeks and will have up to thirty days after to sign up for the Selective Service. I have heard that so far the local Draft Board hasn't touched anyone under nineteen. Stan's feelin' worrisome, he's twenty and finishing up Junior College short of a 'B' average. Allen's completing his first year of Junior College but holding a 'B' average, believes the war will end before being called. But by news reports looks like there's no way out of Vietnam without a humiliating loss or another A-bomb! {Redact}..; to wholesale radiate a population again? ...eradicating like rats?! Goodbye to the cold war..!

Looking like a more intense ground battle despite more aerial bombing; and here at home.., marches, sit-ins and draft dodgers to Canada or Mexico as well. More the reason to booze, chase girls and burnout the GTX's clutch ...which is about accomplished. Pop's pretty well chafed staring at a soon to replace part or the storing of a virtually new car in the garage. The new clutch works great, carryon..!

A week later I don't know why but the living room and hallway carpet had looked fine for five years use …so; new grass-green colored laid..? …stepping through the hall/garage door from school. Well okay; so Pop thinks..? It only takes Tina fifteen minutes after being fed that she dumps on it between the living room and hall. Before doing, thankfully he had stepped out for some fresh air, and after getting her into the garage I'm a spinning around heading down the hall to the bathroom for toilet paper then back clamping a handful of hard turd as he's stepping through the front door …and; "What happened..?!" as it's lifted fully camouflaged by the paper.

"I didn't get Tina out the door in time but hey, there's no stain; see..?" answer. He calms down…

The next morning, Saturday, and there she is again but this time peeing! Pop's jumping up from the sofa shouting, "{Redact redact} dog..!!" charging at her.., she all too familiar with his rants trying to escape still dripping as I'm shouting, "Don't..!!!" But he's too quick, kicking her in the hind right thigh! …she crying out a loud sharp, "ER..ARP!!" as her leg is forced beneath her, nose crashing into the hall/garage door, frequent repeat of cries!!!

In a split second I'm brushing past him shouting, "{Redact redact} you; what's wrong with you..?!!" shoving the door open, she dragging herself into the garage still, "ER..ARPing..!!!" Slamming it behind, catch up to her few feet in corralling her plopping myself down on the concrete floor!!! I pull Tina onto my lap.., she nosing up just below my chin constantly licking it as I hold her tight, "It's okay.., it's okay..!!" whispering, she a panic quiver as I gently pet seeing her hind leg drawn up to her belly trying to relax it but twitching back!

All of this and somehow she's waggin' her tail! "It's okay.., it's okay..," subtly petting towards the thigh …she very apprehensive as I slowly reach it and gingerly begin massaging; the repetitive flexing but lessening in concert with the dwindling quivering. But her licks and wags unceasing! "She's really hurting," brings greater burn to my eyes but the amount of rage for Pop is matching, withholding the moisture! Looking back.., wish I had the insight to apply an icepack to her thigh.

For a good hour I'm unable to look the way of the door.., nursing her to put weight on the leg. There's progress but so much collapsing, got to rest. "Stay Tina," opening the door.., passing between him and the television which is on but hardly audible. Fetching her bed upstairs, pass back by to hear, "Good.., and that's where she's stayin'," having to eat that fearing that I couldn't take him in a fight.

Coax Tina into her bed positioned next to the water heater, "Stay..," heading back in for a Pet Chow burger patty. I sit with her slowly breaking off nibble bits and she accepts each. "It'll be okay, girl," whisper. A couple hours later lying back in bed gazing at the ceiling, television off and Tina in the garage, Mom comes to mind after so many years not; "Wonder how it would've been living with her..?" …nodding off.

Days gone by, am sitting at the desk at a back corner of Mr. Lipkin's classroom which I teacher assist, and am looking to the front. He's up there behind another relaxing back facing his students. It's quiet, they're taking a test. Then suddenly he loses his balance, the chair with him in it tumbling back just below the chalkboard as he clumsily reaching back tries to break the fall..! Their attention caught by the ruckus, the class breaks out in laughter as he jostles to quickly rise! It pretty much goes quiet again with some residual giggles after he has regrouped. Saying nothing, Mr. Lipkin is obviously embarrassed. It happened so fast, he was back up before I could make a move to help. Feel bad for the guy.

Although Tina's gotten better, she appears handicapped favoring that hind leg with bit of a limp and caving in at times. I often take her for walks and massage the thigh. When she tries to run its stretch is less than the left's causing a spine-bent trot. Doesn't run up to and jump curbs without hesitating.., just a foot high! There was one time when she didn't even clear it, rolling back off like a log into the gutter.., pitiful. When she hesitates too long I help her up. Don't believe I can ever forgive Pop for what he did to her. The grass color of the new carpet had to confuse her, and she's fourteen years old. Won't even take her to a Vet.

I'm taking drives by myself a lot, finding my way into Long Beach parking and walking through Nu-Pike Amusement Park along the shoreline south of Ocean Blvd. Don't know what I'm looking for but a tattoo isn't, many parlors roundabout. Turned eighteen three weeks back without fanfare, but got the muscle car!

Not far from Nu-Pike, just a short walk, is a triple-X movie theater and one evening while Pop's at work am finding myself out in front apprehensive but more inquisitive.   Sitting at the back wide-eyed still, the glimmering exposé is putting out enough light to dimly expose the theater's interior and am seeing that there's only a handful of other patrons spread throughout the hundred-plus seating, most sprawled back with silhouettes of top halves of their heads and legs shrouding seatbacks in front of them. Can hear snoring from one. Maybe lately these screen scripts are what I've been looking for; no harm, no foul..? ...but can only take so much of the frenzied conclusions.   Those portrayals nonetheless, walking out into the cool air and noise of the Boulevard, have been planted in the garden of covetousness amid all the others that have brought forth their fruits; the new seedlings.., a little later tended to while showering.

Two days later, a Saturday afternoon, I'm cruising back from roaming the beaches without the guys, leaving Torrance into Carson when again I see off to the left the U.S. Armed Forces Recruiting Station with emblems of four Departments of the Military mounted over its entrance ...slowing chewing over, "Probably shouldn't put off any longer signing up for the Selective Service."

I vaguely remember first catching sight of it long ago out of the corner of my eye but then was just a part of the scenery going by. Amazing how the front has grown prominent.., almost as if becoming haunted by it or jetting out more 'n more to trip up my car. Just passed, I U-turn and pullup parallel a few feet short of it.

Noticeable just beyond the GTX's right front fender is a curbside A-frame sign with a drawing of an old white guy with long wavy white hair protruding back from beneath a white top-hat with a blue ribbon circling adorned by large white stars. Sporting bushy white eyebrows, a thin white mustache and goatee, he's wearing a white long-sleeve shirt under a blue patriot-style coat topped off with a red bowtie; is known as Uncle Sam.

A stern expression, he's pointing at me with large print beneath saying, "I WANT YOU FOR U.S. ARMY **NEAREST RECRUITING STATION.**" I gaze at him for a minute beginning to realize that war isn't too far off for me the way things are going --then, get out circling the front stepping up the curb and pass by…

Entering and then pausing, I see a waiting area containing two rows of six chairs each facing one another, and within each row is an end table dividing three by three the chairs. Right-angled surrounding to the right are two walls full of posters that dramatically portray America's military might, and advertising for each Branch therein. Surrounding likewise to the left are two small offices within each of two walls, each office having a window with its Branch's emblem decaled upon. There is though a hallway opening that's corner-separating those two walls. A fellow is seated here in the waiting area with a clipboard on his lap filling out some form.

The Navy's open-door office is empty, the Army and Marines' have closed door conferences going on between two guys each. Just then approaching into my left periphery is a fellow dressed in semi-formal blue that had exited the Air Force office; "Can I help you?" he asks.

"I'm here to sign up for the Selective Service," answer.

"Sure …take a seat, I'll get you the form," he instructs. Handing me a clipboard holding the half-size card purposed for signup, "When you finish you can leave it in the tray over there," pointing.., "or hand it to one of us freed up recruiters which would be best so to be checked," he concludes.

Finishing, I can see that he's still the one freed up. The other fellow with a clipboard didn't heed his advice and left. Seated behind his desk, that recruiter notices my approach and flags for me to enter, "Make yourself comfortable," he offers adding; "Finished the application?"

"Yep," handing it to him over the desk as I take a seat.

He has four stripes on his light-blue short-sleeve shirt, a plastic nametag that reads, "Willis," and a dark-blue coat also with stripes that's hanging in the corner behind.

Like in the waiting area, the left and right walls have posters affixed but there's this large framed one up behind him of a USAF fighter jet banking left this way from a sizeable white cloud backdropped by clear blue sky. A pilot wearing a white helmet with blacked-out visor and an oxygen hose protruding is turned more left peering out the cockpit; a real dramatic still-shot!

"Mickey William Farrens;" Willis says gazing at the card then raising his eyes to me as I'm nodding, "Well ...it looks good. Your Selective Service card showing your draft classification should arrive by mail in a week. If you move contact the nearest Recruiting Station there," remarking then; "Do you have any questions?"

"No," back to him.

"Okay; thanks for stopping in!" he says rising and extending a hand.

"Sure..," I reply shaking his hand thinking, "I had to."

Turning for the door he stops me with, "Oh; here's my business card. You might want to hold onto it," squinting with a grin.

"Okay; thanks," with a quick peek at it nodding then continuing on. Outside, pass by the A-frame whispering, "Not today, Sam..." U-turn from the curb and head for home as, "Turn around, look at me...," fills the stereo speakers. Window down, elbow on the sill ...cool breeze, the GTX cruises through an intersection as its traffic signal goes from yellow to red. I'll let Pop know what I've done. A week later he hands me the draft card, I to hand him a different one not too far down the road...

There's a couple of weeks left to graduation and my report card might look hellish! Yep, the first Semester 'D' in Physics has turned into a suckier looking 'F'! ...but P.E. saved the day going from 'B' to 'A' finishing out my final year with a 'C' average and able to make the Graduation Ceremony; not a hellish outcome after all seemingly to me...

With a melancholic face he signs the card and spins it down onto the coffee table, pauses leaning back on the sofa turning to gaze out the living room window. Then turning to me he says, "Our townhouse has been sold through the Sales Office at the Community Center, was shown during times when you were at school."

Thinking that the carpet must've been replaced for that; "Where to next..?" I ask.

"Eugene, Oregon," he answers.

"Where..?" by me.

"Eugene, Oregon," by him.

"Why there..?" I ask.

"Gonna take some time off from Longshoring, probably retire due to my back increasingly bothering me as you know, and the change in scenery might do us both some good," he returns.

I ask; "When..?"

He answers, "The Monday after next, after your graduation next Friday."

I'm thinking; "So soon?! ...just super..!! ...my buddies?!! ...I hate the guy..!!! But makes sense, today's Friday the 13th!! That's the miracle?! ...some miracle!

After the weekend the report card is returned to school at the beginning of homeroom. Four days later, Friday, with hundreds of parents filling the football stadium nowhere is Pop seen at the Graduation Ceremony. Diploma in hand, I swiftly peel off my cap and gown stacking them on the chair where I sat during the festivity --then, trek for the curbside GTX across school leaving sounds of celebration behind, lonely crossing from the last building over the grass yard to the curb not looking back. Crank over the engine but sit here couple of minutes soul-searching; "What's been going on..?" occupies my skull abutting; "What's ahead..?" staring out the windshield but hard to focus beyond the polished hood's front edge. Reaching to the stereo I volume up and adopt as my standard, "I don't care!...I don't care!...I don't care!" set forth by Creedence Clearwater Revival's Porterville cut, shouting it over 'n over as they do ...rolling away from the curb, "I Don't Care..!"

Arriving at Scottsdale, Pop has collected a dozen used boxes of various size from grocery stores. "We're gonna take the weekend to gather up what we want to go with us in the cars," he instructs adding, "everything else will go with the Mover's Monday to be delivered when we're settled up there."

"I got to contact the nearest Recruiting Station when we get there," telling him.

Monday 2 p.m.; bottoming out from the mountain pass through Gorman, the Rambler ahead of me is about dragging its bottom, more so on Pop's side. The window behind him is down with Tina's snout hanging out. Just ahead is the Interstate 5/Highway 99 fork and will go left onto 5 continuing north through California's central flats. Hours later but to make it a two-day drive, we shoot through Sacramento and finally stop at its fringe to layover grabbing a bite to eat then find a cheap motel.

The next morning and filled with breakfast we continue on, on 5 North, eventually crossing the Oregon border; all the big 'ol Redwood trees along the way, really neat going through Grants Pass. Early evening are cruising into Eugene and locate a bit better motel.

Just like it's been, many of the days over the next two weeks I'll take out on my own exploring but not yet for a Recruiting Station. Come upon a High School where its oval track is near the road and I feel like jogging some laps to exercise out all the stress.

Fatigued after a few, I mosey into the grass center and stretch out on the comforting half-inch tall blades gazing up at the clear blue sky. Turn my eyes some from the sun's rays but the warmth, "God, this feels good," relaxing back.

The first week here we take in a theater movie starring Peter Sellers, "The Party." Pop sits a little way's down next to the aisle and so do I across from him two rows back. All during the flick he is seen laughing his head off, so much louder than the rest of the packed audience! …constantly wiping away tears. The scenes are quite funny but much more is his carrying on! Frankly, he seems like a different person than I've known and is good to see him that way, sense of humor.

We've been trying to find a permanent place to live but no luck, and by the end of the second week the Rambler's about dragging its bottom, more so on Pop's side. The window behind him is down with Tina's snout hanging out as we're heading south on Interstate 5 back to Southern Cal., Yes..!!! Funny; almost seems like it's been a vacation and even as recurrent thoughts are purging, tossed stuck to building fronts and other things passed, three shapes keep converging within as if having some sort of kinship, the Recruiter's business card, the draft card …and my final report card.

Friday evening of July 11th '69, we're in a Carson motel. I'm looking forward to reconnecting with the guys! Have got to find an unfurnished apartment first. Monday about noon we finally locate an over-carport two bedroom in a horseshoe shaped building that looks good …and, is only a block and a half down from our McDonald's meetup on W. Carson, alright..!! …but we have a problem, big problem, they don't allow pets.

"We'll take it," Pop says to the Landlord.

A gawking look; "What?!" to Pop.

He mimics that it'll be alright. Getting into his car leaving out, "We'll put her temporarily in the same kennel as before for the trip to New York until I can get the Landlord's mind changed," he's conjured up.

I'm thinking, "Remarkable! You're out of your {redact}in' mind..!! …they won't..!!!" angrily eying him, the longtime indoctrinated word finally surfacing with my slant.

"What? Don't look at me like that! It's a done deal," he rebuffs.

Back at the motel he gets on the phone to the Mover's arranging for a tomorrow afternoon delivery of our furnishings …then, calls the kennel to arrange boarding Tina in the morning. I feed and take her for a walk sickened by the going's on. As she and I meander about though, am gradually coming to realize that at the apartment there might not be a good stretch to walk her except along W. Carson; and when she dumps in plain sight would have to nudge it into the gutter with the edge of a shoe scraping it clean against the curb? Wish we hadn't taken the place although so close to McDonald's.

"Don't worry.., Tina will be well cared for," the lady kennel attendant pleasantly says as I poke a couple of fingers through the chicken-wire of the sizeable outdoor pen stroking the bridge of Tina's nose, her eyes locked on mine. Turning about walking away with the lady and Pop down the lane between pens, I can hear the sound of Tina's bark joining the chorus of others left behind; man.., am I bummed…

I don't even stick around at the new place to see the furnishings arrive. Walk on over to McDonald's …and, it's great seeing my buddies hangin' there as I grow closer..! "Mic'..?!!" they all yell with big smiles.

"Yo …right back at you!!" matching theirs flippin' hand-slap-five's..!! …except for Marty.

"Where's your wheels..?" Allen asks.

"At home. We moved into an apartment just down the street," answer.

Luke; "Oregon wasn't happenin'?!"

"A loser. Glad to be back!" I respond.

Stan adds, "Us too.., our number had dwindled even more! Marty moved up to San Jose while you were gone."

"Bummer;" I reply ...then, "Gonna grab me some chow; are you hangin' for a while longer?"

"Sure..yeah!" from nearly all.

I stroll on over to the order-window and as I'm pulling up behind another placing his order, can see it's Archie inside taking it..! He sees me and a quick thumbs-up to each other!! My turn and laughing, "Hey dude, cool.., you're working here!"

"Yep; can I take your order, dude.., I mean sir?!" laughing back.

"A couple of chissburgers, large fries, medium coke and put them on my account!" ordering.

With an in-your-dreams type grin he replies, "Sorry, no can do on account I'll get fired; want extra chiss on those burgers?"

"No, no extra chiss, Ronald McDonald," laughing slapping the greens down on the counter.

Sliding the sack to me, "Here you go, sir..dude," with an Alfred E. Newman grin.

"Thanks.., on the flipside, Archie McDonald!" respond laughing.

"On the flipside, Mickey Mouse, I mean sir!" right back at me with a lesser laugh so not to get fired.

Setting the sack of grub down on the ground in front of Stan's wheels he says to me, "You can put it on the hood."

"Thanks, but I'll work from here;" respond --then, "Split the fries guys..," handing them to him.

Finishing up my meal, Kyle says, "We're gonna cruise the beaches; want to Harley chick with me?"

"Thanks, man.., but I'm a bit zapped from the day, gonna go back and flop," answer.

Stan leads out rappin' his engine.., goes left; then Allen rappin' his followed by Luke likewise and lastly Kyle ...so funny, seat cheeks hanging both sides lets loose the dual pipes! With Coke cup in hand, I head for the apartment.

Entering through the open door, the Mover's are about done. The box spring and mattress in my room are leaning up against a wall. With Pop's help fifteen minutes later everything's found its place. Before leaving the room he says, "You know.., now that I'm off work we can do some things together."

"Like what?" I ask.

"Oh ...maybe bowling, the shooting range or take in a Dodger game," he answers.

"Maybe Pop but I'm too tired right now to think much about that," remark back. The next day we go bowling.

The day following, I want to go check on Tina. She's already at the front of her pen as the attendant and I approach.., barking loudly with the other hounds; then seeing me she goes quiet but spasmodic, tail whipping all over the place and peeing as I enter! Also is wanting to jump up on me but kept at bay while still releasing! I eventually stoop allowing her to jump on me and she just can't stop licking! She's a shiver! "Good to see you too, girl..!"

"Haven't seen her lying in the bed you left, always crouched at the front of the pen ...and, she's not wanting to take food," the lady informs.

Holding Tina, she's noticeably thin. I look over at the bowl that's full and try to coax her to eat from it but she won't. "I'll retrieve some healthy snacks for you to try handfeeding. Usually that gets them going," am told. She takes some but not enough to feel optimistic about her, is still beside herself with excitement wanting to nestle tight.

"It's still too soon. She'll begin to eat from the bowl when she gets hungry enough. Don't worry yourself," am advised. I sit with her for a half-hour more. Like before, it's really difficult to leave her behind. At the apartment, "I visited Tina. She's not wanting to eat." Pop sits back quiet on the sofa staring at me slowly nodding showing a slight bit of concern.

I hold back just short of a week visiting her again. When I do, she appears more thinned. Time together goes as before but I'm not liking the situation. "We'll keep trying our best to feed her," am told. At the apartment, "Pop, maybe you ought to go see for yourself," laying it on him. He doesn't and I don't want to do things with him as a result. Stretch my allowance to hang with the guys, "Groovin'..." along with so many more rhythm our beach partyin'!

Two weeks later am once more approaching Tina's pen and; "God?! ...what am I seeing..?!! ...is that her..?!!!" feeling instant despair for her as I'm hearing, "She just won't eat! Not taking at all well to this environment no matter how much we try to ingratiate ourselves..!"

Her mannerisms are like before except she's nipping at me instead of licking! Continuing to think, "Oh God..! ...she has starved herself not wanting to take food from anyone but who she loves..!!" So skinny feeling bones as I'm trying to stroke her so to calm her..!!! ...but she is delirious constantly nipping to connect.., not for food but affection!! "Over fourteen years of togetherness torn from her!" feeling guilt.

I stay here for at least an hour more holding.., whispering.., trying to get her to eat. But she's too far gone and won't, although now somehow a few licks between all the nips. My eyes are blurred by water ...drips, the guilt; "What have I done to her..? ...or allowed..? How much longer 'til I leave her behind again..?"

Eventually I move through the gateway keeping her from, and mindfully begin to appeal, "God, please don't let Tina die before I get back tomorrow..!" Stoutly shutting the front door behind, "Went to see her again and she's dying!" boldly to Pop.

"What do you mean..?" he asks.

Answer, "She won't eat going on three and a half weeks, they can't get her to!!"

He inquires; "What do you want me to do..?"

Quickly back; "What..?! ...get her the {redact} out of there..!! Have you talked with the Landlord?!!"

"Yes and won't budge," he answers.

Bolder to him; "Why don't you go see her, afraid of how she'll look to you?"

"Don't need to, I believe you," he subtly returns.

"So that's your response?" bitterly challenging him.

"Partly;" he squinting --then continues, "I know it hurts to see her that way but it's time to man up to the inevitable.., her time with us has passed. She's had a lengthy life, a good one because of you," he undertones.

From me, "You've given up on her; haven't you?" nodding bitterly ugly eyed.

"Not really," slowly shaking his head side to side, "but we're not moving," stilled and then; "Are you going to keep seeing her shrivel away..? ...abandoned to starvation..?" challenging back.

Am thinkin', "You pinhole!" while rebound saying, "What else can be done..," spinning away trying to calm, then back taking slow deep breathes and sternly, "Make your point…"

"Mic'? She needs to be given relief," his facial turning to minor benevolence.

I puff squint slowly nodding in awe; "I'm hearing that from you..?" mindfully.

"Maybe coming from me doesn't rest well but realize that people do such out of love if you know what I'm referring to," eye to eye he concludes getting up and leaving the room.

Lying back on the bed, radio down low, "<u>One is the loneliest number that you'll ever do..,</u>" is making it hard to capitulate to his mindset but as it's ending I head out to the kitchen where he is washing some dishes and, "Okay," say to him.

He responds, "I'll arrange it for tomorrow with a Vet, prolonging will only make it rougher," continuing to wash.

"Are you going to take her?" I ask.

"If that's what you want?" is his reply.

"No.., but want to spend some time with her before going over," answer.

He asks; "Goin' it alone?"

"Yeah..," answer.

He just nods lifting the last plate out of the spent wash water.

An hour later I divulge, "Think I'll give Archie a call.., to see if he'll meetup with me here and ride over to the Vet's."

"I understand," he replies.

Archie agrees to but it'll have to be after he gets off work at 3:00." Am thinking, "Jeezze, what a great friend!" Pop arranges for 3:30...

Emotions are mixed although mostly sad carrying Tina out of the kennel practically nothing but bones, nipping and licking but ceasing growing closer to the car, placing her in the front.

Beforehand, I bought a package of bologna stopping off at a park to spend about an hour offering her small chunks but she rejects them.., just staying squatted alongside moving her head gingerly about as if to know the moment soon to come. The silence shrouding is so defiant, wanting to separate us; the alien vacuity of it while she appearing blithe and brave despite being frail. Turns perpendicular to me and rests her chin on my thigh, I gently pet...

"Thanks, Archie, for coming along," say to him starting for the Vet, he riding shotgun, Tina peacefully squatted in the back. Walking through the Clinic's front door carrying her, he trailing, am immediately escorted to an examination room as he stays behind in the lobby.

"The Doctor will be in shortly," the lady assistant advises. Sitting quiet, I let Tina mosey about circling the large exam table trying to hold onto what Pop said, "…people do such out of love," for solace; but watching her explore, all thought is beginning to leave me as though becoming braindead.

The Doctor enters and introduces himself as she gives him a few shin sniffs. He stoops; "So this is Tina?!" lifting her chin petting her forehead.

"Yep," from me.

"Mickey, go ahead and place her on the table," he instructs turning his back to me as I do. She becomes very nervous, I trying to keep her calm, "It's okay, Tina.., it's okay."

Back still turned he says, "You'll need to keep her squatted and head facing forward."

Managing to with one hand beneath her chin and the other petting her forehead 'n down along the back, "It's okay, girl.., it's okay."

He turns around with small hair clippers in hand telling me to hold her firm. Tina's eyes are turned back to the sound of it while I keep her snout forward lowering myself closer, "It's alright, girl.., it's alright..," as he trims a little patch from her thigh. He briefly turns away and back with a syringe in hand saying, "She won't feel a thing."

Tina goes from looking back to at me eye to eye --then oh so slowly closes hers as she gently surrenders all the weight of her head onto my hand and, is twitching tiny wags of her tail.., all in soft stilling concert as I subtly lower her head to rest on the table. He with a little smile remarks, "She wagged her tail.., have never seen that before, amazing…" I don't know how to respond also hearing him say, "She'll be properly cared for..," except to rapidly turnabout and exit, darting tunnel vision through the lobby out the door to the car …Archie fast catching up!

A familiarity with the route back, the car is in trauma-autopilot; I.., still tunnel visioning straight ahead..!! Out of the car, up the stairs shoving the front door open blowing pass Pop 'n into my room slamming its door behind and, start loudly wailing..!!!

…Year and a month to Johnston.

8

"She's gone." From Bill to Sam.

Wailing.., "She's gone, Tina's gone..!" It's probably an hour later and am pretty well haggard, dried out. I head to the bathroom to splash some water on my face. Mosey to the living room. Pop is sitting quiet on the sofa, the television on but low volume. He says, "Want you to know that it has been arranged for her to be placed in a pet cemetery," as I gaze out the dining room's side window.

Somberly bobbing my head for a half-minute then, "Guess I ought to call Archie and apologize for dumping him," remark to him.

He replies, "If it would make you feel better but he understood. Archie appeared at the front door not far behind and we chatted briefly then he left."

"Had to hear me crying," comment back.

"So what?!" he responds and adds, "You got a heart and fourteen years is hard to shake."

Archie answering my call, "Sorry for the abandonment, want you to know how much I appreciate what you did," say to him.

"Hey …it is all good, man..! No need to apologize.., glad I was there but sorry though it was Tina's time," he responds.

"You are a buddy," I remark.

"You are too," he returns.

Friday late morning, August 8th; am pulling away from a Palos Verdes overlook to the ocean after an hour of reflection. Now that she's gone, things said by the guys the last few weeks are of foregoing thought, "A couple of them are considering signing up for the Navy or the Air Force."

Cruising back to the apartment the Recruiting Station is directly between where I am and there. Revelation of the Battle of Hamburger Hill just has not rested well; "Who wants to risk dying taking ground only to soon relinquish and all the while hated by peers back home for being there in the first place..?!" the Recruiting Station now ten minutes away…

As before, I U-turn and slowly pull up to it. More so do not like Uncle Sam pointing at me for the Army but still am not sure which way to go, signup or wait to be drafted. Pop fought during World War II in the Army.

Wouldn't you know it entering? I'm approached by the Army Recruiter but suggest to him that I would like to first visit with the Air Force one who currently is in a closed door conference. "Take a seat, shouldn't be long," he says and turns away. There are two other guys waiting to be seen, but not by the Army apparently. They soon enter together into the Navy's office.

Fifteen minutes pass.., then Willis exits his office turning left towards the corner hallway, the fellow that has been talking with him following, they turning down it disappearing. A couple of minutes later Willis comes up to me and; "Can I help you?"

"It was about three months back that I stopped in to sign up for the Selective Service," answer.

"Oh yes, I remember but it's..?" by him.

"Farrens," I reply.

"Right! ...back to see me?" by him.

"If you have a few minutes?" I return.

"Sure do, go on in..," gesturing for me to pass by. He closes the door and, "Take a load off," as he rounds his desk. Seated; "Well, graduated from high school..?" he asks.

"Yep ...all finished," answer.

He asks; "What's next, Farrens ...and your first name again?"

I respond, "Mickey ...or Mic'. Junior College but been thinking about going into the Air Force, or maybe Navy."

"I take it you're classified 1A for now?" inquiring of me.

A couple of quick nods affirming then, "Have heard that I have up to turning nineteen to decide whether to enlist," to him.

"Mic'.., there's a change coming by year's end and that's all I can say about it, but let me ask; What was your overall grade point average?" from Willis.

Reply, "A 'C'-plus."

And from him; "How far out to your birthday?"

"Awe ...eight months," answer.

He continues; "Any hobbies?"

Nod that I do ...saying, "My car."

"Oh yeah, what is it?!" he asks.

"Plymouth GTX," answer.

He remarks, "Alright.., muscle car!"

"Yep," back to him.

Willis adds, "I bet you keep it running really good!"

"Really good!" and nodding to him.

He nods back and in mellow tone, "Flies..," squinting.

I likewise gesture back.

He asks; "Can you see yourself keeping that flying?" angling his head up and behind a bit to the wall, to the only picture hanging on it of the banking fighter jet. Staring at it for a few seconds.., begin to nod approving.

"Look ...Mic', the Air Force wants a guy like you; will teach you a craft, put you in a career!" he asserts as I look back down at him then back up to it subtly broadening my eyes ...and, back to him with no change.

Willis is a good fisher. Sensing a tug on the line he inquires; "Mic'? Without any commitment, can you spare an hour to take an aptitude test ...to see where you are best talented?   There are four parts to it: Administration, Electronics, Mechanical and General."

Pausing a few seconds.., then, "Yeah..sure," answer.

I follow him down the same hallway that he and the other guy beforehand did, and entering a room see him apparently taking the test. A little over an hour later I hand mine to Willis and he asks; "Call you tomorrow to give you the results..?"

"Yeah..sure," I reply despite tomorrow being Saturday. We shake hands.

"Take care, Mic'," he says and I back to him, then turn away.

Peering through the windshield at the A-frame, I start the engine and mull over, "Going from Bill to Sam; maybe it will be better?" ...U-turning from the curb. The traffic signal that the GTX cruised on by three months ago after leaving him behind has this time brought it to a red-light halt.

Devoid of any emotion, "<u>Love... can make you happy...</u>" comes on and for some reason can think of no one but Kaylee again. Seems as if any 'n all that have been a part of my life are being blanked out by her within the words of the song. Go figure..? ...nothing has ever come about between us and I realize now that nothing is; why then is she the only one of mellow imagining a companion? ...traffic signal going green.

Sliding back at one end of the sofa, Pop at the other, "I stopped by the Armed Forces Recruiting Station a couple of hours ago," tell him.

"And..?" from him.

"Took an Air Force aptitude test," furthering to him.

We're just sitting quiet.., a minute by --then, "Son; even though I'd miss you.., it might be the best way to go. The climate in this country, its messed up way to fight a war. Some twenty-five years ago we had resolve.., a destination. Stopping us to Berlin..? …over eleven million men got us there, and Tokyo, with million's more women back here in factories supplying us; how could we have not succeeded? Vietnam..? …what the {redact}'s going on over there..? If the Air Force is gonna teach you a trade.., seems smart to enlist."

I weigh in, "Might be perceived as cowardly."

He responds; "Cowardly..? Those burning draft cards or dodging to Canada, that's cowardly. Besides, there's no guarantee you won't see Vietnam anyway; and if you do, what do you do then?"

"What do you mean..?" I seek.

"What do you do..?" he reasserts.

Drift into answering, "Guess I will carry a rifle.., fight."

"There's no guessin', Mic'. You'd be in a foreign country where far more people want to see you dead than not. You guess? …you're dead, probably taking your comrades with you."

Interesting, after telling him I took that test he didn't ask why or why now..? …just told it like it is. With that, gazing forward with hands clasped on my lap, I eventually say, "The Recruiter might be calling tomorrow to give me the test results."

He nods.., it going quiet …then, "Thanks for hearing me out, think I'm going to take a walk."

"Over to McDonald's..?" he asks.

"Probably," answer.

"Here.., five bucks to get something to eat," extending to me.

"Thanks," taking it.

He nods.

About a quarter way's strolling down W. Carson, I pause and think about Tina the last time I walked her at the motel before going into the kennel, "I need to visit her grave soon." At the Golden Arches the guys aren't there, nor is Archie working. I take an outside table-seat and eat slowly, the world blowing by...

The next day am hanging around the apartment mostly in my room listening to a lot of tunes and eying some television; so many thoughts swirling, uncertainty trying to prevail. Going on 4 p.m., Pop's been whipping up spaghetti with meat sauce, the aroma drawing me out and leaning against the kitchen entryway, "Smells good," say --then the phone rings! "I got it," turning to go for it.

To my ear and mouth; "Hello?"

At the other end; "Hello.., this is Staff Sergeant Willis calling from the Armed Forces Recruiting Station for Mic' Farrens..?"

"This is Mic'," reply.

"Hey... Mic'; how ya doin'..?!" he asks.

"Good, thanks; how about you..?" back to him.

He responds, "Great..! I got your test results and Mic'? ...pretty decent."

"Thanks," reply.

He says, "And here they are; for Administration 70 percent, General 85, Mechanical 90 and Electronics... 95 percent..!"

I acknowledge, "Neat!"

Willis continues, "Sure are …and it gets better. The Air Force has new state-of-the-art communications equipment comin' on board and Mic'? …we want you to be a part of it! Because of sensitivity factors, I can't describe it but that speaks to the importance of it. It's a new career field opening up and you'd get in early, that means opportunity for rapid advancement in the Force!"

"Wow..!" again acknowledging.

"Yep …but here's the hitch, Mic'? To take advantage of that you'd need to enter the Air Force ten days from now," he reveals.

"Hmm.., ten days..?" echoing back.

"Yep …sometimes that's the pace of things, of new opportunities opening up. If you don't go for it others throughout the country will, snatch it up, shut you out..!" he clarifies.

"I understand," in response.

Bringing the conversation to a close, "Mic'.., sleep on it for a couple of nights …but if it's a go, I need to hear from you by 11 a.m. Monday, and in my office by 1 p.m. to enlist."

I repeat back, "I understand."

Lastly from Willis, "My man …hope to hear from you, take care."

"Thanks …you too," back to him.

"Click."

At the table …spinning spaghetti onto the fork, I fill Pop in on the happenings. Later in bed for the night, am again peering at the ceiling; "Is there a face up there formed by stucco-curds that looks like a military man..?" Songs roll by on the radio but then begins the instrumental, "Time Is

<u>Tight,</u>" and listening through, it chimes me to go for it rather than favoring a reluctance to act. Positively driven, "I'm joining up Monday."

"Welcome to the Force!" Staff Sergeant Willis says resting his left hand atop my signed enlistment slid across the desk, extending his right to shake. As we do, "Am happy for you. I believe you made the best choice;" he remarks adding, "We'll need you back here tomorrow at 8 a.m. to take a physical exam."

"I will be here," reply nodding. Cruising back to the apartment that same intersection as before on W. Carson crossing S. Western has its traffic signal go green before I have to slow, window down, elbow on the sill, breezing through...

Passing by two city blocks there they are on the right, the guys backed in at McDonald's..! Turning in and traversing the sidewalk, they catch sight of me as I lurch the GTX forward. Circle behind the restaurant backing in next to Kyle's Harley, and when getting out hear, "Loser..!" shouted in unison. Wondering, "Do they somehow know what I just did and are calling me that?"

"Losers..!" shout back approaching them.

"What's the haps', dude..?!" from Luke.

"Call me Sir or General, dude..!" answer.

"Say what?!" from him.

"Just left the Recruiting Station, joined the Force.., Air that is..." return, my eyes quickly passing from one to another.

He, Allen and Kyle snap to attention, hands' sloppily rising with palms showing to their foreheads saluting,

"Yes Sir, General Dude..!" by Luke. Stan is just staring at me somber.

"As you were, men dudes..!" order the three, flippin' hand-slap-five's laughing …and to Stan dolefully.

He asks; "Why so soon?"

"Oh …I don't know, seems I'm being led down a path," answer him.

"Man.., got to get you blitzed tonight!" Luke says.

"No can do.., got to take a physical there early in the morning," reply.

"Perfect! Four bottles of brewski in you overnight and you'll show up 4F'n, floored fart-face {redact}ed!" he counsels and all laughing!

"Tempting but probably has been tried," cowardly back to him.

"Awe.., man..?" he tones down.

Stan subtly shaking his head remarks, "Lately, I've been seeing Sam in my dreams finger-pointin' me."

Luke quickly rebuffs, "Sam can go to {redact}, dude..?!" it going quiet for a moment, then after a low puff he adds, "You guys 'been good buddies to me but I've had it with Uncle Sam and Southern Cal. Have had it seein' so often my parents at each other, gonna split east tomorrow to a hefty music festival with a finger-pointin' emphasis right back in Sam's face on the way out..!"

"Where's the festival gonna be..?" Allen asks.

"About ninety miles north of New York City on some farm. I got four days to get there. Am gonna become a flower powered love child lying with Daisy in a field of daisies..!" Luke proclaims.

Stan asks; "Where you gonna get the bread?"

Luke, "There's a trust account left from a relative I can tap."

Kyle then says, "Soon there'll just be us three," with solemn look at Allen and Stan.

The next day I again hookup with them after passing the physical even though noting the back injury. And apparently as he said, Luke is gone.

Four days later the 16th, Saturday night; I ride shotgun with Stan and tie one on taking in a beach party at the cliffs near Rat Beach between Palos Verdes and Torrance Beach. All the brewski I can gulp down provided by the guys as a going away gift, "Chug-a-lug."

There is a bonfire blazin' with three fine lookin' babes wearing hot pants looking our way tease dancin' beside it, synchronized radios roundabout echoing, "It's the time of the season...," and their faces are all a glow..!

I not yet totally wasted, Stan leans over; "Hey.., undefiled? We need to get you hooked up tonight, straightened out before going off to war..!"

Am thinking, "Hmm ...there are three of them and four of us, one being fat; scoring looks like a possibility..."

Then obese Kyle just had to let loose, "Yeah ...if you're lucky, the one an oozy!" ...Allen spewing out beer breaking into laughter, we right there with him as I reply, "Thanks, dude." Wasted I'll get; off to war..? ...undefiled except for hand and mind.

The next morning my head feels a ton, the headache. Pop offers to take me to breakfast saying nothing regarding my hangover. At the café, after ordering, "It is kind of weird; In the gang I was the last to mention Uncle

Sam, the draft or anything else about the war but am the first to go in," comment to him.

"Okay; so what..? They are they and you are you. The choice was yours and not so small of one, live with it. You made your bed, sleep in it. They got to make their own. And Mic' …you better not go into this looking back or else you'll falter, not good in the military," he confides.

Silent, squinting back hearing in my mind, "Walk like a man.., talk like a man..," begin to nod and, "Thanks, Pop," seeing over his shoulder the waitress approaching with plates in hand.

The next morning I visit Tina's grave. As time passes looking down at her stone placard, I'm mellowed into a minuscule squint and smile… again seeing her ease away with the words of the Vet in concert …and then I say, "To the very end.., you wagged your tail. Rest now …Tina."

I leave out and drive around a bunch, the last day in the GTX and am blastin' the speakers..! "I'm the wanderer..," … "Where have all the flowers gone..?" … "Hot town, summer in the city," and "This is the worst trip I've ever been on..," are among the variety overdrivin' my self-awareness cruising the coastline, window down, elbow on the sill, breezin' along...

The 19th, induction day. I did not expect it, is a surprise.., Stan's a knockin' on the front door! Brings a big smile to me, "Hey, man; how's it goin'..?! Come on in..!" to him.

"Good!" stepping in, Pop greeting him.

It's not long before he and I are moseying to McDonald's.., sharing a large order of fries and a soda for each. Archie's not there but he called last night to wish me well.

"Glad you stopped by, Stan," say to him.

With bit of a smile he returns, "Had to.., a lot of good times.., many years 'good friends."

Subtle nods with likened smile and a slow, "Yep.., good times.., good friends..," reply.

Then he says, "Tomorrow, I'm gonna visit the Air Force Recruiter."

"Cool.., maybe our paths will cross in Basic;" responding to that --then, "Be ready to take an aptitude test. There are four parts to it: Administration, Electronics, Mechanical and General."

He nods.

I continue, "Funny; I scored best in Electronics …95%, multiple choice and I guessed at everything. Knew nothing more than wall sockets, switches and light bulbs," grinning.

A grin joining, Stan asks; "Do you know how many deeks it takes to change a lightbulb..?"

"No..?" grin growing.

"Three; one holding the bulb, the other two twisting the stepladder he's standing on..," he delivers, we both breaking into laughter.

"That's my speed..!" I remark as we flip hand-slap-five's.

"When are you headin' that way?" he asks.

"In about three hours, got to walk in there by 5:00; didn't pack hardly anything in a tote-bag," answer.

"What happens to the GTX..?" he asks.

"Don't know, it's in Pop's hands," I reply returning; "What about yours..?"

"Sell it ...or maybe give it to Denise," he answers.

Back at his car Stan takes me into a quick light hug, then backing away, "Take care, see you on the flipside," he says.

"Thanks.., you too; the flipside," back to him.

4:30 p.m.; window down, elbow on the sill, slow breezin' but Pop's window is up. Other than the hum of the engine it is quiet, buildings' tunnel-visioning by; and approaching that S. Western Avenue traffic signal, red goes to green. We pull right up in front of the Recruiting Station causing Sam's A-frame to be just behind Pop's door. Standing the other side of the sign, he says, "Son; not best at long goodbye's," eye to eye neutral expression, I subtly nodding back.

He fleetingly continues, "Write or call when you can," with me maintaining the nods.

Then he puts a hug on me, I lightly hold.

Backing away from me, "Take care of yourself ...Mic', do me proud," he ends.

"I will; love you, Pop," turning about for the entrance.

There are eighteen of us standing with hands' up taking an oath to the Country; half-hour later, are midway to LAX riding in a stubby greyish-white bus. At the Airport, we group up with more recruits in greater number from other area Stations. A bit after 7:00, takeoff. The jet is full nonstop to San Antonio but only about a fourth are Air Force.

Peering out the window at thirty thousand feet, am feeling more 'n more inclined to heed to what Pop said about not looking back.., not falter. What was exchanged between us after Stan left and before leaving for the Station is facilitating forwardness, having said to him, "Sorry only used the GTX for nine months," with his reply being, "It's alright, there's gonna be a new hot-rodder in town!"

Cruising high-up keeps me thinking, "I made a good decision," leaning the seat back taking a slow relieving breath, drifting out…

We touch down at S.A. International short of midnight. There're two midsize Air Force busses parked right outside the Terminal, one looking already full of recruits that arrived shortly before from other parts of the Nation. We Southern Cal. fifty take up the other's remaining seats being the most and off we go, heading out on Terminal Drive catching some Freeway for Basic Training.

Maybe a bit over a half-hour we are slowing and being flagged through a gate passing by the small shack with a large sign affixed reading, **"United States Air Force, Lackland Air Force Base - Air Training Command, The World's Largest Training System."**

The driver dressed in solid green fatigues sporting three stripes on his short sleeves, a green baseball cap and black boots is, akin to the bus he's close following, shooting through like a Formula One Racer at Monte Carlo shouting, "A minute from now when pulling up to the mess, shake a leg off the bus with your belongings doing what the Sergeant outside instructs!" The brakes' jerk-screechin' us to a halt, door slicing open, "Go!! …go, go, go..!!!" he yells.

The only thing I brought along not contained in the tote-bag is a light windbreaker which hadn't been put on being quite warm in L.A. and seemingly in the 90's here ...and real humid. Sitting at the back curvature on the passenger side in the bus, I didn't feel like sightseeing another L.A. from the Airport to the Base ...so, had rolled up the windbreaker and propped it as a pillow aside my head tilted against the wall to doze a little.

Hastily rising while a bit groggy, of course I am the last in line bottlenecking down the aisle hearing, "Go! ...go, go..!!" With just a few guys left in front of me to offload, I realize that my windbreaker isn't with me ...so, rapidly turnabout to get it ...and back around with it seeing an empty bus ahead except for the driver whom as I get halfway to him is loudly voicing out the door, "Straggler..!" ...then grins.

All are grouping beyond the fatigue dressed guy outside, and as my foot hits the sidewalk he is gawking at me five feet away with the backs of his hands on his hips nonchalantly uttering, "Well; who do we have here..?"

"Mickey..," I answer in like resonates.

Appearing puzzled.., nonchalantly he utters, "Oh; just Mickey?" growing a grin looking aside and over my shoulder to the driver, then back as I am detecting where he is going with this. Not gonna allow, "Mickey Mouse," to get started...

I reply, "Farrens ...but go by Mic' Farrens," eye to eye.

"Farrens..?" his voice firming.

I just nod acknowledging.

"Tell you what, Farrens..? Get back on the bus.., go all the way to the end.., turn around.., come out and we will do it again," he instructs.

As I'm doing I'm wondering; "What is the guy's problem?"

Foot hitting the sidewalk, "Well; who do we have here..?" again from him.., many of the others showing sizeable grins.

"Farrens, sir..," reply steady flow.

"Farrens ...what?!!" he shouts, feeling the moisture of his breath.

"Farrens, Sir!!" shout back.

"Fall in, Airman Basic!" he orders. I just had to be the one. Been standing silent off a bit to the right observing.., is a guy with four stripes whose nametag reads, "Brewer."

I do so and turning back, the shouted one loudly informs us, "I'm Tech Sergeant Larson (five stripes showing) and from now on nobody calls me Sir..! You address me as Tech Sergeant Larson or just Tech Sergeant; do you understand..?!"

"Yes, Tech Sergeant," with some adding, "Larson."

"Okay.., let's do it again and keep it simple," he orders.

"Yes, Tech Sergeant," all back to him but of course not respecting loud enough ...so; "I can't hear you..?!"

We repeat at the top of our voices!

He continues, "Okay.., here's the drill. It is a quarter after 1:00 and you're going to be fed breakfast. Stash your belongings alongside the buses and form a line behind Airman Basic Farrens at that door; do you understand..?!"

"Yes, Tech Sergeant," at the top of our voices!

~ 183 ~

"Woe.., cool.., I've become important," thinking as he's shouting, "Go! ...move it..!!"

The door is propped open, "Take 'm in, Airman Basic," neutral expression he orders.

"Yes, Tech Sergeant," I return a bit louder than him.

Walking alongside a wall to the left, the hall vastly opens up to the right easily seating five hundred. Noticeable some twenty feet ahead, the wall ends and aligned with it is the front of a running buffet, an ongoing shelf protruding some to slide trays along.

Drawing close, oh man.., can see the steaming hot breakfast; am really hungry but I stop at its beginning because the serving utensils are buried at the opposite ends of the big 'ol sunken square pans, and there is nobody on the other side to dole out..! Ponder; "Reach over the hot foods for them, and how much of each item to self-serve up..?!"

The line of guys behind are irking, "Farrens, get going, the food's getting cold; go man go..!" So, I do...

Five strips of bacon ...next, big 'ol scoop of scrambled eggs plopped on the plate taken from their stacks at the onset. Tray on the move, "Yes!" cubes of country spuds ...next, --he's blastin' through a swinging double-door the other side of the line-counter, a guy in tan semiformal uniform touting four stripes chargin' towards me yelling; "Want the {redact} 'you think you're doin'..?!!"

He snatches my plate away and also grabs the tongs from me that was gonna be used for the toast --then, reaches for the spoon used for the spuds and begins methodically sectioning away amounts from the pile on my plate! Next, does the same to the eggs --then, reaches for the bacon tongs and plucks three of five strips off..!! The radical's nametag reads, "Phillips."

Right about then am hearin' shouting gettin' louder, advancing up the line; "Who's holding up the procession..?!" from Larson.

"No one now, Tech Sergeant! Just some misunderstanding," from the anal staring across at me extending the plate back.

Larson at my ear; "Looking for more trouble, Airman Basic..?!"

Taking the now lighter plate turning my head a bit to him, want to answer, "{Redact} no but the guy's a moron..!" ...instead I only reply, "No, Tech Sergeant!"

He instructs, "When you get your drink at the end, start the seating at that corner table, first chair, Farrens!" pointing to it.

"Yes, Tech Sergeant!" respond.

There is a P.A. system within the hall, speakers' roundabout.

Parked, going for the fork, "<u>Sugar, ah honey honey, you are my candy girl...</u>," comes on but not too loud. Can hardly believe what I'm hearing 1:30 in the morning right off the bus; in the military? Think, "Surely, the Air Force isn't candy{redact}..?" ...but it does turn the tension taking a slow deep inhale and likewise out...

With the last of the guys lining the counter, I'm two-thirds through chowing seeing the Tech Sergeant over there loudly voicing, "Come on, move it..!" Following the last of those with a clipboard and pen in hand, he stops short at the front of the table, "Listen up! In five minutes beginning here with Farrens, I'm going to dismiss you out to the busses one at a time alternating back 'n forth across the tables with all on his side boarding the front parked, the other side on the one behind. Gonna do it at a pace so that the last one seated eating has a fair amount of time to do so. When I point to you.., without hesitation standup and loudly state your last name.., without hesitation and loudly; do you understand..?!"

"Yes, Tech Sergeant..!!" by all.

"Then when I say, "Go!" to you.., move it stashing your tray through that conveyor window (pointing) hightailin' out the exit!" he concludes.

As I'm finishing up am thinkin', "Batting a thousand, two for two, Larson and Phillips; hope the average dwindles to near zero. What does Brewer, still silent, play? Got to watch for traps."

"Farrens ...go!" he loudly says. Am up and a couple of paces away hear behind a name stated, then, "Go!" and so on 'n so forth. I take the first window seat behind the driver, guys filing in and about fifteen minutes later with some sixty aboard, Larson hops on grasping the poll at the top of the steps telling the driver, "Go..!" as he braces himself looking forward.

Just like before, it's Monte Carlo; bodies swayin' holding on as the bus corner's right, then left, again right and screeching to a halt a minute into the ride in front of an old looking two-story wooden barracks, one of several lining the road. The other full bus which Brewer is on pulls up behind us in front of their next-door barracks.

Larson loudly instructs, "Listen up! Because it is late, we won't group up outside the barracks. Go right on in taking the closest available bunk.., left bottom...left top, then on the right alternating side to side. Set your belongings on the one you take and then line the aisle next to it facing the barracks' front! Don't want to hear a sound out of you! Go! ...move it..!!"

With all quietly lining the aisle of the open bay abode, Larson outlines, "Okay..! I'm gonna spend the night here in the upstairs office behind me but will not be your Training Instructor, T.I. for short. This is not my assigned Squadron. The one you were to have had an accident that will keep him out during your training. A permanent T.I. will arrive in two weeks. Therefore, Staff Sergeant Brewer who is the permanent T.I. next door has graciously volunteered to float back 'n forth but mostly focus on his trainees.., unfair as that might sound. So, I want to know who here is the oldest?! That one will have charge over the rest of you as Staff Sergeant Brewer's assistant, answerable to him not you." By process of elimination, twenty-year-seven-month-old Krause is the poor soul so entitled.

There is a footlocker at each end of the double bunks, at the head of my lower one and at the foot for the one atop; fifteen double bunks in a row both sides of the aisle. "Turn in...in your unders, you'll be given seven hours to sleep; if you can? ...daylight arriving much sooner. Stow your clothes on top of your footlocker..!" by Larson.

Resting back atop the blanket due to the heat and humidity, "God.., all the feet-stink beginning to permeate the place..! ...and heard, whimpering resonating throughout from several." I'm caught surprised by that but though am unable to expend sympathetic thought for their anguish because I am too {redact} tired …losing consciousness. Days' ahead, the crying will diminish.

Don't know how much sleep was had, but, "Rise and shine..! Out of the bunks now.., now.., move it..!!" yelled from the chipper Larson standing nearby. "Farrens..? …first into the showers taking your soap. Five minutes in and out, then into whatever clean clothes you brought! The rest in sequence from your bunks follow him! Grab a towel from the stack on that chair going in and stow it dirty in that large gunny sack beside the chair once dressed! Don't want to see wangs swingin' in the air! There're four showers …so this is gonna be a smooth operation! When dressed.., back into the latrine to shave and brush your teeth using what you brought! Your Recruiter should have told you about those items! There're four sinks also! A smooth operation; right..?!" by him.

"Yes, Tech Sergeant..!!" chorused back.

"Good; Go Farrens..!" ordered. Lastly; "Krause? …you are going to supervise!"

"Yes, Tech Sergeant!" Krause returns.

A half-hour gone by, Larson's shouting; "Farrens and everyone else?! There's a gunny sack in your footlocker. Put your filthy clothes in it, then it on top the locker with your baggage brought next to! Then line the aisle and wait!" Soon to a fourth of us standing he says, "Gather around!" at my bunk. He quickly takes us through making the bunk only to unfurl it all in a pile, "Get started!" to me and the rest, they turning for theirs. He repeats to the next fourth standing ready, and so on…

Half-hour later all peeved by the sloppiness of made beds, "Fallout in the street, move it..!!" The same moment are Brewer's trainees and we're all treated to a brief course in close-order formation; side rights', side lefts', about faces' and saluting, then marching drill …sloppily picking up pace headway to the mess hall for lunch, "Hup …one, two, three.., hup …one, two, three…" With stomachs decently filled, "Hup …one, two, three..," sloppily to the barber for near balding.

Next, assembly-line shots in both arms and similarly through the wardrobe supply factory; entering, sprint tailoring …moving along seeing sewing machines stitching away at my fatigues' form-fit lengths, three sets neatly folded. Those, underwear, cap, boots, jacket and a duffle bag exiting.., a load to carry for sure!

A bit less sloppy marching back to our barracks, "Ping..!" is irregularly but often heard from cap wearing Basics outside their barracks, mockingly emulating the sound of a guitar pic pricking the stubbled scalp. The cap always on outside. Good thing only one haircut will be needed during Basic! Other than a better march to and from dinner, the rest of the first full day is spent remaking our bunks which were stripped while gone; replacement stacks of blankets, sheets and pillowcases left instead. Subsequently, time is used for searching the new issues for tiny manufacture's inspection tags hidden in several spots throughout each garment; the proper way to fold and store underwear as well as strict hanger spacing for fatigues and jacket on the rack; also the storing of toiletries and odd items.

Larson shouts, "In the morning after breakfast, you're gonna detail the barracks inside and out for afternoon inspection. While at attention lining the aisle, all of your clothing will be thoroughly investigated for tags; any found..? ...you'll eat as after lunch dessert!"

Prior to lights' out we again shower and brush teeth establishing the sequence hence forth with shaving in the morning. I don't quite know why but am turning in with an unsettled stomach. Maybe it is chef moron's mess hall grub the culprit? Might be the reason why it's called, "Hell's Kitchen."

The next morning, I and Airman Basic Hernandez from El Segundo are assigned to clean the office and wax-buff its floor, but what I went to bed with is now full blown! Stomachache, nausea, and uncontrollable shivers skew my effort. I head downstairs to fetch a shoeshine rag from my footlocker to make the buffing task easier, also bringing the jacket to wear to knockdown the chills although it's in the 90's and humid.

On our knees swirling a shine am trying to keep down what little bit ate of chef moron's breakfast but about to throw up! "Hey, man.., you don't look too good..! Better go to the doctor's..," Hernandez says.

Reply, "Think I will; you can handle this yourself?"

"Sure ...man.., go," he returns.

Standing, I rollup the shoeshine rag and stuff it in one of my jacket pockets, descend the stairs hanging it backup. Staff Sergeant Brewer is next-door with his trainees ...so, finding Krause, "I'm really sick," say to him.

"You sure are..! Let's go next-door," he leading on out.

Brewer looking me over.., gives directions to the base infirmary saying, "Try to get back before the inspection."

"Yes, Staff Sergeant," by me.

As I turn away, hear him say to Krause that it is time to fallout for lunch. Seems I will miss that for goodness..? …apparently not the only one affected by Phillip's mash potatoes! Looks like at least a couple of hours here. Eventually am given a shot in the rump and meds to take with me, also a limited duty note for the remainder of the day and tomorrow.

Arriving back at the barracks I've missed the inspection but am told by Krause that Larson and Brewer are waiting upstairs for me. I approach the open door seeing Larson straight ahead sitting opposite-side of his desk peering at me not too pleased. I stop and knock on the wall next to the doorjamb.

"Enter," boldly by him.

A couple of steps in snapping to attention still with the foul stomach, "Airman Basic Farrens reporting, Tech Sergeant!" announce as loud as I can.., Brewer out of the corner of my eye sitting with a grin.

Silent.., Larson stares at me for the longest time with slow agile nods, squinting in concert. Then he tilts a bit to his right gradually pulling open the top narrow drawer aside. Reached in begins raising his hand out grasping a rolled-up shoeshine rag; the one I put in the jacket pocket..? He is gradually letting it unfurl as his hand slowly rises…! …I choking a swallow anticipating its end to exit one of these days…

Then he and Brewer burst into laughter! "At ease, Farrens..," Larson laughing tears' out! "You won't have to eat it; but, what's the story..?" he asks.

"Oh …man, Tech Sergeant; I was feeling really sick and wanting to expedite buffing the office floor, fetched it out of the footlocker but did not think to put it back, just rolled it up shoving into my jacket pocket," answer.

Grinning, looking over to Brewer he remarks; "What to do with this guy..?"

Quickly I intercede, "Got a note from the Doctor, Tech Sergeant!"

Looking it over; "Farrens..? You slid by this time …but limited duty this soon can cause screw ups taking the rest of the Flight (barracks group) with you," he responds.

"I understand, Tech Sergeant," affirm back.

"Alright; for the rest of today and tomorrow you are going to straggle behind the Flight everywhere they go.., to mess, drill pad …everywhere, and to keenly observe the training until rejoining. From then on your detail will be to police up outside the barracks," he orders.

"Yes, Tech Sergeant," reply as he is putting the note in the center drawer.

"Take your meds..," handing me the rag --then, "Dismissed!"

"Thank you, Tech Sergeant," and about face, out the door...

Descending the stairs am thinking, "Awesome..! …picking up a few cigarette butts outside will be the easiest detail while others indoor tradeoff cleaning the latrine or on their knees buffing the barracks floor." It is also the last time I will see Larson. Thereinafter, Basic isn't troublesome. I get use to the pace, the shouting, endurance rapidly strengthening but not for all…

The several weakest ones collapse in the heat during calisthenics or lengthy marches although consuming lots of water and given a bunch of salt pills; or are they saltpeter..? How could they not want us at our best? But there're some fine lookin' WAF's (Women's Air Force)..! ...more the reason to take cold showers; or saltpeter?

Krause cadences marching and seemingly is doing a good job as we follow Brewer's bunch everywhere. Although not said, our Flight has taken it upon itself to outdo his. A week and a half into training is when the first marching evaluation by Base Command takes place at the parade grounds. The last ones to.., we pass by the viewing stand corralling all the Brass, "Eyes'.., right!" by Krause. From there we proceed to lunch.

An hour after that, Brewer steps into our barracks congratulating us for best evaluated marching Flight but that is all that is said, turning around exiting looking somewhat steamed; Why? A minute later we're all cramming up to the open windows facing his barracks hearing him over there laying into his band of brothers..! We cannot help but to breakout in loud cheering and laughter, dancin' around high-fivin' each other as the cussing across the way continues..!! ...Krause doing an especially good dance..!!! That is our award for being the best, so we think...

Two days later, an hour before lights' out, in walks Brewer with this African-American five-striper dressed in semiformal tan. The dude looks like a black puma, sleek lean muscles with veins poppin' out of his neck and forearms; wouldn't want to be Vietcong crossing his path in the jungle!

"Flight? Line the aisle facing front!" Brewer yells. A moment later, "It is my pleasure to introduce Tech Sergeant Towns.., Samuel Towns and he is your permanent Training Instructor!" Brewer reveals and stepping aside.

The Tech Sergeant with his dress hat tucked under an arm centers himself and smiling, "Thank you, Staff Sergeant Brewer. Men..? I am honored to be your new T.I. and for now that is all I have to say other than see you bright and early!" That was it, sweet and simple, the two exiting into the dark. We all looking at each other echo, "There went the dance; who knows what envious Brewer might have said to him?"

Morning comes too soon but we all for fear of the black cat hustle our rears readying to hear his first order! Centered once more; "Men..? Again I wish to express the privilege that it is to take over this group! I know of your marching excellence and have otherwise heard nothing but good things about you; who would I be to mess up a good thing? If it hums, let it be. If a squeak starts, I will first hand an oil can to Airman Basic Krause. If it breaks, I am here to fix it. Krause..? ...step forward next to me." With both facing us, "A shoutout for the good job he's done..!" by Towns turning to him. We let out, "Hurrah..! Hoof, hoof, hoof..!!" as he gives Krause a firm tap on the shoulder.

The Tech Sergeant continues, "As you were. Krause, thanks. Men..? By what you achieved at the parade grounds, whenever we arrive at the mess hall the Flight waiting next to enter, and all behind it, will have to standdown letting you pass ...I guarantee it." Again we let out, "Hoof, hoof, hoof..!!" Man ...he emits a confident easygoing manner, kind the way Gil did.

Marching is now a real trip, seeing out of the corner of my eye off to the right Towns struttin' in fatigues wearing a Park Ranger style hat and hearing his cadence, "Ya...up, one, two, three.., ya...up, one, two, three..," at the rhythm of, "<u>Duke...Duke...Duke.., Duke of Earl.., Duke...Duke,</u>" struttin' right along with him. We're the groovin' Flight, it's all gonna be good..!

After dinner, we are given time to write to family and friends. My two are brief, one to Pop and one to Stan. To him, "Hey, buddy; how's it going?! Okay I hope. Man.., Basic's a trip! Got this cool black drill sergeant. He's more like a pal, not a rear. Makes us feel like singing Duke of Earl when marching. Getting in good shape! Half the guys in my barracks are clowns, but the WAF's (Women's Air Force) when passing by are real knuckle biters! Think things are gonna workout. Miss you all back home. Write when you can! The return address is on the envelope but only good for another two weeks, time's a flying. Take care and tell the guys hey for me! Mic'."

Moving right along --when out of left field four days later am called up to see Towns. He informs, "Your father is on Base to see you."

Surprised; "Really?!" respond.

He remarks, "Yes, Farrens.., and Base policy is no visitors before graduation but somehow he got clearance to momentarily see you. He is waiting over at the parade grounds. From the time you leave here to reporting back, thirty minutes is all you got; is that clear?!"

"Yes, Tech Sergeant," answer.

He ends, "Go, dismissed!"

Walking at a stout pace but not so to arouse higher rank on the way, or miss saluting Brass, it's a few minutes to the grounds seeing the GTX across the street parked parallel curbside and Pop's back to me leaning against its front fender apparently gazing out over the grounds.

Beginning to circle the front end; "Pop..?!" a bit over medium tone to him.

Quickly turning to me; "Mic'..?!" likewise from him as I round the front to an abrupt halt two feet away.

He extends a hand and shaking it, "What a surprise..! Good to see you but why the visit?" to him.

"Was a bit bored ...so, thought I'd take a trip to Texas in the hotrod to see where Crockett made his last stand, the Alamo..! ...and if was possible, a stop by to see Airman Farrens. Good to see you ...son; how's Basic treatin' you?" he asks.

"Good, Pop," reply nodding in accord.

"Good..," joining my nod and, "neat Base..," he comments quickly roaming his eyes. Back to me he asks; "Got time for a bite to eat?"

"Awe ...sorry, Pop. Was only given thirty minutes round trip," answer.

"Too bad.., thought you could drive us," he remarks.

Respond to that, "I wish a bite together could happen, not enough time ...but a ten minute spin around a few blocks behind the wheel can..!" as my eyes widen.

Bringing a grin he tilt-nods for me to go to the driver's side and makes an about face to the passenger door, must be thinking like me.., "Shoot ...there's no trouble ahead, go for it!"

I scrunch down so cruisin' along... anyone looking our way won't be able to see if I have stripes on or not. Emitting a prideful face am musing; "What other Airman Basic has done this, or ever will..?!" window down breezin'.., so is Pop!

Pulling up back at the grounds I look at Pop and, "Thanks for bringing the GTX."

"Of course. It's a hoot to drive," he replies.

To him, "Forgot to ask; did you get my letter?"

"When was it sent?" he asks.

"Three days ago," answer.

"Probably sitting in the mailbox;" he says --then closes, "You better get goin', Airman. Take care of yourself..."

Nodding, "Will, Pop;" and, "love you," turning away to hear behind, "Love you too."

Bookin' back to the barracks am reckoning; "How great was that..?!" but is quickly banished by a half-hour having come 'n gone, and in the nick of time, "Reporting back as ordered, Tech Sergeant!"

"Fall in," he then orders.

A week to go to graduate Basic, I receive a letter from Stan saying he is entering the Air Force Thursday, October 9th ...a week afterwards, bummer.

The 1st; day before the graduation parade ceremony, we all head back to clothing issue to have Airman stripes stitched on, including the semiformal tan uniform and formal blue's issued amid the course. Returning, man.., the barracks' a buzz with Basic ending joy!

An hour before dinner the Tech Sergeant comes up to me and says; "Airman Farrens..? ...the start of your Tech School has been setback two weeks. In the interim you will remain here and be quartered over at Temporary Hold. After the morning's ceremony and returning to change out of tan's into fatigues, go ahead straggle to lunch and afterwards report to Tech Sergeant Franklin at Temporary Hold; got it?"

I answer, "Yes, Tech Sergeant," realizing I might have a chance to see Stan!

"Wish you the best, Farrens," he closes with.

"Thank you, Tech Sergeant," reply.

Next afternoon, am entering an outer office at Temporary Hold. A secretary, male and Airman also, is at a desk. "Can I help you, Airman?" he asks.

"I am to report to Tech Sergeant Franklin," answer.

"Wait here," he says and knocks on the door behind him.., mostly entering an office with a hand remaining on the half-opened door. Stepping back out, "The Tech Sergeant will see you now, Airman."

"Airman Farrens reporting as ordered, Tech Sergeant!" in front of the desk with another African-American opposite side looking kind of like Towns, cool..!

"At ease ...Airman," he says then asks; "How was Basic?"

"Excellent, Tech Sergeant!" reply.

He returns, "Good;" then, "Tomorrow 7 a.m., having finished your breakfast by then, report to Staff Sergeant Phillips there at the mess hall for K.P. until you rotate out."

{Redact}! mindfully and obviously my expression.

"Is there a problem, Airman?" by him.

Me, "Oh awe…"

He interjects, "Well …spit it out, Farrens!"

"Awe.., no, Tech Sergeant," by me.

He responds, "Apparently there is but you're not willing to divulge. Look; there is another detail available but because of your security clearance and specialty course I went ahead and took the liberty assigning you that; but if you prefer, janitorial all the barracks with one other guy can be switched to ...but the toilets are to be spotless."

Am wondering; "What the hey did I do right to deserve such great choices..?" giving my answer, "K.P."

"Alright.., you're quartered in barracks two. Retrieve your belongings from your training barracks and settle in. You're a free straggler while here, but there ought not be a need to see you in my office again; right?" Franklin advises.

"Yes, Tech Sergeant," reply.

He, "Good. I'll flag Staff Sergeant Phillips to expect you on time. Dismissed!"

6:30 a.m., amid breakfast, from behind he's at my ear whispering; "Well.., enjoying your breakfast, Airman Farrens..? Coffee is to your likin'..?" Just wee bit squint forward slowing my bites, I remain quiet as the moron continues, "You want to be my newest assistant rather than head potty sanitizer, I'm flattered."

No one's seated close by, I am on the end. My squint the same and still silent, he circles around knuckling straight-arm onto the table facing me with a donkey rear's grin and says, "You're in a good place, Farrens..," subtly nodding and, "gonna make sure how you look and smell ...well, when the rousing lasses come sashaying through for their breakfasts.., you'll be between two other guys at the counter extending scrambled eggs scented with the fetching hand fragrance of bacon grease while properly attired in a grease stained tee shirt with hangin' dog-tags. Will supply you with plenty of bacon fryin' time. Wink at the gals going by..! And the ripe pong of garlic and onions to take home each evening, plenty of peeling time."

Staring at him am thinking, "Not such a moron after all.., sure know how to humiliate someone; no.., is still a moron. I'll get through this…"

I've been receiving military pay and a couple days later make my way over to the Commissary looking for some sort of bar soap to counter the built-up mess hall odor, but not setoff the Staff Sergeant more. I gain preferential help from a store clerk; "K.P..?" rhetorically by her.

"Yep," I still answer with a slight smile.

She says, "Believe we have just what you need..!"

"Great, thanks..!" reply to the sweet woman.

Strolling back to Temporary Hold am thinking, "If I'm still here next week, am going to try to find out if Stan arrived and able to be visited."

Monday the 13th; wow …a change of heart in Phillips? Only work up to lunchtime and after chowing, a shower and into clean fatigues, I head on over to Base Administration/Personal to see if my buddy is on Base!

To the pretty clerk …WAF Sergeant In blues, "I am due to transfer out from Temporary Hold soon and my hometown buddy might have arrived on Base last Thursday to start Basic Training. If so, I sure would like to locate him with possibly a visit."

"Wait here a minute," she replies turning from her desk for a door behind, entering an office after knocking. She returns handing me a slip of paper with his Flight location noted, "About seven in the evening is best to try for that but no guarantee you'll be allowed to see him by the rank in charge, good luck though," she kindly says.

"Thank you, Sergeant," to her.

He's quartered in the newly built two-story brick-stucco barracks and walking down his floor's hallway is like passing by rows of prison cellblock doors with peepholes.

Three good knocks on his. Moment later a Staff Sergeant steps out asking; "What do you want, Airman?" After repeating what the pretty kind WAF had suggested, "Five minutes is all you get for the visit, I'll send him out," am told.

Looking through the peephole seeing him traverse the lengthy bay, there he is twisting up from a footlocker to face the Staff Sergeant; Stan, all pinged..! But standing at attention it appears as though he is being cited the Riot Act! I turn away from the sight. Moment later the door opens and, "Hey.., buddy..!" with a big smile to the Ping with no pork chops; but he's all tense, a distant look with no smile, leaving the door cracked open. His eyes are jostling back 'n forth between it and me but mostly concerned about it. Becoming weirded out, "Hey..Stan, it's me your pal Mic', man…"

"Good to see you …Mic', but I got to get back in," he replies.

"Hey.., we got five minutes …it's cool, man..!"

His response is, "I better get back in, was good seein' you again."

Squinting …real slow nods, "Okay; was good seein' you …again, take care..," say to him looking at his back, the door closing…

Standing here quiet.., am trying to wrap my mind around our relationship; "What just happened..? What have they done to him?! He's not a whimperer at night; is he?! No.., not him."

My emotions not bringing peaceful resolve ...I whisper, "It's time to move on man.., not look back," silently leaving the cellblocks behind ...and, not to see him ever again. Three days later am gazing out the window of the packed Air Force bus heading due north on 281 to Wichita Falls.., Sheppard AFB.

> ...11 months to Johnston.

9

Technical Airman; or..?

The outstretched plains are passing.., causing my thoughts, my feelings, to transition from the cool Stan I once knew to whom all ahead might become kindred spirits given the mind-tweak attachments of the last two weeks; the window mirroring an Airman with a bit of hair parted…

Kind of funny, there had to have been others in my graduating Squadron that are entering the same electrical course but I must not have been in the right place at the right time to hear of them. If is so, such knowledge was also missed at the daylong K.P. stints, none of relationship detailed.

For sure had to have been some spread throughout all the Flights that trained up to yesterday's graduation; wonder who all riding the bus might be classmates? Now arriving at the new Squadron hearing of a newcomers' briefing in an hour, will likely find out then. But before it while all the others were being assigned quarters, I was ordered to report to the administrative NCO (Non-Commissioned Officer) in charge, just a little way's off, so to be assigned a barracks as the new "Yellow Rope" leader of its Flight, relieving the current one graduating to his permanent TDY (Tour of Duty).

Handing me the Yellow Rope to be attached atop a shoulder and circle beneath the armpit, Staff Sergeant Leverman outlines, "This time next week that barracks will mostly be cleared of its graduates with some remaining until theirs, you taking responsibility as it begins to gradually refill. In charge.., you'll form up your Flight with the others to march it to all meals, to 'n from the central gathering location for tech schools, and all other marches required. Barracks' inspections are weekly with the best one thereby awarded privileges; think you can handle it, Airman Farrens..?"

"Yes, Staff Sergeant," answer gripping the 'Rope tight.

He continues, "Good; your tech school starts Monday and is the longest in duration, nearly ten months, and you're one of three chosen out of the class to lead a Flight. In about a month the current "Red Rope" Squadron leader will be graduating and Farrens.., that position could be filled by you."

Leaving his office toting my packed duffle bag heading to the assigned abode to meetup with the current 'Rope am thinking, "What a mindblower..! Holding back from throwing hot coffee in the moron's face two weeks ago to quite possibly overseeing a Squadron..? ...only in America, only in the Air Force..!"

Twenty minutes later I meet nine other electro-whizzes that am gonna spend the next ten months with but none of residing in my barracks. It is also at the newcomers' briefing that we submit a list of seven preferred TDY's after graduating, which was foretold of at enlistment, and am weighing, "Let's see.., 1st is Norton AFB, CA ...2nd, March AFB, CA ...3rd, Myrtle Beach AFB, SC ...4th, Charleston AFB, SC ...and back again 5th, McClellan AFB in CA ...6th, Homestead AFB, FL ...and lastly again in CA, Vandenberg AFB. A pretty decent lookin' dream sheet as it is referred to."

Monday; am settling into the classroom with ten fellow students, the one more being a Staff Sergeant to become a course instructor. I am awestruck by all the light-blue colored computer lookin' machinery horseshoeing from half of the left wall around the front to half of the right. Also at the front is a same color podium having three emblems affixed; the top one is *autodin*, below it ...**DSTE,** and below it is a shield denoting SHEPPARD TECHNICAL TRAINING CENTER with a tall thin robotic **Star Man** stretching out his arms aside, and crisscross orbiting his waist are a jet plane and rocket.

The machinery is DSTE, Digital Subscriber Terminal Equipment; the specialty course number and title: 30650F, Electronic Communications and Cryptographic Equipment Systems Repairman. Ahead.., are multiple two and three-week subject segments beginning with two-week Basic Electronics.

At the end of it two weeks later, a Friday, my barracks has filled only to half and one other is about the same with their new Yellow Rope, a second start 30650F set to begin his first segment with nine others Monday trailing our class moving on to its second. There'll be one more student joining his group. Somewhere between Ohm's Law and Joule's for DC (Direct Current) circuits, I short-circuited into numbskull mode and got lost..!

An hour prior to letting out for the weekend, textbook prepping for the second segment, I am called out of the class for a sit-down with --or rather a dress-down by-- Training Center Brass, a First Lieutenant waiting for me in a small conference room. "Take a seat, Airman Farrens," he orders. Subtly parking myself he continues, "You flunked the first segment test, the only one to. I don't mean barely flunked it, but big time. Good grief, Farrens.., how'd you end up in that specialty field, dumb luck..?!"

I don't know what he is seeing but my face has the feeling of going AWOL! All I can do is just sit here quiet for he took the words right out of my mouth gawking at him all dumbfounded. Don't want to tell him that I guessed at all the multiple choice electronics questions on the pre-enlistment aptitude test.

After grinnin' and shaking his head awhile, he gets serious and lays it out, "Okay, Airman Farrens.., here are your new career choices for at least the remainder of your enlistment. Either get your act together in the 30650F specialty restarting with the next first segment class, learn the equipment and pass all tests with flying colors ...or you can be a lifer mess hall chef's assistant; which is it, Airman..?"

It's crashin' in on me, "{Redact}..! ...would work for more Staff Sergeants like at Hell's Kitchen, peeling garlic and onions..?! Not supposed to be looking back..!" I answer, "I'll get my act together, Sir!"

After squintin' and nodding some, he says, "Monday morning, restart with the second class. That's all.., dismissed!"

"Thank you, Sir," about facin' and getting out the door as fast as a worm can...

Man.., do I pick up on the DC jive and two weeks later top the class on the test, and it won't be the only time. Whisper to myself, "This {redact} is easy!" The second segment of study appears a no-brainer also.

The Monday following acing its Friday test, after marching the troops back from dinner, I am called into Staff Sergeant Leverman's office who has stayed over to see me, "Aut..ohh..!"

He commences, "Farrens.., I was apprised of your change in school and why. Am also aware of your outstanding turnabout, good for you. But that's not the main reason for calling you in. Because your barracks is not quite two-thirds full, I'm going to disperse the Flight amongst the others with you joining up with Cranston in your class, topping off his barracks which is currently three-quarters full with some of your guys. Although your inspections have been above average, the last two being his first two have been the best ...so of course, he is still Flight charge with you backing him up. I know the guys moving over with you have some allegiance to you so they need to adjust right along with. Except for the Red being in with a Yellow, no other Flight has two Ropes. You're keeping yours for three reasons; to give him well deserved relief at times because of best inspections, the other two are due to three weeks' time-in-grade (rank) over him but more so by what you did. When the going gets tough, the tough get going! You did that."

"Thank you, Staff Sergeant," reply with a slight squint and nod.

"For sure, Farrens;" and he goes on, "You also will be available to march other Flights when necessary but you're not a boy going about asking if that's needed, or at the whims of other Ropes, just available. Otherwise.., you're a free straggler for the rest of your days here; any questions..?"

"No, Staff Sergeant ...thank you," I reply.

He nods with an affirming grin knowing that I want to let out a cheer --then, "Dismissed!"

All of the eight barracks are old style wooden just like our Squadron in Basic, but these have two floors with each having four quad-rooms lining both sides of the hallway and one to two bunks for Ropes in the front upstairs room over the latrine/showers, sixty-six guys topping off. Approaching 'Rope Cranston's room after my Flight had cleared out, am hearing at low volume, "Easy to be hard," coming from some music device.

Out of courtesy I tap on the doorjamb waiting to hear his voice to enter, or if not after a few seconds will do so anyway; but, "Enter," is heard.

"Cranston, I presume..?" by me.

He nods and, "Farrens, I suspect," relaxing on a bunk with his back upright against the wall.

"Yep.., classmate," breaking into mellow laughter.

He is sliding into also --then, "Welcome to my barracks..!"

"Wow..," chuckling a back-in-your-face response adding, "so I've heard…"

"This is my show.., gonna keep it first class..!" he remarks.

Slowly reducin' to a snort-gurn grin nodding …am thinking, "Jeezz… Cranston, you're not an Airman First Class yet," and replying, "Well okay.., sir..dude.., call on me when it starts becoming second class.., I'll be around."

If over the next eight months I march Fights thirty times, that'll be an exaggerated figure, but not going to allow myself to become bored. Will stop and chat with whomever I can as often as I can, laughing away..! …and stroll wherever, saluting the Brass occasionally. The thing is.., there are Vietnamese guys crossing my path that are all decked out with metallic ornaments; have not seen a one dressed in fighting duds …so, I salute anyway even though they might be grunts like me, good practice. Don't want to mess up this good thing going, got to keep doing what's been done in class.

I did not make Red Rope but George Skaggs in our class did; a tall thin redhead plastered with freckles yielding from the hollers of Kentucky, Red on red. The dude's always smiling, nothing bothers him.

With another month in the books, we're allowed to have our own cars on Base, but I recently received a letter from Pop with a photo enclosed showing him leaning up against his new Chevy pickup with a cabover camper on it that he lives out of; was given permission to park as his home base in a Gardena casino's lot so long as he gambles daily. Bad memories of the backseat of Mom's car. The GTX and Rambler station wagon were traded in. Am not interested in anything to drive other than the GTX.

Skaggs bought in town this big 'ol beat up '65 Olds 88 4-door V8, a real smoker but hauls when gunned.., and on a Saturday he and I take out headin' north crossing the Oklahoma border bending west towards Chattanooga cruising along the vast buffalo plains with windows' down, elbows' on the sills, and man.., herds of buffalo all over not far off the highway! "Bet you can't get within a hundred feet of one," he challenges me.

"Pullover," I return.

There are about a dozen grazin' some two hundred feet afar as the brakes screech the 88 to a halt. One big 'ol bison is split off nearer to the road and is eyeing me as I meander closer to it. My steps are becoming measured foot in front of the other because that beast is not moving its head, pinned on me.

Oh so slowly.., "Think I've made it to a hundred feet," when {REDACT...}, it's chargin'..!!! ...mad dashin' to the car but about three-quarters to it, Skaggs hits the gas kicking up roadside dirt..!!! Running so fast I'm bent back from hips up not wanting to look-see behind..!!! "Stop, you hillbilly..!!!" yell.

He does hearing him laughing, but as I'm about to get ahold of the doorhandle, again he darts away laughing his head off..!! "Gonna kill you, Skaggs.., stop..!!!" from the top of my lungs.

About forty paces down the road finally does for good! He's a laughin' 'n laughin' as I'm pounding on his shoulder! He laughs out, "You won but we didn't say how much the bet!"

I burst into laughter with him as he floors it leaving the 'ol bull in the dust; then calming I remark, "Figured you're a man of honor, left the amount to you if I survived..?! {Redact}.., that was rowdy!" shaking my head.

"Lunch is on me," he replies calming but we both with residual chuckling.

"It's good wearing civvies and not unload in them while being chased by half-ton of hoofs," I reckon and again we bursting into laughter.., elbows' on the sills breezin' leveling off cruisin' speed with straight pavement ahead and plains of buffalo still on both sides not far off…

One of the guys in class is married and his wife rented a single level one-bedroom apartment in town to be with him through tech school but like the rest of us, he must be in nightly for bed check. A weekend though does not go by without us having a cookout there mellowed by some brew. Located a rural liquor store that doesn't card us.

The end of July and well into enjoying the days of summer with a month remaining 'til graduation, I hookup with three others in the Squadron, one with a car, for a Friday late evening outing. We locate a dive on the outskirts of Wichita Falls to chillout. The place is crowded but we commandeer a table as it's being vacated.

The loud country western music coming from the juke is good and the skimpy cowgirl dressed waitresses …woa, the lungs! And Texas gals on 'n off the dancefloor..? …easy on the eyes, real easy..! Only four months after turning nineteen and not carded, am having a good 'ol time tipping up bottoms of longnecks gazing at them all...

"Hey.., checkout the two brunettes at that table!" one of the guys says, acknowledged by us other three. "Let's hookup with them!" he adds.

"There are only two of them," I remark adding, "and we only have an hour and a half 'til bed check."

"Plenty of time for a prior bed check with the one on the left, you three fight it out over the other!" by him.

"Okay.., do your thing but we're on the road to the Base by 9:30; got it?" I enact.

"Hey, I got the key to the wheels," he trying me.

"And I have two stripes, don't recall seeing anyone else here that does," simplifying things. Was promoted shortly after my birthday.

"Okay, 9:30 ...no sweat," he replies, then heads on over to their table. Few minutes later they are joining us.

For the next half-hour we're a partyin' mostly wearing out the other one by us other three alternating turns on the dancefloor while he's making his move. Then, when the ladies go to powder their noses, "We're gonna follow them to Cassie's place!" he exhorts.

One of the other guys says, "Look, man.., time's getting tight, just get her phone number for a later date."

"No, man.., I'm in bed with her!" the yearning one proclaims.

I respond, "You want it to happen, give me the key," staring him down, the other two as well. He hands it over.

Twenty minutes later we're all stepping into her one-bedroom squatter's flat without any refreshments. The one that the three of us shared dances with is fairly blitzed and tired, lays over stretching out on the upholstered sofa as the couple head into the bedroom. We three guys find chairs to park, gawking at the one passing out seven feet away facing us resting her head on a curled up left arm, the right one straight along her topside hip.

Sunshine is lookin' quite pretty.., soft white skin, rich dark shoulder length hair and passionately shaped in her white button down blouse and denim jeans, sensuously bare feet with toenails painted the same color as her hair and matching fingernails. She looks so sumptuously peaceful with her eyes closed ...because of her knockers! ...tryin' to bust out with every slow inhale..!! So plump, the cleavage, one breast resting heavy upon the other!!!

Waitin' ...waitin' with, "Whole lotta love," invading my mind and thinking; "We got to endure this trying to dismiss what's going on the other side of the bedroom door..?! God.., I have to have what's in front of me..! The other two can sit here all stoic but not Mic'..!!"

Subtly slip out of the chair stealthily closin' --then stop looking down at her wondering; "Where do I start with the whims of rushed affections for Amanda and Roni a recall fueling to engage her..? ...a rise having begun. But a half-hour won't allow for anything other than manhandle her ...and, this conversely isn't the atmosphere to exaltingly get to know the one who danced her heart out with us three. What is happening to me..?" turning to head out the front door, the rise lowering. "Hopefully the other two guys are in the same frame of mind." Five minutes later one steps out, and after five more so does the other. "We'll give him five minutes to propose to Cassie," I state.

Time having passed, I quietly enter back in and gingerly wake Sunshine so she won't be startled awake by what I'm about to do. Brashly knocking on the bedroom door, "Zip it up, we're out of here in a minute with or without you..!" loudly deliver.

As I am turning over the engine, the straggler is stumbling out the front door clumsily tryin' to get his shoes slipped on. All we hear heading back to the Base is how neat a soulmate she's gonna be 'til he rotates out! Great guy. Sitting on the edge of my bunk slipping the shoes off I muse, "Got close but still undefiled."

The last Thursday in August of '70, "Okay troop …big smiles," the Photographer says to the posed twelve of us and the General Dynamics Instructor surrounding the podium with DSTE the backdrop. In the graduation shot is the husky handsome one standing top left.

Of course the Air Force has the sequence down pat, handing tech school completion certificates to abundantly happy semi-professionals before receiving the marching Orders to our first, maybe only, TDY's. In a few minutes we will lay hold of them. The anticipation; "Which place from my dream sheet?!"

Gathering in a nearby unfurnished room with Staff Sergeant Leverman who was already here and holding a cluster of envelopes, he says, "Here they are, men..!" and begins calling out our names. A few ahead of me having opened theirs react contrastingly, two letting out ecstatic vibes while one somberly stares at his unfolded sheet. Then.., "Farrens," is heard and the secured mystery Order is extended..! Out of the envelope expanding my first, maybe only, assignment I see, "Johnston Atoll," quickly wondering; "What is a Johnston Atoll..? ...and where is It?!"

All are jubilant except for two more. We muted four aside, some will see England, Japan, and Thailand, a sky high one to Hawaii with the remainder staying Stateside. Us four..? ...one headin' to Alaska, two to Vietnam; and me to what and where..?!!

I'm asked by one of the joyous; "Where're you headin', Farrens..?!"

"Johnston Atoll..," I answer.

Instantly another of the happy is laughing in my face; "Oh no.., Johnston Atoll..?! I've heard of that place! ...a coral speck out in the ocean! Hundreds of guys but no women there! Don't drop your soap in the shower!! Arrive a King.., leave a Queen..!!!"

Two weeks leave coming to all and consensus is, "Can't wait to get home to family!" "<u>Don't it make you want to go home,</u>" a motivation to be heading that way for some rest, but as I'm stragglin' back to the barracks my TDY weighs heavy, appraising; "What home is there for me to return to..? Pop had written that he'll put me up in a motel close to the poker club and provide a rental car. God, that's home..?!"

The next morning am on a bus to Los Angeles, an eleven-hour trip. At Its Terminal, "Welcome home, Mic'!" by Pop with a quick hug.

"Thanks, Pop, a sunny day..," back to him bushed.

"Good to see you," he adds.

"Same to you," I reply.

Outside in the back parking lot, "Well.., my home on wheels..!" approaching ten feet to his camper.

"Cool.., Pop," with a smile.

"Take you on a tour," he offers with a big smile. We enter a side door and, "Have a seat, take a load off," as he is stashing my duffle bag up on the cabover bed. Then opens all the curtains parking himself on the short, cushioned, bench-seat across the tiny dining table from me. Striving with all the things heard-said by my classmates about their homes, "Guess this is mine..," goes without saying.

He asks; "How was tech school?"

"Decent," I answer.

"Taught you a trade..?" rhetorically by him but I still nod yes.

"So, where you headin' from here?" he asks.

I respond; "Have you ever heard of Johnston Atoll?"

"No.., haven't; where is It?" by him.

Answer, "Not quite sure …but somewhere on the equator in the Pacific I've been told."

He, "All the years after the war being a Merchant Marine circling the globe and never heard of it; a new base?"

Me, "Don't know, haven't heard."

"For how long..?" he asks.

"Understand it to be a year," reply.

"Oh;" he reacts diverging, "Shortly after my visit with you in Basic, a couple of Secret Service Agents came around asking a load of questions about you, me, others and the things you did while growing up. They said it was just a background check for a security clearance."

I acknowledge, "Got a Top Secret Security Clearance."

"That's good, a feather in your hat," he remarks --then; "Hungry?"

"Yep, but something lite, the bus ride has left me a bit fatigued," answering him goin' on 8 p.m. but still daylight.

"Okay, then to the motel. We'll rent you a car in the morning," he concludes and I nod.

The Gardena Inn is where I'm put up and man.., the sounds of prostitution comin' through the wall for the next thirteen nights will taunt me to seek out that action because of what lies ahead. To purchase a lady of the night before the experience of being Alcatraz buttonholed, for sure seems the lesser of two evils becoming defiled.

The next morning am driving a Dodge Dart, miss the GTX but this gets me around, especially to the beaches where I bodysurf the waves, stroll the lengths weaving between sunbathing babes on beach towels and along the boardwalks eyeing bikini clad breasts and bottoms wishing for a night before girlfriend to send me off.

I spend a lot of time with Pop at the Four Queens Poker Club in Gardena, in his camper playing chess which he beats me at every time. We often eat in the Club's restaurant, their patty melts a favorite. Not allowed to go into the casino not being 21, probably for the best.

With Stan in the past, don't feel like searching out the rest of the gang but maybe I'll stop by Archie's..! Decide to wait until 5 p.m. so to catch Gil at Scottsdale's entrance, but pulling up to its hut there's another guard who tells me that he's moved on. Slowly rolling towards Archie's lane I pass by Kaylee's thinking how grand it would be for her to be the girlfriend sending me off to Johnston Atoll.

Mrs. Rollins at the front door, "Archie just started his Sophomore year back at Cal State Fullerton;" she says adding, "I will let him know that you stopped by."

"Thank you, Mrs. Rollins," to her and.., the last time to enter Scottsdale. How a year changes things, three of my best buddies withdrawn.

Now a Wednesday, the day before bussing north to Travis Air Force Base to process back in, I'm standing over Tina's grave, also for the last time. Later, the rented car returned and entering the motel room as Pop heads out of the parking lot, am having to accept, "Well.., the last night here and once more not gonna find myself lying with a woman; the purity of Kaylee at work, or a higher power..?" Early next morning having breakfast with Pop; "Sure you're gonna make the 4 p.m. reporting time?" he asks from across the café table.

"Yep; Greyhound from here to San Francisco to Fairfield, then Travis main gate at 3:15..," answer.

"Got your tickets on you?" he asks.

Nod acknowledging.

"Lots of good sights if it travels up the coast," he comments.

"I didn't think to check the route but if not, more sleep time to Frisco," I remark.

"You're okay moneywise..?" he asks.

Back to him, "Drew from the bank three hundred dollars." He's aware that over the last twelve months I had saved up nine hundred dollars from military pay, also that he is named the beneficiary on my Bank of America checking account.

He brings up, "I still got the hundred bucks you left me when you went in; do you want it to add to the three hundred..?"

"No, it's yours.., but I have a favor to ask of you," in response.

"Go ahead," he replies.

"I don't know how things are gonna go at Johnston but probably won't need most of my pay out there. Would you be willing to send me a hundred bucks each month so I can have my entire paycheck go directly to the bank? Will pay you back with interest when I return," propose to him.

"Yes …but without interest, just let me know as soon as you can your mailing address for there," he returns.

"I should have a paycheck waiting at Travis but will try to have it deposited," conclude with him nodding a few times. Throughout the conversation I couldn't find myself confessing the fear that's grown during leave about Johnston but think it might have been showing…

Just before going into the bus terminal is the same between us as was at the Recruiting Station.

Man.., the bus is right on time, pulling off into a turnaround in front of the Base's main gate with several antiwar protestors lining each side of the road. The MP Sergeant posted directs me to Deployment and Mobilization to process back in. The NCO Clerk there scans my Orders, "Johnston Atoll;" he says with a neutral look …then, "Gonna get you out quick so you can enjoy weekend downtime in Hawaii."

Having not known that It is a stop-off on the way, "Thanks, Sergeant!"

"No sweat, Airman First Class. There's a C-141 leaving at nine in the morning for Hickam that I'll hop you on. Plenty of time to down a big breakfast. It's a six-hour flight arriving about noon their time. You'll quarter overnight here in transient housing;" handing me a key with an attached tag showing building and room number …then, "Here is the flightline gate number," writing on a slip of paper …continuing, "and a Base map where they're located," pointing them out …adding, "the mess hall is here. Although you're off duty 'til Johnston, wear your fatigues from here to in-processing at Hickam; clear so far..?"

"Yes, Sergeant," answer.

He informs, "I'm seeing backpay available to you."

"Thought so, Sergeant. I'd like to have it deposited in my bank account as well as entire future pay," request.

He suggests, "You might want some pocket money out there."

"Pop's gonna send some each month," reply. A few minutes later the pay transfer arrangement is completed.

Lastly, he says, "FYI, there will be Army onboard to Nam. Conversation might not fit in with yours but maybe so due to the nature of JA. Good luck, Farrens."

Somberly I return, "Thanks..," and turnabout wonderin'; "What the inferno did he mean by that..?!" adding to my fear…

Making my way to transient housing I stall to browse the map for the possibility of a Chaplin going on 4 p.m. There's a location denoted not too far away. Approaching it the building is like all others, not Church looking but has a posting over the door reading, "Base Chapel." I step into a front office where a WAF Sergeant greets me; "May I help you?"

"Yes. If not too late, I would like to visit briefly with a Chaplin," answer her.

Just then a tall thin African-American Captain in tans enters from an adjacent door apparently heading home, I coming to attention! "As you were," he says to me.

"Chaplin.., Airman First Class Farrens just walked in asking to visit briefly with you if not too late," she conveys to him looking at her.

Turning back to me, he smiles and says, "Certainly.., follow me." In his office standing he extends a hand, "I am Chaplin Malone," with a welcoming voice.

Grasping it, "Pleased to meet you, Sir," I reply.

"And to you as well..," as he rounds a large desk adding, "please have a seat."

"Thank you, Sir," taking one of two across from him.

He having seated; "Now, what can I do for you..?"

"Well, Sir..." --quickly he interjects, "Chaplin."

"Chaplin.., I'm on the way to a place that has me really scared," tryin' not to lose it.

"Vietnam?" he asks.

"No, Johnston Atoll," answer and pausing as he slightly gestures as if he doesn't know of it, then, "and I've heard something troubling about it," my eyes beginning to whelp.

"What thing..?" by him.

"Guys' getting sexually assaulted," the flood gates openin' dipping my head, two weeks of escalated fear draining. A few seconds of silence ...then notice a box of Kleenex being slid to me.

As I draw one from it; "Brother Farrens, who did you hear that from..?"

Answer, "A tech school classmate when receiving my Orders at graduation;" sobbing like a wimp ...adding, "I can defend myself against one but not the many."

At a mellowing pace, "Look.., sadly there are times when someone alleges something not knowing firsthand if true, don't take it to heart. We must not let evil have a place to impede the grace, the mercy, of God ...nor diminish the work He has given us. Haven't been to Johnston Atoll so I cannot tell you what to expect from others; but to be predisposed with ill-fated thoughts..? ...doesn't serve you," he counsels.

I raise my head squinting soakin' in his words as my eyes begin to dry.

He continues, "Maybe it has happened, maybe not ...but you must not proceed there crippled by fear without fact, evidence! I want to share a Bible verse so to strengthen you to cope. From Ephesians 3:16 ...That he would grant you, according to the riches of his glory, to be strengthened with might by his spirit in the inner man."

In return taking a deep breath, "Thank you, Chaplin."

He asks; "Do you go there nonstop from here?"

"No, there's a weekend layover in Hawaii," answer.

"Great..! I suggest though.., that instead of rigorous pleasure events, rent a car and gradually tour the Island ...possibly all the way around," by him.

My eyes broadening ...nod in agreement.

"These are perilous times, brother. More so than not, finding peace within comes by those slowing moments to realize God's love for us. I want to end in prayer that those moments will be afforded you," he concludes.

Following the prayer, "Thank you, Chaplin Malone, believe I can make it now."

By him, "You're welcome, brother Farrens..."

Friday, September 11th, the C-141 touches down noon at Hickam AFB, Honolulu. There were no windows on the transport to view what could have been beautiful sky and ocean mellowing along the way ...so, slept most the trip as others did rather than focusing on interior walls or the pallets of combat supplies filling the back half.

I offload with half-dozen Air Force and about three dozen Army, process in like at Travis. As before am provided temporary single occupancy quarters being relieved of duty until Monday and again, can be in civvies. Can go anywhere I wish and stay out as long as I wish, but be on that flight in tans to Johnston Atoll Monday 8 a.m.!

What's different is I'm handed commercial airline tickets for Aloha Airlines out of Honolulu International to the Marshall Islands, Guam and circling back through Samoa but first touching down at Johnston eight hundred miles southwest, a weekly commercial stop-off. Was told I could have been put on one of the daily windowless C-141's for the following day but the Clerk having had a good week wanted me to go in style..! Am thinkin'; "You know..? ...these process-in Clerks are real decent guys, a weekend vacation here.., then a commercial flight out with Stewardesses..! ...the last time to see babes for quite a while...

Settle in and going on 2:30 am in civvies strolling around the Base making my way towards the ocean. The place is beautiful.., eventually coming upon Mamala Bay Drive and crossing it, pass by an outrigger restaurant with a large outdoor pavilion that looks out to Hickam's own beach. Am quite hungry but think I'll trek back to the front of the Base, turn towards Honolulu and stop off at the first fast-food restaurant I come to.

After chowing decide to rent a car. I drive all around Honolulu seeing Diamond Head not far off going for Waikiki in between. So much to see but as I begin to grow tired, also begin to recall Chaplin Malone's advice.., so I start back for the Base to get a good night's rest for an early morning takeout to circle the Island.

Starting out clockwise, zigzag highways and roads trying to hug the coast while not in a hurry to get anywhere. As the mountains begin closing in on the right, connect with a seaside highway that'll guide me all the way around. The little villages dotting the coast but man.., it's the waves, what breakers..! And in the real.., the celebrated Banzai Pipeline just south of Sunset Beach stomping the pictures and videos of it! Nothin' like seeing the massive curls, them breaking, and hearing it all, feeling the breeze, firsthand up close..! Introspectively, "It's good to be alive, living the dream…"

It took 'til dark to tour Oahu, sampling several times along the way tidbits of Polynesian cuisine. The palm trees for as far as you can see swayin' in the breeze, and a pineapple dish on every menu not to mention tan bikini dishes gracing the sands..! "Awe …to live a beachcomber's life," whisper...

I return the rental and make my way back to the Base. Tomorrow am gonna bodysurf and tan a little, walk through some of the swanky high-rise hotels blanketing the hillside overlooking Honolulu, and end my vacation relaxing over dinner at the outrigger restaurant that views Hickam's beach, the surf and horizon sunset. Good thing I withdrew three hundred from checking..!

Sunday evening after a full day am sitting at a lengthy parklike bench-table in the restaurant's outdoor pavilion as the sun's near set, gazing the menu. The table had appeared to be full of patrons but I was welcomed to fit in with one side of them nestling open a gap. The friendly ambience, cordial conversations. "What will you have..?" the pretty Hawaiian Waitress asks.

Trying to decide, "Hmm.., the Pacific Salad pictured looks really good, so does the Island Style Shrimp! Wonder if I can down both?" comically suggesting.

"You can take leftovers home," she remarks.

"Okay, both..," I order.

The folks surrounding, also feasting, are grinning and one fellow says, "Sounds like you can't go wrong..!"

Nodding with a smile I reply, "Ending an active day, saved room for this to remember."

Oh man.., it's really good..! Start out fast, then some twenty minutes later am slowing for a mid-break with so much left. The sunset was great and talk turns to me, eventually asking where I'm heading from here..?

"Johnston Atoll," answering. Responses are likened to Pop and the Chaplin, not heard of it.

As those around gradually depart bidding me fond farewell, I gingerly continue to graze, eventually seemingly spaced in solitude enjoying the feel of the subtle saltwater breeze, "All is well," mindfully.

Then a fellow having lagged behind the others, seated a ways down the table but apparently in ear-sound length, has risen from his fill and closing to pass by me the other side of the table --then stops and turns to me owning an eerie grin, "Just left there.., headin' home. Hope you survive unscathed, but probably won't," he imparts, turns and walks on leaving me wonderin'; "What the inferno..?!!"

…Half-day to Johnston.

10

Can use a beer if old enough.

Gazing out am believing that… that guy is firsthand evidence of the violation ahead.., but I'm not goin' AWOL. The fear is now as before but I must continue to rest to realize God's love for me. Won't try for a beer though wanting one …or two.

Moseyin' back to transient quarters, I'm trying to gather some memories to muster up courage but find myself in no-man's land surmising, "Joined the military to defend the Country from foreign foes but; gonna have to defend myself from my Country men..?" The night goes by without finding sleep, in no-man's land…

8:05 a.m., Monday, September 14th, 1970 …taxying. The Boeing 737 is virtually full of Hawaiian men, women and a few children. Looks to be a half-dozen Caucasians aboard including myself, but the only one in uniform. The four Stewardesses are lovely lookin', a Caucasian and the other three appearing Hawaiian, but am unable to connect with their charm having stared at the ceiling throughout the night, so just close my eyes hoping for some sleep.

Rolling to the start of the runway, the Captain comes on the speakers outlining the stops and flight times. First, Johnston Atoll in two and a half hours. Am in a window seat, right-side near the back.

Thoughts have finally fatigued me enough to go a bit deep into sleep giving it up that I'll worry when the time comes.., then fight. Probably a couple of hours have gone by and beginning to sense a gradual descent just as the Captain again on the speakers announces such.

Am slowly cracking the eyes open blurrily lookin' both ways out the portals but only see ocean. Shut them for ten minutes more, then open blurrily again …drifting my gaze to the right and through the portal; "What is it I'm seein' a mile out..?!

A tiny rectangle flattop floating on the water with a thick black line running the middle of its length!!
Exiled..!!!"

Passing by circling clockwise, once more the Captain comes on, "Ladies and gentlemen, we're starting our final approach to Johnston Atoll. Please return to your seats and remain in them until again reaching cruising altitude. This'll be a ten minute stop 'n go for those deplaning, touchdown in ten minutes. If this is your destination, the crew of Aloha Airlines thanks you for choosing to fly with us and we hope to see you again soon."

Slowly steadily nodding; "Ten-minute stop 'n go..? …figures..."

Exiting the turn for landing, I lose sight of it …but now lowering to about ten feet above the water, ripples are shooting by..! …then a flash of dry white surface aside the edge of black runway and a quick drop, jolt contact, rapid momentum-lean forward as turbines go full reversal joined by on 'n off hard braking..!! …abrupt worry; "How much runway's left?!! …goin' off into the water?!!!"

Maybe two football field's length to this side of water's edge with what looks like a frontage road running along it as we near coming to a stop at the Atoll's corner, even intervals of hard braking all during touchdown. Might've been more distance to water's edge but not totally comprehended with the tumult back 'n forth leaning.

Now entering a tight U-turn and to midway through… the same distance to water, but coming out… the Atoll is opening up with this four to five-story, all concrete beige, building nearby dominating the view. Square.., it has large corrugated sidewalls with no windows.

Again the Captain, "For those deplaning, welcome to Johnston Atoll. Its 10:22 a.m. local time and a sunny eighty-five degrees with light winds out of the northeast. About two minutes after coming to a stop, your baggage will be placed at the base of the stairs. Again, thank you for flying with us today and we hope your stay here is a pleasant one."

Entered the view when he began his greeting was the start some hundred feet away paralleling of a string of connected single-story shack-like buildings with much taller multistory dorm-like concrete ones backdropping, some tight gaps will begin to appear.

Then not far along is the onset of a slew of all white guys growing to what looks like a hundred plus.., congregating mostly in front of what looks like the Terminal just behind the not so tall Control Tower. Nearly all are in some variation of uniform; most in baseball caps, short-sleeve fatigue shirts and cutoff fatigue pants, white socks and tennis shoes. Some are dressed similar in civvies tee shirts and shorts, some without caps.

They're all staring our way cheering, waving their arms as we pass by a couple of plane lengths --then U-turn again and halt in front of them, looking across through the left side portals. "{Redact}.., they're not all out to welcome me ..are they?!" troubled…

Stepping into the aisle am noticing four Hawaiian guys ten rows up entering it as the side door is being opened by a Stewardesses who then retreats like the other three to make room to pass. As the first exits, the crowd goes motionless and quiet; "Maybe because there're no Hawaiians out there..?!" nervously supposin'.

Too soon comes my turn, clearing the door seeing nothing but a hundred or so grim faces looking at me. A pathway has been made for the four ahead as I lift my duffle bag lagging a bit.

Closing in on it; "What's going on? None are lookin' at me but focused beyond..!" bewildered. Entering it am still ignored --then, there's a sudden roar of cheers and raising of arms..!! Quickly I turnabout to see the four Stewardesses trading off at the top of the stairs with joyful smiles waving..!! ...and as they tightly join for a finally, I turn again and go on to enter the Terminal.

Though the sign over the door denoted, "Detachment 1, 15 Air Base Wing," apparently for Johnston, the process-in NCO behind a desk looking at my Orders voices, "Detachment 1, 1957 Communications Group, you're in the right place," with a donkey rear's grin. Despite that, am quite relieved that the mob outside was interested in the ladies, now disbursing filin' past a window facing the Atoll's interior as turbines rev to taxi.

He gets on the phone; "Staff Sergeant Leland..? Airman First Class Farrens has arrived;" pausing ...then, "Will do..," he ends hanging it up saying to me, "That was your Supervisor. He'll meetup with you in a half-hour. That door leads out to the main drag and directly across are three four-story dormitories. Wait in the bottom lounge of the one farthest to the right;" he orders and then, "Welcome to the Rock," returning to his former grin. That was to be my incoming briefing.

"Okay, thanks ...Sergeant," with a drawn out nod, bland facial.

Out the door turning right; "Where did everyone go..?" mindfully. Passing a small gymnasium then a mess hall, I look back left for approaching vehicles and seeing none cross the road at the first dorm passing it and the second ...then, down a sidewalk between it and the third.

Midway on the right is a door that I pass through into a brief hallway with a stairwell dead ahead and openings on both sides, coming to see that the one on the left accesses a hall, and to the right the lounge apparently...

Like was so quickly along the road, no one else is in here. Windows run both sides of the large room, light gleaming in. There're several black vinyl lounging chairs sporadically spaced, ease back into one facing opposite of where I entered.

Impacted by a comatose brain, am stoically peering straight but not comprehending anything other than the deadening silence ...except though, there is an echo revibrating within the sphere attached to my shoulders; "What is this place..? ...what am I doing here..? Can't grasp.., can't grasp.., numb..," with no notion of time passing.

Then suddenly I'm jolted out of my disbelief stupor; "Airman First Class Farrens..?!" by a Staff Sergeant passing my right from behind and turning to face me as I in no-man's land utter; "Yes..?" lookin' up at him.

He is wearing a light-green cap, short-sleeve fatigue shirt with E5 stripes, knee-high cutoff fatigue pants, white socks and tennis shoes. Introduces himself, "I'm Staff Sergeant Leland, sorry for the wait," with a brisk but disarming delivery extending a hand.

"That's okay, Staff Sergeant Leland," return likewise rising to shake it.

He remarks, "Except when Brass is present, call me Serg for short and I'll call you Farrens, real informal out here."

I nod agreeing as we turn for the doorway.

"Glad you are finally here," he says smiling, I continuing to nod with the beginnings of a smile as he adds, "I've been here for three and a half months, and DSTE installed two months ago. I'm a KW-7, KG-13

Crypto and Teletype maintenance guy; DSTE..? ...hands off for me although placed under my care. Its General Dynamics Engineer was here the first two weeks of installation, gone a month, then back for a week and abandoning me two weeks ago."

I join in, "We were taught pc-board-swap repairs for those Crypto machines as is mostly for DSTE."

"Of course it makes sense that one of the walls in our office is adorned to the ceiling with printed circuit boards!" he remarks, we breaking into light laughter. Then, "I am on an hour lunch break. ...Hungry?!"

"Sure am," answer.

"Good ...let's get your stuff over to your temporary quarters, then head to the mess hall. About mid-afternoon tomorrow your permanent quarters should be available. We'll get a call when so," he outlines.

A brisk nod by me.

Passing the two dorms I did before, we diagonally cross the road and continue up beyond the Terminal and a Post Office ending the string of buildings. A left see-thru of about fifty feet reveals the flightline. It is the wide blacktop runway that I saw from the air running the length slicing this place in half. Quite surprisingly, we are walking by an outdoor theater! Scanning ahead mostly to the right, all the terrain between anything manmade looks lifeless.., just super fine bleached sand; no grass, trees or shrubs in sight.

Next on the left is a short-length single-story building, motel looking with two doors, and near abutting its other end begins two rows of multiple two-story apartment style buildings, one row adjacent the road with the other being aligned with this short one nearer the flightline.

Going no farther than the first door, the Serg unlocks it and we enter a fairly decent, clean, studio type room with bathroom, a tiny frig and two-burner hotplate. I plop my duffle down beside the full-size bed and he hands me the key saying, "Welcome to JA," and nods to the door.

Heading back towards the mess hall he asks; "Where do you call home..?"

"Los Angeles," answer and in return ask; "And you, Serg..?"

"Boise," he replies.

I nod approving; don't know why..? ...just do.

Passing the Post Office again, he tells me our mailing address.

Entering the mess reveals a half-dozen rows of tables seating what looks like twenty each. A typical style buffet counter but; "You got to be kiddin' me..?!" mindfully. One after another.., hamburgers, cheeseburgers, hotdogs, fries, hefty subs and chips..! Condiment bar with whole leaf's of lettuce, tomatoes, onions and pickles..! The fruit and salad bar.., several items ...bookoo dressings..! And the desserts.., cookies, cakes and pies..! An ice cream machine.., vanilla, chocolate and strawberry with syrups and toppings to draw from..! This mess puts Lackland, Sheppard and even Travis's to shame, no wonder the crowd's gulping it down..!!

Can't help but to lag behind the Serg. I squeeze in a spot across the table from him. The guy next to me grinning asks; "Sure you filled your plates enough..?!" rhetorically.

Answer anyway a bit cocky, "Believe so.., maybe could have piled on more but didn't want to waste."

Between gulps the Serg tells me that here it's all you can eat.

Again the guy next to me, remarks, "Each evening is a different ethnic theme, tonight is Americana, the steaks..! Not gonna describe tomorrow's Italian, or the breakfasts every morning..! …got to see for yourself." He continues, "All nonmilitary functions are contracted out to a Firm called Holmes and Narver, providing such as the professional chefs. Nearly six hundred skilled civilians, virtually Hawaiians, are employed out here. There is a tailor to get your fatigue pants cut into shorts but leave one full length. Also, a fairly sizeable BX (Commissary) to buy white socks and tennis shoes if didn't bring along."

Gesture that I hadn't.

Another fellow weighs in, "You'll need to be careful not to get scraped. The ground is coral-sand mix and coral in the wound will begin to grow."

"If you do, get over to the dispensary to be flushed out," the Serg advises.

Nod acknowledging, then I ask; "How many of us are out here …military?"

He answers, "Around four hundred, all Air Force …well, except for one."

Grinnin' I ask; "Why's that?"

He replies, "He's Coast Guard maintainin' the transmitter on Sand Island across the channel."

Chewing a wad of fries I'm rationalizin', "Thousand total on this speck!" and then swallowing ask; "Where does everyone sleep?"

He, "There is enough housing spread throughout, mainly the northeast quarter;" pausing and then says, "Take your time and enjoy lunch but I have to get back to work. If you want, stroll around the place. I'll knock on your door at 7 a.m., get plenty of rest." The Serg is about 5'10", slender at maybe 170 lbs.; has brown hair protruding from beneath his cap, brown eyes and overall exudes a country demeanor; looks to be about twenty-eight years old. He rises and then pauses, gives me directions to the tailor shop and BX.

Back to him, "Thanks, Serg. Think I'll visit them before dinner."

As others leave out I get friendly, "See you around, Farrens..."

Heading back to the room to retrieve two fatigue pants for the tailor, I stop by the Post Office, abled there to get out to Pop a brief letter with JA's mailing address. Entering the tailor shop a friendly little old Hawaiian is working. Leaving for the BX with cutoffs underarm, going slow, it dawns on me that like at the mess packed full, other than some Hawaiians seen while walking along, there're none else out here except white guys but gonna give that time. Still a whole, feel anxious about this place ...flat place. Loss of equilibrium. Nothing but ocean, nothing but ocean. No women but seemingly no inordinate vibes swapping; will give that time also staying vigilant, on guard.

The BX is amazin' given its size! The stereo electronics available, and photography, fishing equipment and scuba gear, etc. Low prices for it all..! Clothing section, and comparatively disproportionate is the large layout for beer, wine, and hard stuff! But am only nineteen. I buy a light-green cap, some white socks, white tennis shoes and cool lookin' shades at neat duty-free prices still leaving me half of the three hundred after spending nearly that much in Hawaii.

Back at the flat there is an electric clock on the nightstand reading ten after three. Won't unpack everything 'til my permanent quarters tomorrow. I feel like laying back to unwind, try to shake off the lingering sensations of abandonment and condemnation. Think I'll set its alarm to an hour and a half from now, some shuteye before dinner. The front curtains are drawn, none at the back. Going under... ...deep...

Suddenly, I'm startled to wake up by the sound of screaming jet turbines fast approaching! The backwall is progressively vibrating but I'm frozen by the charging racket amid the grip of sleepiness..!! Got to get the {redact} out of here, fast!!! ...the aircraft's out of control veering to slam into here..!!! But as I jump up dartin' to the door, the screaming shoots by settlin' into taxying idle..!! Quick shiver, "{Redact}, that was scary!"

Its four o'clock. Will come to find that daily last landings occur about now, none overnight to allow for sleep. Think I'll stroll a bit more before dinner. Locking the door behind, ten paces is to the sidewalk and I go left moseying on past the end of the two-story apartments to road's end coming upon an immaculate Olympic size swimming pool! Looking through its fence; "Is it closed..? No one's using it; strange..," mindfully.

I lookoff to the right, to what distance is to ocean the other side of a merging angled road some hundred feet away. About twenty feet beyond its opposite edge is a massive fat area stretching both right and left, maybe one and a half football field-length going right and three times that to the left, same distance to water as to the right. On it to the right are structures that give it the appearance of rocket launching.

Stepping onto the road I continue left strolling some minutes looking about but am becoming more attentive to the fenced-off portion of the flat that's drawing closer, my steps becoming worrisomely short due to the unfolding revelation, stopping about thirty feet from its corner. Barren.., it is capped with more densely packed coral-sand, or cement; its entirety surrounded by chicken-wire fence topped with barbed-wire.

Sidestepping to the opposite edge of the road from it, I can easily make out the first several of many small square signs hung on the fence running its length and recognizably circling projecting foreboding images. There are two types alternating. One is white bodied with words in black reading, "CAUTION," below it, "Radioactive," and below it, "**Stay Back 20 Feet**." The other is yellow bodied with black lettering, "**CAUTION**," below it, "**RADIATION AREA**," with a red three-prong radiation symbol nestled between the two statements.

"All that's radioactive..? ...some four to five acres..?!" am tryin' to grasp peacefully; with a sense of safety..? ...feelings of wellbeing..?!

Backing up some dozen feet more from it, I turn and head for water's edge walking on the unfenced portion staying parallel to this end's chicken-wire.., closing on a double-gate in it nearby the water. It is adorned no less ugly than the rest of the crowning, "Great..!" Start back the route I came and turning left from the pool, peer down the main drag comprehending this place's overall isolation, and a fairly good idea of the oppressively wee neighborhood in which to exist.

Walking the same side, on the right nearer the flightline, I go on past the mess hall until coming lastly upon the NCO Club but don't enter being underage. Man ...the thought, "I'm on this atomic dot in the middle of nowhere and can't score a beer..? ...keeps fresh what that guy at Hickam's outrigger restaurant said last evening; meaning the radiation..? ...or mentally; both..? Wonder if anyone had ever been told of the radiation before being shipped out here..? Of course ...not, AWOL if had..! How to unwind without brewskies..?"

Slowly shaking my head, "Man..? ...the depression that wants to set in," moseying back to the mess. At lunch the guys didn't seem all that bummed, but not all that thrilled. Maybe meals are neutralizers; "Steaks this evening..?"

Again; "You got to be kiddin' me..?! ...but no..! The T-bones and Sirloins are real ...right before my eyes, just like the guy next to me at lunch hinted! Grilled onions and sautéed mushrooms to top; the baked potatoes, butter, sour cream and chives! Mashed potatoes also, with white and brown gravies! Steamin' green beans, corn, and carrots! Hot dinner rolls! The fruit, salad and dessert bars like at lunch! Sodas, iced tea, coffee, and chocolate milk as was then also! How can this be, way out here..? Not seein' this getting old ...is countering the depression. What to take? T-bone with toppings, baked potato with the works, green beans and iced tea this time!"

Subtly parking, I do not see the Serg anywhere. Nonchalantly start diggin' in, and, a sense of acceptance comes easily by the lethargic vibes heard roundabout. Then instantly déjà vu, "I've been here years ago, but don't know these guys..."

"What? No; ...it's not necessarily the here and now but more so the feeling of shackled diminishment that has transcended time; from when began, cannot remember. And.., there is a troubling vein of imprisonment, reverberant ugly scenario of isolation, a blur of long-ago befriending loneliness that's putting me in bit of lockbrain mode.., eating on instinct listening to the seemingly stoic renditions of back home. Got to somehow shake off this feeling, but trying splits me in two; one prone to fight-or-flight, the other viewed as capitulating. Mixed emotions. Starting with the landing, this place has rollycoastered my nerves. See no way to jump off the tour ...but instead, keep holdin' on for moments of straight coasting to regroup, rest, stay unassuming. Owning that.., mellows me back together."

One at the table asks; "How old are you ...Farrens?"

"Nineteen. Not yet drinking age," I answer.

All around are grinnin' as he spiritedly begins to say, "Farrens.., there's no drinkin' age; where do you think you are, the States..? Enjoy soldier..!"

I'm caught to the quick in that I'm soaking up gladness by that freedom, nodding slowly wanting to match the size of his grin ...but instead, resign to an acknowledging cool one so not to come across as a guzzler.

He continues; "A bottle of beer..? ...two bits. Pint of Bourbon..? ...only six," keeping my soakin' it up gesture.

"Drink all you want as long as it doesn't interfere with your duties," another remarks.

An affirming nod, though with a distant gaze at him.

As those two rise from the table he concludes, "NCO Club is at the end of the road to the right out the door."

"Thanks," looking up at him.

Sitting awhile longer as others rotate through ...am thinkin', "Don't believe I'm gonna nip so soon at the bait to visit the Club.., give off a skewed nature that I can't cope ...or am easily swayed. Anyway, I'm really pooped."

A quick relieving deep breath slowly closing the front door, then back-floppin' onto the bed whispering; "A JA Mic' face up there..?" White linoleum panels with densely speckled pinholes makeup the ceiling, no discernible image of me. Think, "That's okay, have had enough for the first day but better not shut the eyes, got to shower then early turn in.

Felt good washing off the sundried salt. I set the alarm for 6 a.m. if not waking before. It's too hot to be undercovers. 7:30 p.m. ...vision narrowing.., blurring...

Eyes opening.., the clock comes into focus, 4:50 a.m.; "Jeezz.., nearly nine and a half hours sleep..?" A weirded mind.., "Wasn't a nightmare, still here." Despite being well rested am still beside myself about this place, of what all lies outside the door. Because of the reenergizing sleep though, I feel like a bulwark to whatever else JA gets in my face with. But what to do until Leland shows..? Do not want to hang in the room for two hours.

I step outside up to the sidewalk and pausing, take in the morning's dark although there's a mere yellowish glow shining down a third of the main drag from the horizon right, and from that direction a light-warm saltwater breeze. Those with the morning's silence and silhouettes of lights that can be seen dotting the Atoll is keeping me centered peacefully. Standing in new tennis shoes and socks, cutoff fatigue shorts, short-sleeve fatigue shirt with A1C stripes hangin', and a light-green cap atop, "This is quite nice," meditating.

I think there's enough time to stroll to water's edge of one end; but which direction, northeast towards the sunrise or southwest again beyond the pool? Now closing on it I veer right …then, left continuing on the angled road but {redact}.., "Gonna have to skirt the radioactivity!"

Staying on this left side of the road, estimate that it is thirty feet parallel running the chicken-wire fence. That humongous sight is imposing! Find myself goin' it slow passing.., a fearful respect as if it's a cemetery for those buried due to some tragedy. The eerie stilling quiet blanketing its entombing slab engenders a haunt that in there… is a plot reserved for me.

At its end I leave the road heading for the west corner and soon reach the sedating ripples rhythmically splashing at the base of the five-foot high boulder-laden seawall, and pulling up take a slow relieving deep inhale …and out.

Emerging east daylight a contrast to this end's night sky is gleaming white the foam of tall breaking surf against a subtle curving barrier reef, its greatest feats appearing about a mile out are also closest to here. The noticeable arcing of it moves away from this spot as the leftward going line of foam dwindles with distance to its submergence. View of the reef's circling right is blocked by the Atoll but appears similarly to move away from it.

But 'ol man! ...back at Banzai Pipeline..!! Beyond the reef the oncoming current is defining a midpoint in it near an eighth of a mile to the right where rad ten to fifteen-foot curls are crashing on ...then, serenely reforming into the two-footers splashing below. Takes all I can to turn from that mesmerizing dramatic force becoming subtleness. Passing back by the radioactivity, won't ever again take this route to there ...unless commanded to, and then... might not.

Breakfast am sitting across from the Serg remarking, "The cooked to order omelets, the bacon and sausage, scrambled eggs ...but these biscuits and gravy with so many chunks of hamburger, the Denver Omelet will have to wait 'til tomorrow..!" with a sizeable smile gawking down at the plate, OJ and coffee sittin' beside.

"Good start to the day..," he affirms.

"The food's great, Serg ...but, I started my day with a walk and saw two things that seem so at odds with each other..," reply.

"What things?" he asks.

"Big 'ol waves breaking a mile out and acres of radiation nearby," I answer.

He's quiet for the longest time focusing down ...then, "The coffee's especially good this morning," remarks raisin' his cup to right below eye to eye.

Believe I got the gist ...but just one question though entering on shaky ground; "Were you made aware of the radiation prior to leaving for here..?" a hand paused beside my cup, index finger looped within its handle ...still eye to eye.

Gradually lookin' back down spiking two squares of spuds he counters, "Wasn't made aware of the Prime Rib Saturday nights..," slowly inserting them into his mouth …eye to eye.

A slight puff grinnin' with subtle nods, my cup is raised at a likewise pace. Nothing more need said.

Taking last sips and empty plates, "Bit more time for seconds; or are you ready to meet DSTE..?" he asks.

"Ready for work, Serg," reply.

Out the door going right, the multistory building first seen at touchdown is quickly coming into view beyond the tip of the last four-story dorm. With a brief point to it, "That's JOC, Joint Operations Center, our eight-hour home away from home," he presents.

Entering, first off is a Sergeant MP rising behind a semi-circle counter. Am introduced to him. Moving on, "Our comm operations is on the third floor. I'll take you on a tour of the building after we check on the equipment," the Serg says as we begin climbing a stairwell.

Exiting it, we go a few paces down the hall to a secured room. He shows me the keypad entry code and we enter the Crypto room containing a floor centered rack displaying a top row of three KW-7's mounted, and below it a row of three KG-13's; one of each's front panels is lit, the others sitting idle are backups. Off to the side are two Teletype machines for handshake linkup with a distant site, probably Hickam, when we and they synchronously change our crypto codes soon to happen. "They're a blinkin'," he says.

"Sure are..," I concur.

"Let's go across the hall to the DSTE room. You can look it over while I come back to change the two's crypto codes …then I'll rejoin you," he instructs.

The DSTE room is large with light-beige linoleum flooring …and there it is right in the center, the blue beast; all devices near standard refrigerator dimensions except for the IBM cardpunch and line-printer likened to a stove's.

As Leland turns back for the Crypto room I proceed further into this one first halting in front of the punched card reader, then punched paper tape reader, the CCU (Common Control Unit), then paper tape punch, cardpunch, and lastly the line-printer.

It all looks in order.., clean. The CCU indicators are blinkin' away signifying incoming data transmission as the cardpunch is tappin' along in concert generating a recorded pile. Off to my right next to the wall is a console keyboard/paper tape punch for transcribing outgoing messages to the tape reader.

As I am circling the devices, in walks an Airman First Class chewin' some gum and carrying paperwork. He approaches me saying, "Hello Farrens.., I'm Zemke, Communications Operator."

"Hello Zemke, I'm the new DSTE Maintenance and Repairman," in return.

"I know; Staff Sergeant Leland mentioned you. I work out of Base Command, Comm Operations. Welcome to the Comm Center," he replies and then goes on telling me that he's been on JA for seven months and was trained by the General Dynamics Engineer to operate DSTE, coordinating all message transmissions on it. Is also the

Transcriber. Although holds a Top Secret Security Clearance, he is not authorized to access the Crypto room.

"Would you like a piece of Dentyne..?" extending the packet after adding one to that already in his mouth.

"Thanks," taking one.

"Well.., better get to transcribin' these outgoings," he concludes.

Zemke's about six-foot tall, slim, matte white skin with black hair; appears a bit drawn, shaky with a tinge of alcohol outdoing what he had before adding the piece.

I return to the front of the equipment taking a few steps back scoping its entirety; seems to be operating just fine …good. Then the Serg is approaching left; "Working okay..?" he asks.

"Yep …but need to begin the preventative maintenance routine," answer.

He responds, "Let's go back across to our office."

Next to the Crypto room, it is not entry code secured just as the Comm Center isn't. As is the rest of JOC, there're no windows. Two desks within are positioned perpendicular to each, one's top cleared of anything and the other is obviously the Serg's …and like he said, printed circuit boards packed in their shipping cartons are stacked high as well as tech manuals, a bookoo pile of DSTE replacement parts, and small cartons of lubricants; and standing next to the wall is a black briefcase containing precision tools and gauges.

There's a standard metal locker closet against the wall adjacent his desk, and next to it a short table with a cabinet sitting atop containing a hundred small clear-plastic drawers. Only twenty show parts in them apparently for the Teletypes ...as he's opening the locker.

About a fifth of its space is occupied with KW and KG circuit boards. "The rest is for yours, cabinet drawers also. I'll make room for your tech manuals next to mine beneath the table," he offers.

All I can do is nod much approving.

Also in the office is a floor safe for storing both the daily changeout crypto code-cards for one crypto device's card drawer, and likewise the crypto grid-maps for spaghetti pin-wiring the other's swap-out block. Due to the safe is why the office doesn't need to be entry secured. Soon I'll be given its combination so to alternate days of swops.

"Ready for the tour..?" he asks.

"Sure ...Serg; I'll begin organizing this when we return, and get a handle on scheduling maintenance," answer.

Half of one floor is for MP (Military Police) offices and the other half for the Rocket Launch Control room, we not having clearance to enter. Another of the four floors is Base Command and Logistics, another Administrative Support and office supplies as well as JA's telephone system and radio station.

Upon return to our office the phone is ringing. "Your permanent residency is ready for move in, bit sooner than expected," the Serg says hangin' it up.

"Cool," respond.

"Tell you what, Farrens; you are located on the top floor of the four-story dorm farthest from here, closest the mess hall. It is laid out in cubicles with yours the fifth on the left from the end door that faces the mess. Go ahead now and make your move around lunch taking an extra hour to settle in. See you back afterwards," he instructs.

"Okay, Serg..," reply and turn for the door.

Lugging the duffle over a shoulder, I slowly turn the second floor's outside landing after first flight of stairs; again the next and at the fourth's, pause to look out over the string of rooftops and.., what a panoramic of ocean to horizon! ...but hardly anything of JA a contrast, just flightline and three water or fuel storage tanks beyond the rooftops, then a frontage road, all intertwined with static coral-sand flatness.

Scanning both directions of the main drag, and what else can be seen, I catch glimpse of a handful of guys scattered about. Weighing; "Thousand out here..? Where is everyone..?! Well.., still a half-hour before the mess opens for lunch."

Manage to traverse the doorway. It closing behind the interior dims some with its swing and; "You got to be {redact}in' me..?" ...curtains my height line both sides of the aisle. Approaching the fifth one on the left am noticing a break between it and the next after, about the width of the brief hallway I entered yesterday the second dorm down. Across from it, instead of a curtain, is a same width interior wall having a closed door labelled, "Latrine/Showers." Peeking left after a step passed my cubicle's spanning curtain, can see that the break is a descending stairwell.

Stepping back and slowly sliding the curtain quarter ways open, look in comprehending the depth not much more than its width. Am furnished a bunk with one side touching the left panel-partition wall and its far end touching the backwall. There's also a nightstand with small lamp, a metal locker closet at the opposite backwall corner, and abutting this side of it a low but wide four-drawer dresser a little over arm's length from me. Really cramped space...

And am thinkin', "And it just keeps gettin' better..." Though there's a solid wall to the ceiling on this break side, the panel-partition the other separating me from my neighbor at curtain height has a two-foot opening remaining to the ceiling like all the rest, "Great.., fart sounds and smells shared again. Thank goodness for the bottom tilt-out window..! Definitely gonna have to decorate this Alcatraz cell."

It only takes a half-hour to unload into the drawers and locker closet. Clean bedding is stacked at what will be the foot-end of the bed, and after making it I sit back against the head-end's wall stretching my legs out crossed over. Squintin' at the curtain a few feet beyond the foot-end ...muse; "What criteria did some ninety-day wonder sitting cush Stateside use to send me here..? Maybe if I had listed Nam first on my dream sheet, I'd be kickin' back in Rio. Well.., at least am not in Nam; but the radiation..?" Several seconds gone, then couple of nods with a sarcastic grin, "Just another turn of events, Airman First Class." Hearin' the stomach growl, rise to head for the mess.

Back at the office after chowing, the Serg is away ...so, I begin organizing all the DSTE stuff with maintenance scheduling in mind. He now entering ...says, "By the way, received last week your OJT (On-the-Job Training) outline with sequenced tests;" inclining his head to the other desk, "The packet is in your desk drawer, bottom right." I pullout the sizeable cellophane wrapped packet of course material. It is remedial to Sheppard's classroom training that must be completed in phases for a promotion.

As it has been so far, conversations crossing the dinner table are monotonously pitched in sync with meandering dissectin' of entrées. It puts me in dreariness as if am a new arrival inmate walking down the dead silent cellblock to his cage just before a mass prison break, calm before the storm. The look on some quiet faces are that of last abstracts of gloom as eyes sink below the surface of quicksand.

I'm at odds because the lasagna a third of my plate, spaghetti and meatballs a third, and two slices of loaded pizza the other ...are quite delicious! But as tastebud comparable the Italian is to last evening's spread, it somehow doesn't affirm a selfsame feelin' of wellbeing, or keep buoyant hope of redemption; an undermining already of the mess hall's appeal? Can't be the skillfully prepared cuisine, or the guys, it must be me ...but, am also hearing opposing words within, "Keep your wits, Mic', you're here for a year. Stay true to yourself..."

Before heading back to my cubicle think I'll drop by the BX to get flip-flops for the shower, a plastic soap case also, and see what's available to decorate the walls; just browse around. Easily come across the first two, then seeing a few models ...oh yes, an alarm clock although may not need it because of sounds of others waking.

Moment later am slowing up to a tiny section of framed prints varying in size up to 11 x 14 inch. Interesting.., eight out of twelve depict some sort of seafaring vessel with a few having people aboard sailing or fishing; three prints of solitary island beaches and one 8 x 10 of a coastline rock-cliff with a slight bluff jettying out and lighthouse atop. Maybe the Air Force is tryin' to keep us from being bummed out thinking too much of home. The only one with any kind of structure, I reach for the lighthouse print.

"Well.., looks like that is all that will be hanging for a while," making my way to the register. But not far from getting there I'm comin' upon the book 'n magazine section and, YES! …there they are..!! …issues of Playboy and separate Playboy calendars from which luscious excerpts can plaster the walls..!!! Reaching for a calendar… am thought caught, "Might be too soon, ought to try to keep from fervent hand acts."

Being stalled, I'm recalling some from before that off to the right is music stuff. Neat little AM/FM stereo receiver/record player with a pair of tabletop speakers; for only twenty-four bucks..?! Thinking, "Don't believe it'll get stolen; but you know..? …might be competing with other tunes playing throughout what is essentially an open bay." There's a large pair of padded headphones that look just right; for only four bucks..?!

…And the 78 rpm Rock albums; seventy-five cents each..?! Gonna take three with the system, Creedence Clearwater Revival, James Taylor, and Tony Orlando & Dawn but first got to free up at the register what I'm already carrying. Anxiously toting the duty-free load out the door, was only set back thirty-three and a half bucks..! …cool shopping spree…

Making the top landing, thankfully the door's propped open and entering see midway down the aisle two fellows in civvies chatting. They then catching sight of me, one that is short and stocky grins asking; "Gonna make it, guy..?" with a rasp Bronx accent.

I reply, "Yeah...thanks, I'm right there," lookin' over that way.

Shouldering the curtain open, I gingerly let it all slip down onto the bed. Slide the curtain back closed. Within a half-hour, going on 8 p.m., all the components are unboxed and hooked up sitting on the dresser leaving space aside on the right for stacking the albums, and having enough room the other to lean the picture against the wall. To the pillow is an easy reach for the headphones.

Just as I am taking a seat at the edge of the bed to kick off the shoes, rest back and spin CCR, a couple of taps are rippling the curtain. Rising and sliding it open, "Hey guy; welcome to the Rock, Schlitz..?!" smiling, from the one that offered help.

I've noticed low buzz comings 'n goings since arriving back, and despite pausing ambivalent ...still respond, "Thanks, don't mind if I do..." breaking into a smile stepping into the aisle.

"Fitzpatrick from Jersey.., Fitz' for short," introducing himself.

"Farrens from L.A.," connect gripping the opened cold brown bottle, tappin' the tops.

"What's your field, Farrens..?" he asks.

"Electro' Comm and Crypto Repair," answer and in return; "Yours..?"

"Motor Pool," he replies.

I nod a few slowly. Though from Jersey, Fitz' somewhat resembles the crass New York City lower eastside gang leader 'Slip' Mahoney of the TV Bowery Boys, but a bit stockier.

"Toured the Rock..?" he asks.

"Some," I reply.

"Come on, I'll show you one half ...then the other," he offers.

An eye-widening expression by me of, "What..?! ...how..?!" but I go with it giving a 45 degree head-tilt. He nods for me to follow.

We mosey out onto the landing at mess hall's end, still some daylight left. From there he points out additional places that I didn't know of starting beyond the NCO Club's northeast end of JA, just catching the transmitter tower portion of Sand Island not being blocked by the other dorms; it a half-mile across the channel.

Slowly rotating left to right, near three-quarters of JA's seven feet above sea level flatness 'been scanned ending at that massive fenced plot. "Five acres of radiation poisoning..," he says slowly tipping the bottle to his mouth.

All I can do is gaze squinting at it somberly shaking my head side to side, then tip my bottle. Lowering it as I lean beside him on the railing; "Fitz'? ...what the {redact} is that doing there..?"

He answers, "Don't really know.., nobody does.., never been told by nobody, never will..."

"How is that?" asking.

He puff-chuckles and, "Let's walk to the other end," slowly turning and reentering. Not many steps along he reaches for a curtain, the third on the right. Veers in and opens the small frig bending in, then still bending extends back a bottle; "Another one..?" he asks.

"No...I'm good, thanks," answer.

At the other end we relax as before, staring out this time at the northern length ...and, "Look around Farrens; what strikes you the most?" he asks.

Answer, "Acres of chicken-wired {redact}."

From him; "Really?!" ...then, "Expand your vision."

Taking several seconds, "The long barrier reef and ocean for as far as the eyes can see," adding.

He; "How does that make you feel?"

Me, "Oh.., I don't know, probably trapped.., abandoned."

A forty-five degree twist towards me, I likewise to him, he subtly nods with, "Somewhere down the road to obscurity.., this place became incidental, except to the Generals.., who want to keep its radioactivity shrouded in secrecy. By virtue of that, we're oblivious to the rest of the world; who gives a {redact} what you and I think about our exposure to Plutonium..? ...our constant fear of that..? ...especially since the NCO rank-in-file and some Officers nearer to it," gesturing to the apartments, "being more exposed but having more in stature to lose, don't speak out."

I; "Plutonium, for sure..?"

He, "No. Also haven't been told it is but makes sense; nukes exploded in the Pacific..?" silence taking hold. Then he breaks it remarking, "In Nam.., I believe the warriors are clothed and carry M-16's so to take on a visible, non-static, enemy; most likely can retreat to relative safety; got each other's back. What clothing's been issued us to block invisible, statically camouflaged, nuke-rays..? ...weapons so to take them on..? ...or given a treaded path to flee the inundation..? How do I... got your back, you... mine, comrade..?"

"I don't know, comrade..," answer with growing resentment for the Air Force.

Slowing even more, Fitz' rhetorically asks; "Chicken-wire fence; if that's shielding, then why the signs warning to stay back twenty-feet rather than to just keep out..? ...trickery, playing us for fools..?"

I can only puff-chuckle nodding at the absurdity, then also rhetorically; "Wonder which came first, the chicken-wire fence or the passing road distanced twenty-feet conveniently marking the rays' end..?"

After tipping my bottle the final time, I likewise utter, "Puzzled; as a morale factor why, if really contained, there isn't an intake briefing upon arrival where then the bordered radioactivity is revealed and conveyed that the rest of the place is deemed safe..? Think they would want us at our best."

He's laughing.., "Comrade; don't you get it..? ...briefing by whom..?! By whom of credible medical knowledge..?! ...and would put his behind on the line claiming our lives aren't being shortened by daily inundation..?! ...daily for a year..?! We won't have early onset of cancer or sterility..?! It's part of the shrouding to only have medics out here. Hey ...put yourself in Doctor shoes. Being told ahead of time you're gonna be reassigned to a mile and a half by three-quarter Plutonium radiated flat in the middle of the Pacific; wouldn't you say no way Jack..?!! For fear of you resigning your commission and/or going public; what could the Force do to you..? I just went over halfway here, haven't seen or heard of a Doctor…"

I, "This place is far more likenin' to a forward combat base than the resort Hickam in Honolulu. All the nukes tested in this ocean to kill the Commies but instead it's sittin' here putting our lives at risk without the least capacity to fight it off..?! What the {redact}..?! …we're the enemy to the good 'ol U.S. of A..?!!" We're leaning here with the slightest shakings of our heads side to side owning donkey rears' grins.

Both 'bout ragged out, and bottles' dry, he's bringing it to a close, "Its Military City Hall; whata we do..? …alarm our loved ones so they become embattled with nimrods..? What added distress then for them..? …to be informed of our involuntarily confinement in a psych-ward unaware that the sedation is covert, and are told some quack story about us..?"

Answer, "I don't know, Fitz'.., seems like a lot of time and effort on Government's part."

He condenses his angst brought by the Service, "Alright; here's the short 'n sweet version. Good 'ol Fitzpatrick died at sea. Allegedly had withdrawn for a week becoming disoriented before seen a way's off jumping into the water. By the time he could be reached, the sharks had taken him under. During Uncle Sham's internalll investigation, all his comrades were lined up in the aisle for in-your-face opposing remarks (I'm fast-forwarding to my turn.) but none were given."

Near whisperin', "{Redact}, Fitz'.., I'm having a sickening hypocritical image…"

He; "What?"

I, "We're all in this, alone…"

With a slight quick reflex, "No;" gesture perceived as against our plight and not me, he likewise, "Can't escape our isolated radioactive habitation, nor complain."

Silence again taking hold …then, "I have this feeling, but not a feeling, can't put words to it but am not liking the headache," confide in him closing my eyes.

He empathizes, "Hey.., comrade …don't stress, I know what you're experiencin'; it has come upon us all, right from the get-go. The first two words that were passed on to me describing it.., "Fear {redact}ed." Straightening up looking at me, "But the Force isn't totally unsympathetic. It is graciously supplying a nuke-ray antidote.., the endless low-cost alcohol necessary to war on. Dose as needed. Medicate until you drop at night, wake to die another day. The third word shared, with one less letter than them combined.., "Forgotten..," and although similar but with one less letter.., "Forsaken." Shortening words do not dumb down our 4-f condition, meds do. Having near halfway still to go, more so believe it best to keep on hand in the frig a good batch of antidote, ought to keep taking the medication…"

Then as he turns for the door …I ask; "Does this place even have a mission..?"

Opening it …twists his head back; "Who the {redact} knows..? Never been told that one either, but scuttlebutt is a rocket's soon to be shot off;" tilting it to enter saying, "Can spare another dose if you want."

"Sure.., be by in a few minutes but want to take in more of the breakers," respond. Here alone peering out, "This vantage point is great, curls' soothin', but that peripheral eyesore so close is annulling, unnerving..," mindfully, still with the headache needing another dose.

Sorrowfully not being considerate of time passing, Fitz' is stepping back out, "Here ya go..," he says extending a bottle adding, "I got to get down Trinity-J and sack out."

Respond, "Thanks, comrade..," then; "Trinity-J..?"

"Mixed med solution of each a shot of Jack D., Jim B., and Johnny W.., otherwise affectionately known as 'The Kindred Spirit,' dosed seldom except when I'm being bound tightly by 4-f, which every night you'll catch wind of from someone administering," he answers.

"Will resupply you tomorrow, Fitz'," inform him.

"No, comrade..?! First night's doses on me," he replies, seeing him as a kindred spirit.

Following him back in I see a few others gathered in the aisle chatting friendly low key, two holding beers, one some sort of cocktail, all acknowledging us as we pass. Not noticed all that much until now, the more inward we go the more pungent the smell of alcohol.

Sitting back against the wall with beer in hand and headphones on, am taking slow deep inhales shutting my eyes as CCR begins, volumed just right to put me a cruisin' in the GTX. Then Porterville perspective.., "I don't care..!!!" Put on James Taylor, "In my mind I'm goin' to Carolina..," unwinding me bringin' some peace of mind.., beginning to imagine I'm there...

Stretching out atop the blanket still in day clothes as the album's last cut begins, I lower the empty bottle to the floor, and ending few moments later, the phones next to it as the record player automatically shuts off. Eyelids' gettin' heavy but with each blink to final closure is a glowing mindsight projection of a large rectangle flat angled eleven o'clock from me. Goin' unconscious…

Nineteen. First night of dosing, three hundred sixty-three more to go…

111

Most do dose, most don't fish.

Two more days go by having found out that Zemke occupies the first cubicle in from the door across the aisle and religiously doses Trinity-J every evening after dinner, steadily comatosin' to lights' out, showering in the morning. Two months back with proposin' to his waiting heartthrob in mind, got a 'Dear John'.

From then on he withdrew socially off duty and in concert has been slipping workwise, though for the few days seen in the DSTE room not all that noticeable, just the alcohol breath winning some over the Dentyne. Have heard that he has been reprimanded.

Man..; what else can the poor guy do..?! ...stuck way out here and the {redact} doin' what she did, how convenient. What a heart..? ...makes me kinda glad I didn't have a girlfriend to send me off. From here on out Kaylee's off my mind; but Amanda..? ...or Sunshine..? ...well.., were also non-starters but still good to keep around should the need arise.

What can anyone say to Zemke to ease his mind..? ...that she's a loser..?! ...more fish in the sea; way out here..?! I haven't yet heard that there's a Chaplin on JA. Probably not. What would he preach..? ...that God is so loving bringin' us here to rest our heads on pillows ...and get nuked..?! That such a love for us has turned the chicken-wire into solid lead..?! This is a real hellhole and no amount of preachin' will bring a change.

Five days gone, first Friday and after a good Oriental dinner; what to do..? I have held off buying a frig even though still enough in pocket to do so. Ought to wait for the bucks from Pop. I did buy a Styrofoam ice chest, bottle opener and two six-packs of Coors; one in the chest, the other in reserve. There are ice machines on the first and third floors, trash cans outside for empty bottles.

DSTE's doing fine cruisin' into the weekend on standby ...but; what to do..? Begin dosing again with some of the guys on the ward..? ...or wait to take in the John Wayne western in about an hour and a half at the outdoor theater. Neither seems that good. I haven't stepped into the NCO Club yet.., believe I will.

Walking there really feels good, working off the full tummy. Might go on by but now at the entrance, steppin' in. Sitting at the bar with a Rocky Mountain in hand, I turnabout scoping the atmosphere. There are three tables of Blackjack going on, and one has an open seat. Sauntering up to it …I ask; "Open..?" to the five players.

"Sit a spell," the one dealing says.

It's a dollar game and am filled in that the first in a round to Blackjack off the dealer has the option to buy it for five bucks, providing he has afterward a remaining bank of twenty. If it's not bought, then the option passes to the next if also Blackjacked. If no one else has, then the dealer retains it. Whenever the dealer's bank falls below ten closing a round, the deal must be auctioned to the highest bidder having a remaining bank no lower than twenty bucks. I'll come to find that the deal is prized! The chips regardless of color represent a dollar and are exchanged at the bar. The place more resembles a saloon than a cocktail lounge.

I bought thirty chips and with twenty-six left in front of me including the bet, Blackjack..! Double payoff and buying the deal, twenty-three is in my bank. Have won fifteen when another hits it, breaking even overall in the round. With five more selling the deal I turn from the table reaching down to the floor for my brew, then leaning back up catch quick periphery sight of a hand pulling away from my stack..! "Hey …what the {redact} you doin'..?!!!" eye to eye.

He is just sitting there quiet, then drops his sight. I'm looking around at the others as they remain quiet. Am thinking seein' two less chips than I ought to have, "Man.., I want to lay into the guy..!! …but don't know his rank..?" A round is dealt, peeved..! Lose, so I gather up the stack and head for the bar, leave out a twelve-dollar winner, minus two…

Instead of going left back to the dorm, I go right, towards east end water beyond JOC passing over the frontage road. Helping to vent, I stare out across the channel to Sand Island and another off to its left further distant. Do not know if it has a name. Turning left going counter-clockwise, I come upon adjacent to water's edge the baseball field also seen barely to the right of JOC from the dorm's fourth floor stairs.

Continuing circlin' the northeast corner, am passing by dorms for the Hawaiians …then, an outrigger café run by them called, "The Waikiki." Not far and off to the right is a short jetty with a standalone house at its tip for the Commander. Those two are the only places with some Palm trees surrounding. Soon, angling left for the dorm, come upon an empty basketball court adjacent this right side of the road that used to be the taxiing loop-around back in the days before JA was expanded; also is the road that passes by the fenced radioactivity. It's a bit late for any pickup games but will check it out tomorrow.

Climbing the stairs on the barrier reef's end of the dorm, I pause at the top landing to again scope out that which was toured over the last hour …and again, skim along the reef seeing those awesome curls --"But {redact}..! …that nuke site..!! …a trumping hot zone to the left hafting again the entrapment on this speck doubling the compression felt!!! Am believing this'll be the last time to take in the breakers from here," slowly shaking my head turning to open the door.

Thinking one dose, but might take two, to denuke my mind starting out with CCR eventually to jam with my Porterville standard, "I don't care..!!!" Wanting to spin

Tony Orlando but not enough time left tonight, for I got to get off this atomic dot with J.T.'s help again, stretching out to, "<u>In my mind I'm goin' to Carolina... Can't you see the sunshine..? ...Can't you just feel the moonshine..?</u>" setting the second bottle down next to the first as it is ending, the phones also. Pj's are gonna miss out once more drifting away.., but that stalking glarin' rectangle penetrating my skull from its one o'clock position is a drag on the trip to Carolina...

Saturday midmorning, there's a pickup game going on at the basketball court, alright..! Five on five with four waiting courtside, will round out the next team. Only white guys are out here, no other race seen about except the Hawaiians passing by. All participants are shirtless sweating profusely, and courtside are two ice chests full of brew. I didn't think to bring any, dah...

"That's okay, next time. Help yourself, and to the suntan lotion," from one of the four awaiting.

Funny; all rank is gone when off duty but steadily getting to know who is what by them seen in fatigues, and the few Officers likewise. The Serg clued me in to salute them of course when they're in uniform, even if not wearing a cap. When passing in civvies, no need to salute ...just greet, "Sir," still respecting.

Up 'n down the court making shots, the fast-paced teamwork, the near crippling windedness.., feels great! For that relatively brief duration of competition, thoughts of radiation poisoning are sweated out. Heading back to the dorm for a brief shower before lunch, I first make a quick BX stop-off to restock the Coors.

Donning clean civvies …am thinking; "You know..? …have found the Hawaiians to be nothing but friendly. Lunch at the mess is hard to pass up but think I would like to see what the Waikiki serves up? Anyway, Prime Rib this evening at the mess!"

Looking up at the menu board behind the counter; "What you like, holly boy..?" from the smiling somewhat elderly Hawaiian.

"What is PuPu..?" asking because there're just names listed.

"Steak," he answers.

Thinkin', "No.., Prime Rib later," and then ask; "Saimin..?"

"Soup, very good!" he responds.

"Okay …that," with a nod.

"Fart, one large bowl isn't gonna be enough..!" mindfully. The mellowing light chicken broth, the long real thin spaghetti, and thinly sliced green onion-stalks a floatin' are a tasty mix, but got to save room for later. Amazing how satisfying this is…

Peering out from the patio that overlooks it is an inlet formed by the coastline, and there is a guy floating around out there enjoying himself. Back at the ward a half-dozen comrades are gathered outside of Fitz's cubicle soppin' it down. I join in popping a Rocky Mountain and ask; "Fitz'..? I just came from the Waikiki and in the cove there was a brave soul swimming; waters' not shark infested..?"

He answers, "It's a swim area protected by shark net. As you might've noticed nobody uses the pool because of its closeness to the radio-dump, the cove is swam instead."

I remark, "It's a real neat pool but what nitwit thought to put it that close to a radiation hazard picturing a hoppin' partying place..?"

Laughter starting anticipating his reply, "Playboy General not havin' to live out here, and inept at nuke containment."

With a chuckling smirk as are with the others; "You know..? I'm really beginning to feel like something other than human," I confide.

He, "Yep, and this junkyard dog is gonna have another Schlitz..," as some hearing that let out, "Woof...woof...woof..," going for more of theirs, Zemke quietly staggering past heading to the latrine.

Again I weigh in, "The space across from me; haven't seen anyone comin' or goin'..?"

Carmichael from D.C. voices, "That's Chi' town Pickler's. A month ago, halfway into his stay, he went on two week's leave like we all can, but must have lost track of time or the way back. Probably got lost taking a slow sightseeing through Canada;" everybody grinning as he goes on, "I'm eight months here and he's the third AWOL heard of so far." Carmichael, recently promoted to Sergeant and opting not to move to the apartments, favors the look of Mick Jagger but not quite as rowdy!

Then Gattis, an average lookin' guy, says, "Pickler.., what a bummer if caught. From JA to Alcatraz. Here's to Pickler on the move in Canada!" toasting, we all tapping bottlenecks as one.

Looking to Fitz' ...I ask; "How close did you come to goin' AWOL..?"

He low tone draws out, "{Redact}, not close.., didn't take it and not gonna. No returning to JA once off. Doin' time nonstop."

Carmichael, "The same here.., and there are many more like us. Typically it's the married that take it …and return, a lot to lose if don't."

"Zemke..?" low tone I ask.

He responds likewise, "At five months he was ready. Thirty days to go to asking for the hand of his squeeze, plannin' on getting the rings going through Hawaii.., got the two-page twenty-one days prior to liftoff. Crushed.., he cancelled leave and began ramping up his dosin', is out by seven."

Seeing him exiting the latrine it goes quiet, but then Fitz', "It's the tuff single that pass up leave; right Zemke..?!"

"Right..," he barely audible …somberly replies going by.

Gatherings like this are frequent, commonly low-key ebb 'n flow to blowoff JA, but have heard that on a few occasions someone has gone ballistic about this place. Disbursing with two hours to dinner, I kick back still feeling a bit beat from the basketball game. Mellowin' another Coors, am pondering six months from now; "Nonstop sightseeing Mexico or… nonstop time here..?" Fitting the phones finally to hear Tony and his babes, but before the vinyl completes I just got to hear again, "In my mind I'm goin' to Carolina..,"

The Prime Rib was excellent, need though to walk off the load but gonna score another from the ice chest to carry along. The offshore breeze feels good strolling along the frontage passing the east takeoff end of the flightline, turning right at the east to southwest corner where off to the left there is a jetty that runs a few hundred-plus feet narrowing nearly to a point.

Coming out of the turn starting down the south length, a short dump truck passes from behind right and distances all the way to the southwest corner where it backs up and tilts its bed. Cannot quite make out what it is offloading but looks like sludge. Just this side of it is a pickup parked parallel but not as far off the road, and no one's noticeable in or around.

At about midpoint of the south length, just short of another jetty of near length to the other, am stopping to sit awhile atop the concrete seawall as the dump truck passes back. Not long thereafter, still gazing out to the horizon, the pickup slowly cruises by. Given the distance between the radio-dump and my cubicle, here... a more welcomed relief with less dosing is felt, questioning; "Why couldn't it have been on this side of the flightline rather than in the vicinity of where we lay our heads each night? So much ocean, it is soothing but... so much ocean."

Introspectively squinting, "Humorous.., the irony of what Pop once said about calling too much on the past instead of imagining the future. What future? ...a radiant one..?! I'm at naught sitting out here needing to dowse nuke-fear. The past is all I got..."

I continue on near to the southwest corner seeing the beauty of a setting sun fading into the ocean horizon. Stop short though thinking I will save that corner for another day. Heading back am seeing off some to the right a pickup parked at the opposite edge of the corner jetty, close to its end. I had not noticed it when parking but maybe is the same one that passed.

It is backed up to the short flattop concrete retaining barrier with the tailgate lowered a couple feet from touching it, and there is a guy sitting stoic at the back edge of the tailgate with his feet propped upon the barrier ...holding a fishing pole. My periphery attention is kept on him as I slowly continue by, losing such turning the corner towards the flightline's end. Been now a week on JA and had not noticed until just then anyone fishing.

It's the middle of the following week and having walked two more times passed the jetty have seen him out there. Believe I will pay him a visit the next time seen. But now this morning having entered the office, the Serg informs me that the Atoll is on heighten security approaching the launch of a rocket tomorrow night. "Cool..," am thinkin' ...asking him; "Is that JA's mission?"

He answers, "That will be the last indeterminately, sending up an astronomy satellite. I've been briefed that after, our posture will be that of readiness to test."

"Readiness to test what?" I ask.

He speculates, "Most likely launches and detonations of nuclear warheads again."

After dinner there are five of us gathered outside of Fitz's cubicle, Zemke again staggering by. After a hit off a brewski ...I say, "Found out today our mission."

Fitz'; "Yeah..? ...what?"

Reply, "After tomorrow night's satellite launch we will go into a readiness to test mode."

Carmichael interjects, "I'll drink to that..!"

Fitz'; "Readiness to testicle what? ...Charlie stormin' JA..?! They'd be crazier than us..!!"

Carmichael, "Drink to that..!" the other two tappin' bottlenecks with him.

I, "Test nuke launches and detonations."

Carmichael, "Won't {redact}in' drink to that."

Fitz', "Picture's comin' clear, that radio-dump is someone's big {redact}in' mistake..."

I, "Drink to that..!" we all tappin' bottlenecks.

Thursday the 24th, 9:29 p.m., a crowd is standing behind vehicles semi-circling between structures at about five hundred feet from the launchpad to watch liftoff. One minute to ignition sirens are blarin' all over the place..!

Loudly the fellow on my right asks; "Bring your sunglasses..?!"

"No..!" loudly answer.

"Don't look at the rocket's thrust, cover its tail with a hand..!" he caringly volunteers.

"Thanks..!" loudly return, and moments later the sirens halt --then, "Ten, nine, eight, seven, six, five, four, three, two, one..." Awestruck, "Remarkable..! ...the blast of it!! ...it's daylight at 9:30 p.m..!!!"

Figuring it is far enough up, I lower my hand seeing the flare of its afterburner obscuring all else of it! Panicking think to myself, "{Redact}, it's falling back onto us ...run..!!!" but the same fellow next to me with his shades on isn't budging, nor anyone else?! Nearly lettin' loose in my pants, "Shouldn't have looked at its flame..!" mindfully.

A couple of days later midmorning, my second Saturday here, am ten minutes into a pickup game having brought a six of Coors to share. A teammate swishes the bottom of the net and I'm on the run to defend the other end skirting the out-of-bound's next to the road --when at midcourt; "Who out of the corner of my eye is approaching..?!" double-taking seein' Chaplin Malone in full tans smiling big at me..!

Slowing up, I veer off the court to a stop a few feet from his halt, and not even thinkin' to salute; "You're here Chaplin Malone?!" breaking into a big smile.

His still the same ...answers, "Yes."

Just then from the court; "Farrens.., what 'chu doin'? Get back in the game..!"

"We'll talk a bit later, Sir..?!" to him.

He subtly nods agreeing.

Back on the court I turnabout seein' him walking away. Trying to get back up to speed, "How neat this is..!" mindfully.

Same scenario as last week, am gonna do the Waikiki for another bowl of Saimin, then Prime Rib for dinner. Pocket money is at seventy-one dollars, no panic yet. Soup's only a half-buck and afterwards gonna scope out the 78's at the BX to add a few more to the collection. Saimin finished ...I push back a little from the table, incline resting and peerin' out to the cove, nobody is swimming. Begin thinkin' about the sight of Chaplin Malone; "The Higher Power has been out here all along but didn't realize it until seeing the Chaplin..?"

But puzzled; "Why send a godly man to join other military, and civilians, subject to secrecy of nuclear harm? What joyful message will he bring on Sundays..? ...that God is wrapping his arms around us, shielding us from the nuke-rays..?! Surely he didn't choose to be assigned here because of our meeting. Anyway, am lookin' forward to hearing his sermons but tomorrow might be too soon for him to start." I rise and head for the BX. Walking out of the store with Iron Butterfly's In-A-Gadda-Da-Vida album, My Generation by The Who, and Led Zeppelin II with Whole Lotta Love track. Might date Sunshine later tonight.

Sunday evening, but an hour later than in the past, am again traversing the takeoff end of the flightline ...and thinking that he might be, there is the fisherman yet again sitting stoic. Anticipating such, I brought along a second Coors and a bottle opener in my back pocket for a friendly intro. Ten feet away in my approach, he has yet to turn to see me ...so; "How're they bitin'..?" a little loud.

Motionless centered on the tailgate looking out, "Pass around front," is his response.

Clearing the pickup's driver-side front fender; "Woe..?!" mindfully, seeing two sharks lying on the deck, one about four feet long and the other is about five. I ask; "You brought those in with that pole..?!"

"Yep," from him.

Me, "Must have been quite a tug of war..."

He, "Yep, but that's the fun in it."

The sharks between us, "I'm Farrens."

"Wynnewood; take a load off," he returns slidin' over.

Rounding the sharks and extending at the tailgate ...I say, "Brought an extra brewski along."

He, "No thanks, don't drink."

"Okay if I partake?" ask.

He, "Go ahead..," as I park two feet from him. Wynnewood looks a year to two older, is about 5'9" maybe 170 lbs. resembling a bobcat sailor wearin' a white tee shirt, dark-blue bellbottoms and same color tennis shoes …but, adorned with wireframe specks comes across as a cool rock 'n rollin' bobcat sailor.

Lying in front of us on the flattop barrier, proppin' my feet at its ledge, is a metal pole with a large hook, and off to its left a neat looking Bowie knife about eight inches long. Next to it is a fairly decent size fish without its head, maybe a five-pounder whole. Don't know what type it is having been cutup in chunks of eight with three gone. "That must be bait there," showing some fishin' knowledge.

"Yep," as he begins reeling in the line.

"Big chunks.., can imagine the size of the hook," I comment.

Clearin' the water and swinging it half-exposed to him, Wynnewood rips the remainder of the wad off tossing it into the water revealing all of the humongous treble-hook.

He remarks, "Can only allow it to be submerged no more than fifteen minutes if a shark hasn't latched on, small fish nip away at it." He maneuvers the hook into another chunk through the gut cavity with about a half-inch of each prong protruding …and continues, "Where I'm gonna cast I have found to be exactly right, goes down about eight feet and well-spaced between coral-heads."

I ask; "What happens when the shark takes it, gets snagged..?"

He replies, "Can if you don't know what you're doing. The finesse tug of war lettin' its force run outward but not turn left or right into the coral, nip tugging to wheedle it completely around and reelin' in with a bit of tension before it turns to run again. Always keep some tension on the line to tire it. Either you'll tire out losing all of your line or it to become souvenir jaws." Smiling he then says, "Funny when it's cruisin' on in more, resting, that it doesn't have the slightest clue how pretty its pearly whites are gonna look hangin' on the wall."

The line sitting idle waitin' for a hit, he reaches back into a small ice chest lifting out a bottle of Coke. Also in the bed is a spear made up of a yellow broomstick with a rope looped firmly through an eyelet at its top end, and three narrow foot-long sharp-tipped spikes bound firmly at the bottom spreading outward. Next to it is a round plastic pail with a shorter rope tied to its semicircular wire handle.

As he pops the bottle cap I inquire; "Wynnewood, where're you from?"

"Cape Elizabeth," he answers.

I, "Not familiar."

"A small coastal town south of Portland, Maine," he completes …then; "You..?"

"South Los Angeles," from me …then ask; "Been on JA long?"

He, "Ten months."

Half-dozen seconds passing …then, "Two weeks for me," from me.

He remarks, "Kinda figured.., hadn't seen you around 'til lately."

"Quite convenient having the truck," from me.

"Yep, don't fish without it," from him.

~ 275 ~

I ask; "What do you do?"

"Radar Tech," from him …then; "You?"

"Comm maintenance and repair," answer.

He nods …then says, "If I didn't have to work tomorrow, would stay out longer taking in the brightening stars," reelin' in the line going on seven o'clock.

Cleans off the hook laying the pole in the bed. Both standing, he shoves the remaining bait in the water then goes over to the two sharks and jams the Bowie hard into them centered an inch behind the eyes. Hoists the four-footer parallel atop the barrier and begins eviscerating around its mouth. Goodness, what a bloody mess hackin' away but looking to enjoy it, eventually separating the jaw with all teeth intact from the carcass, jagged flesh adhering all around the jaw! Gives the now benign predator the heave-ho splashing about ten feet out. With hardly any breaths between, Wynnewood's at it again with the five-footer; then holding its jaw up, "Right on.., gonna look good on the wall..!" Laughin' he asks; "Think you can out distance my toss without falling overboard?"

I kinda laughing with a don't know gurn, "Give it a try..," grabbing its tail and whirlin' around like an Olympian ball 'n chain thrower …then, there it goes..! Splashing.., "Yeah.., right out to yours..!"

He lowers the roped pail a couple of times over the barrier's ledge filling with water and outward splashes clean the barrier's surface of surgical scraps. Then the jaws spread open are tied at one end of a strong nylon string, and its other end to a one-inch diameter steel washer which is then wedged into a carved notch halfway amid the barrier's top; the string running straight within a carved groove to the ledge and over, jaws ending up submerged about two feet. He concludes, "I'll check on these this time tomorrow to see if they've been picked clean by the small fish. Want a lift back?"

I, "Sure, thanks..."

At the dorm I drop our empty bottles in one of the designated trash cans outside the north end of the building and take in a shower when one comes available. Leaning back against the wall in sleepwear with the nightstand lamp lit dim, I take a hit from a Coors and begin recapping the shark fishing episode. Not much later I don the phones and go for another brewski to dose, but then realize, "This one can wait 'til tomorrow," putting it back into the ice chest.

With fifteen minutes left to lights' out and having listened to Iron Butterfly's In-A-Gadda-Da-Vida album, I begin spinnin' J.T.'s turning the lamp off and eventually am easin' into, "In my mind I'm goin' to Carolina..," lowering the phones to the floor as it ends letting the player auto-shutoff. Sliding flat, eyes' blinking to final closure.., again unveiling is the mindsight projection of the white rectangle angled eleven o'clock to it...

Monday the 28th, two weeks from the day of touchdown; after work I stop by the cubicle to relax a half-hour before dinner. There is an envelope sitting on the bed, mail delivery. Opening, two one-hundred-dollar bills are nestled within a folded paper ...and unfolding, it is a letter from Pop wherein he says that the extra hundred is sent to last until his first of November sending of a hundred, aligning to the first of each month thereafter; to let him know asap if I received this. Tomorrow I'll sendoff an acknowledgment, then buy a frig.

At dinner starting off taking a sip of iced tea, I begin to think about the Chaplin, our paths having not crossed since that first time but by now should of, haven't heard of any church services either. Couldn't have been a figment of my imagination; veering off the court up to a ghost..? Believe I'll look him up.

The next day I stop by the terminal to see if there is any info on his whereabouts and come to find that he's gone, stayed only a day for a look-see. Well.., guess he did a do-drop-in while on Hawaiian leave but got the {redact} out of here as fast as he could because of nuke-rays..! As for me.., no longer fear being buttonholed.., just sterility and a shorter life due to radiation poisoning. Puff-chuckling; "Wonder if he'll at Travis counsel a swop in fears to other transient souls outbound to this atomic dot..? ...or play ignorant to keep it secret. Of course, he'll be under orders to by the Generals. Powers stronger than the guy on high? I really appreciate what he did for me but because of this, have lost all trust in God. Believe I'll look to see if Wynnewood's fishing this evening, will only take a brew for me."

Passing by the flightline's end, there he is off in the distance. About ten paces to leaving the road onto the jetty, a pickup pulls up from behind on my right and, "Hi there..," from the driver with his arm resting on the window sill, short-sleeve shirt displaying a Military Police band and E4 stripes above it.

"Hi," back to him.

He asks; "May I get your rank and name..?"

"Airman First Class Farrens," answer.

He, "Well.., Farrens, I assume you hadn't been told that bottles can't be individually held walkin' along, they must be in a sack or six-pack carrier."

"Hadn't been told," subtly shaking my head.

He rhetorically, "It's a broken glass safety concern, and we can't have a bunch of guys strollin' allover swaying bottles ...you understand."

But I reply anyway, "Makes sense."

He remarks, "A little civility ...you know."

Am thinkin', "Okay guy, get off it ...but gotta let him do his cop thing," only nodding ...then, "Was just headin' over to that fisherman friend, but here's the bottle."

"Wynnewood? Go ahead and take it with you this time, drop it empty in the back of his truck."

A slow nod with a slow, "Thanks..," by me.

He drifts onward honkin' his horn a couple times ...declaring his superiority.

A few feet to go to the truck; "How they bitin'..?!"

With the handle of his fishing pole firmly lodged in a square hole atop the bed's sidewall this side of the tail end, "Just got here, cast not long ago," he answers putting a pair of pliers in a small tackle box on the other side of him. But then the line's hit, the pole a smooth arching with the reel's drag sounding..!

"Yo..!" from me.

Not panicking, he stands and slides around to this side of the truck and works the mired pole out of the hole; props a foot upon the barrier's ledge and begins his mastery over what's at the end of the line. Cool steady as can be, ten months of experience if not more has etched a confident look. Gingerly tightening the drag, "It's only a three-footer, will toss it back," as the shark capitulates from swimming out to in with tension kept on the line.

Less than ten minutes gone by toying with it, "Here ...hold the rod," he says handing me it, then grasping the hook-pole he bellies on the flattop extending it down briefly out of sight and muscles up the shark snagged at a corner of its mouth. Slides it across the flattop onto the deck retrieving his pliers while it's floppin' around.

As he's manipulating the treble-hook out ...I ask; "What type is it?"

He returns, "White-tip reef; see the white on its dorsal and tail fins?"

I; "Have you never been able to land one?"

He, "Not yet, but there was one time when one was a bit over five feet and tryin' to belly it out holding onto the line with one hand and muscling up the hook-pole with the other, nearly went into the water."

I'm smilin' big as he clears the hook from its mouth, then grabs the tail and carefully bellies back lowering it headfirst as far as he can to the water, drops it from there; no Olympian toss, still alive.

Wynnewood leans the rod against the bed on the side closer to his ice chest and lifts a Coke out popping the cap. Joins me sitting on the tailgate I guess for a timeout. Both peering out.., lower my bottle the last time and ask; "What keeps you from the alcohol?"

Squintin' out; "All things equal..? ...this does," he answers.

Squintin' also, am silently putting together the equal things ...then, "I like the work I do, no alcohol there," say.

He, "Yep."

I add, "Otherwise, everything else has dosin' partnering."

He; "Really..? ...do they have to have?"

I, "Well ...hangin' in the ward with the guys shooting the bull, brewskies help us diminish the fear of radiation;" offer up as he slowly nods ...I continuing, "Shootin' hoops.., all seem to be sopping it down; and when relaxing back with phones on to my favorite tunes, mixes to calm the fear," turning my head a bit to him.

He puts forth; "Farrens..? ...no need to be offended by what's gonna be said, just wanting to reason the pros 'n cons of drinking to {redact} off the stress being applied by Plutonium. But here's where I'm at. A guy like you, goin' to bed every night weighted with fear that I'm being harmed by that unrelenting pestilence just outside my window. But I'm not gonna be taken in by the Military's passive immunizing with streamin' alcohol dumbing us down to accept fear, compounded daily, as being alleviated rather than submerged; constant fear constantly drowned while constantly isolated..? Man.., I can't judge my brethren though; drank before landing here but sparingly on peaceful easy occasions, parties and yes, fishin' with friends who could buy. Here..? ...constant fear entraps us to drink."

I remark, "Believe I'm a good guy..."

Wynnewood responds, "Not tryin' to cut into you but if you are consuming two or more bottles a day, you're easily on your way to bein' an alcoholic by the time you liftoff this place; look like it, smell like it, and act like it." Am still squinting out but with an empty bottle layin' flat at my side away from him as he's continuing, "Because we're all in this together, we're all good guys; but, from the moment I first set foot in the dorm to now.., I have seen good guys who got here before me go from drinkin' a couple of bottles a day …casually ramp up in support of 'Screw you radioactivity..!' Not gonna find myself landing in Honolulu also facin' drying-out demons because of winding down the days here drowning presumptive ills due to the exposure; drowning to falsely expand a sense of mental fortitude."

I comment, "Seems to be the in-thing."

Agreeing …he says, "Don't know if you realize it yet but most married don't drink, a few do; and like me some singles don't but most do, which far outnumber all that are stuck here. Ten months now.., looks as if three-quarter's Air Force drink, yeah… the in-thing. Alcoholism flourishing, and it keeps flowing in. But each to their own without judging because of the common threat. You listen to tunes, so do I. You shoot hoops, I read. You drink often, I shark fish often. This is the farthest point onshore from the hot spot."

"I wonder what the Military's overall take on this is..?" question tryin' to reason out Its concern for morale, now and in the future.

He answers, "Whenever questioned at any level, The Military's response will be that they are just giving us what we want, the lesser of two evils; and with that.., are apathetic backs turned on us dismissing the radiation threat. Sorry to say.., don't believe that'll ever change."

Barely noticeable bobs lowering my vision to just over the ledge, the way Zemke is comes to mind and am beginnin' to think, "Might spend the money on fishing equipment rather than a frig." I ask; "What test are your line and wire leader?"

Lightly smiling he replies, "Sixty-pound both." Showing the same type bobs about a dozen seconds pass --then, "Tell you what, Farrens.., tomorrow 5:30 meet me at the southwest corner."

I'm curious but say nothing, nodding, as he slowly up ends his Coke ...then lowering, "Think I'll pack it in for the night; lift back..?"

Nod, "Sure..."

Next day sitting down with the Serg at lunch; "Serg.., okay if I leave out from work a bit early?"

He; "When?"

I, "About 4:15."

He, "Yeah..sure, as long as DSTE's up and runnin'."

I get to the mess just as it is opening for dinner at 4:30. Am able to down a fair amount allotted enough time to by not stopping at the cubicle to change into civvies. 5:05, out the door bookin' towards the NCO Club. Passing it I make my way to round the flightline, passing the jetty and down the south length seeing way far the speck of a pickup parked. Bookin' without bottle in hand.

Reaching it with a minute to spare, I see Wynnewood below at water's edge standing on a large boulder that is one of the many making up the sloped six-foot high boulder laden seawall. He is about four feet aside-left from the base of a dump truck width, slightly oval, smooth surface, cement slide. Turning to catch sight of me, "Come on down..!" he says.

Making my way there …I ask; "How you doin'..,
Wynnewood?"

"Good..," he answers turning back to the horizon.

The sun is angled enough to the right so not to sheen the
ocean surface. Gazing out also …I ask; "What 'chu see..?"

"Don't you see it?" he switches up.

I, "No; what?"

"Let's sit a spell," he suggests.

Both perched against a couple of back resting boulders
and staring out …am beginning to think, "He's
hallucinating."

"Stay focused on the horizon," he says wearing a
peaceful easy smile.

"What does he see..?" wondering. Half-minute passing
in silence, "Believe some jaws…" I start saying --then,
"Shish..!" from him pinned on the horizon.

"Okay..?" mindfully --then; "What..?" mindfully
attention caught. Am seeing from it a shadowing in the
water that's so gradually broadening this way. Not a cloud
in the sky, looks like a near black blanket stretched wide
being pulled just below the surface toward us! "What's
goin' on..?!" I ask.

"Patience, you'll see..," from him.

Gulls are starting to show hovering over the darkness,
Wynnewood with a large smile, I with a can't believe what
I'm seeing look and, "This is amazin'..!" declaring
becomin' quite clear over the next forty-five minutes that
we're being invaded by fish; million or more..? …all types
in various size swimmin' back 'n forth at our feet! …and
in few amount are mostly white-tip dorsal fins piercing the

surface mixed in roaming about. "But what's calling them all in..?!" wondering.

Wynnewood rises and climbs to his pickup fetching from its bed the three-prong spear, but when returning just stands next to me holding it. "What're you waitin' for..?" I ask.

He, "Hang loose for five to ten minutes more."

I; "Does this happen every day?"

He, "Yep."

"Why?" ask.

"Won't be long and you'll know," from him, then sure enough there's the sound of a heavy vehicle's motor loudening.

Looking up the bank am seeing the backend of a dump truck slowing up to the top of the slide, then revving its motor starts tilting the bed. Quickly from Wynnewood, "Step back some!"

Do and; "Woe..?!" ...ton of trashed mess hall leftovers, puke-like sludge, a floodin' off onto the slide whizzin' down into the feeding frenzied turbulence of gluttonous aquatics! The spectacle of splashing fish..! ...the chorus of dozens of excited gulls..! ...at Wynnewood's feet the blurred rush of combat for the fishmeal as he's propped on the base boulder cocking an arm back to fling the spear! The other gripping a length of rope tied to it. Waits for the flood to cease then lets it fly just a broomstick distance into the chaos! Boom..!! ...it a violently shaking..!!! Quickly a short pull to him muscle-arcing out over a shoulder the stompin' two-footer speared..!! "How cool was that..!" awestricken.

"Not gonna be shark fishin' tonight but wanted to show you how I acquire bait," he shares.

Ear to ear smiling, "Hey..man, thanks..!" reply.

The catch still frantically twitching on the spear, he arc-flings it back out off the prongs. Rinses them clean and; "A lift?"

Quick bob back. Arms on the sills a slow breezin'; "Use a fishing partner..?" ask.

He answers, "Welcome it …but, no alcohol."

"Yep," by me.

Nearing the jetty, "Gonna stop-off to check on the jaws," by him. Lifting them out, "Right on.., are ready for some gloss!" he boosts.

"Man.., they're picked clean, just jaws with all the teeth!" heedfully impressed. Continuing on to the dorm I say, "Could use some advice on what all to buy."

He, "When we park I'll take you through everything."

Back on the ward, it's unusually quiet. I get a shower in and kick back to some tunes, low volume, and rerun these last two evenings. Rise with the phones on and take a peek in the ice chest to see if ice needs replenishing, nope. Four Coors are left. Really enjoy them but think I'm gonna slowdown, but, one for the night turning in. Sippin' on it, "Will transition off with the remaining three …hopefully," is the design in accord with this time tomorrow fully shark fishin' equipped. Last song, "In my mind I'm goin' to Carolina..," eyes' blinking to final closure.., rectangle at eleven o'clock…

Days go by pretty much as I foresaw, except, Fitz' and the others are a bit put-off by my weening off dosin'. They recognize though by the couple of jaws shown them that

I'm hanging with Wynnewood the non-drinker most evenings, that shark fishin' regardless has grabbed ahold of me frequently passing by toting rod 'n reel and tackle. No ridicule is tossed my way and actually with Zemke getting worse, seems to counterbalance. They know that I still care about them ...and, aren't convinced I'm losing my taste for the brewski.

Five weeks to go for Wynnewood, passed my fifth. Am feeling like a pro clearing the sea of sharks with him. The teamwork bringing them in pole-hooked by the mouth. Nearly all are returned but this evening two five-footers are lying on the deck, white-tips, availed to give up a jaw to us each. As I'm lowering a three-footer back, Wynnewood taking a break poppin' a Coke, a lanky six-foot tall studious looking white guy with shortcut dark-brown hair wearing specks approaches. Introduces himself, "Milton," projecting a meek but friendly personality. "Arrived JA four days ago," also saying. In return we introduce ourselves with a handshake.

Hereinafter, he'll show up more nights than not bringing a six-pack of Coke to add to the now sizeable ice chest. Won't get into fishing but makes for good conversation, so trifecta. Does take up photography as his main thing and with three weeks left for Wynnewood, on the tripod delayed flash ...click goes the shutter bit after dark. The three of us in the frame standing shoulder to shoulder sporting trophy smiles, Milton by one arm sideward v-flexed is holding up a three-footer by the tail, I with both hands a grip am center straddling a five-footer by its, and Wynnewood has a three-footer by one hand extended out front ...and draping his other grip a menacing lookin' four-foot moray ell, dead..! The three-footer's still showing a bit of life are returned.

But the ell …man; was that the heebie-jeebies..?! Wynnewood thought he had snagged on coral jerking away on the rod, then when it broke loose thought he had lost the leader and treble-hook as there was no drag reeling in. Then he sensed a slight bit of weight thinking a small white-tip got hung-up and cleared, won't need the pole-hook levering it up by the rod. Then breaching the outer ledge sliding toward his and my feet propped on this closer ledge, "{Redact}! …get away!!" he erupts dropping the rod splittin' left knocking a standing Milton back as I'm fast reflexing off right!! …the snake sliding off the flattop going under the tailgate all coiled around the hook 'n leader!!

Rapidly I ask; "What is that?!!" tensely starting to laugh.

"Moray ell, don't let it latch onto a foot, will have to cut either its head off or your foot!!" laughing he spouts, Milton sporting laughter! Ends up having to sever the leader several inches from its mouth, hook still lodged. In return for duplicates of the photographed four critters displayed on the deck …then held by us, Milton gets the five-footer's jaw.

First week of November, receive a hundred more from Pop. Pickler's cubicle is cleared out and Zemke has an A1C coworker that just landed on JA. Scuttlebutt is Zemke's being relieved from Comm duties due to his drinking, relegated to a gofer; Uncle Sam's way to deal with alcoholism, soon thereafter flying him off to Hickam to dry out, then back a couple weeks later kept under wraps still as a gofer with a little over three months left in his tour; Military's skirting of confession that It's fostering an alcoholic out here as the spigot is left on for fear of a swan dive off the fourth floor landing by him ...and for that matter, the rest of us. Am helping out training the new guy, Ellis, on DSTE.

It's funny.., Wynnewood and I hadn't ever dropped by either's cubicle, seemed right keeping it clean to fishing. A week left 'til he lifts off into the sky blue yonder, we're for the moment doing the fishermen's wait sipping Cokes peerin' out, beside each a rod is wedged in a sidewall hole. Milton has yet to show if he will. A couple of small white-tips have been returned. "Only seven days remain Xing-off the calendar," I comment.

He remarks, "Hadn't been doing that."

I; "Don't have one on the wall?"

He, "Yes, but when I got it only circled the expected parole date not seeing it until flipping up the page exposing this month."

I ask; "Then why even have it?"

"It was sent from home, country pictures of Maine," he answers.

I confide, "Broke down bought a Playboy one, but am finding that it's not fitting in with the lighthouse picture and jaw's hangin'."

He acknowledges, "Going through the year.., it became obvious to me that with drinking, gambling and pornography also evolved for many."

Thinking on that for a moment, "Soon after arriving here, played Blackjack the one time at the NCO Club; haven't since, not gonna. Believe I'll take down the calendar, find something different;" I respond, silence for several seconds --then, "Guess those things in Nam are acceptable, maybe expected with the threat of one's quick demise, dodging bombs and bullets, instant traumas. But they're not isolated, we are ...compactly... and can't dodge life-shortening, ill-causing, nuke-rays. If he leaves there unscathed, uncertainty of physical harm isn't taken with him. Constant yearlong exposure to radioactivity; are any of us unscathed leaving here? Not told not.., believe I'll take the uncertainty, the fear, with me haunting tomorrows wherever I go. Glad our paths crossed, my friend.., but I can't begrudge fellow comrades that undertake such distractions, as ill-fated might be."

He, "That's been my hypocrisy. Although resigned to stay clear of those who partook in those things, I've felt like you. All in this together under JA's influence, couldn't judge, couldn't hate anyone for their shortcoming's, just the demoralizing force always in range of sight. Will take the uncertainty, the fear, with me but nothing else except the belief I did the job asked of me ...and, the friendship we developed."

Nod smiling.., another swallow of Coke, "Looks like you'll be home for Thanksgivin'."

He with a couple nods smiling, "We'll probably celebrate Christmas two weeks before it having to move on to Langley." A month back he mentioned that's his next TDY.

"More country than here?" I jokingly.

Still noddin' smiling, "Yep," by him.

Now dark a bit ...I share, "Stars are a sight, never seen so many so densely inhabiting the expanse. Hard to keep looking at the darker it gets.., more appearing.., overwhelming…"

He returns, "Give it time.., you'll get used to it.., absorbing them..."

I ask; "What's gonna happen to all your belongings, jaws and fishing equipment, when you leave?"

Lifting his rod out of the hole reeling in the line …answers, "What won't be carried in the duffle will be crated sent on to Langley. Tomorrow got to get those things over to the guys doing that …so, am bringin' in the line the final time."

Placing the rod back behind him, Wynnewood slides both the spear and hook-pole up between us halting the hook and prong-ends just in front of us saying, "These are yours…"

I; "What?!"

He, "Yours.., to keep the tradition alive."

I ask; "Were they passed to you?"

"No …made them, so from me to you it now begins..," he replies.

"Thanks.., Wynnewood, hopefully it won't end with me," return.

He concludes, "Tomorrow and evenings 'til leaving I'll spend time here, hang with you."

"That'll be great. My Supervisor recently told me that our pickup can be with me most the time," answer adding, "and an ice chest full of Coke will be here."

He, "Cool..," then; "Lift?"

I, "Sure..," turning for my rod to reel in the line.

Like always he cleans his Bowie of only bait residue this time, sliding it back into its sheath but instead of tossing into the cab sets it on the bumper after shutting the tailgate. The barrier's rinsed, I putting the pail in the bed near the tailgate as he picks it up heading for the driver side door. As sufficient as my knife is, it isn't a Bowie. Before reaching his door, I mine, he stops and turns my way; "Farrens..?" ...stopping and lookin' his way. He extends it across the bed stating, "It's yours also."

Caught to the quick; "Your Bowie..?!"

He, "Yes, here.., you know it'll be much easier than what you have to cutup bait and de-jaw sharks."

Taken back, all I can muster is a mellow, "Thanks.., my friend..," grasping it.

He gestures for us to head on.

Sittin' the edge of the bunk after kicking off shoes, I look across to November's Playmate hanging above the dresser. Hands' clasped between open legs just beyond my pecker peering at her a dozen seconds.., go over and slowly lower her from the wall closing the centerfold dropping into the small trashcan. Next, Led Zeppelin II is being tucked away in a bottom drawer storing Amanda and Sunshine with it for the foreseeable future.

Week later, November 20th, am allowed time away from work to see Wynnewood off at the Terminal. Shaking hands, "Take care, Farrens..," by him.

"You too..," by me. Funny; although knowing each other's rank, we never referred to each that way but am wishin' the recently promoted Sergeant well as he turns for the C-141, I to reenter the Terminal.

The next evening backin' the pickup close to the barrier with an easily speared five-pounder in the bed, I shutoff the motor staring at the rawhide shrouded Bowie sitting on the dash.

Moment later.., it's that befriending loneliness tryin'…

12

The five-pounder's head splashes into the water.

$\mathbb{B}$egin sectioning the remaining four pounds into eighths, also tossing the tailfin, thinking about how well Wynnewood mentored, the lonely feeling moving on whispering, "Aside from work this is my main thing. Will there be a protégée..? Most do dose, most don't fish."

Two days passing, three to Thanksgiving; Ellis well by now is responsible for transcriptions. Lethargic Zemke delivers up to him if already in the DSTE room outgoing communiques, and allowed to pull from the cardpunch and line printer incomings. Exiting the stairwell returning from a late lunch, am seeing the Serg standing outside the

DSTE room with Comm Commander First Lieutenant Saurage. "Sir!" to him as I approach.

"At ease, Airman First Class Farrens..," greets me. Staff Sergeant Leland orders me to stand back from the partially open door. In a lurch not able to see in, am wondering the going's on but remain silent.

A long half-minute --then, am stunned seeing an MP carrying this end of a stretcher exiting, one of two known Medics the other end as an IV bag is being held up alongside by the second Medic and.., Zemke flat-out eyes' shut! In tailored shorts, the front most of his left leg from knee to sock is blood smeared, sock and tennis shoe soaked, wrist and hand smeared some with a white gauze widely wrapping mid-forearm!!

Once passed, we three enter seeing Comm Supervisor Staff Sergeant Keith and Ellis gathered with another MP conversing. Leland tells me to check on DSTE staying clear of the dense ten-foot trail of blood droplets leading up to the console keyboard/paper tape punch seeing smeared footprints surrounding it and the chair turned quarter ways, also a pool of blood at the base of its left front leg and small stack of bloodstained papers probably outgoings touching it! Am also told to remain until a cleanup's completed, watching that for an hour conducted by a Hawaiian team with sympathetic looks and purging comments.

Stands to reason due to the fact that all the blood was contained in the room he gashed the outer edge of his arm on the corner of something, maybe the door latch by the trail; not even aware..?! Who knows how long he sat in the chair hunched forward supported by the elbows perched on his knees..? ...hands' slumped according to Ellis. Returning from lunch he saw him there incoherent breathing shallow bleeding second by second drops immediately caught below the knee flowing down.

Ellis panicky, tried to stop the bleeding but not quite able to quickly got on the Comm Center phone calling for help, then back to Zemke trying his best! MP's from downstairs showed a minute later, Medic's five after that, and the Serg soon thereafter from lunch with the Comm Supervisor and Commander on his heels.

The actual account of how he injured himself was never ascertained, too far gone by his alcoholism to even realize. Blood thinned by it causing such a gush! Won't know if he's left the Atoll alive or dead, or at all..? What happened to him after stretchered out to an ambulance is shrouded in secrecy. Maybe will be dumped at sea off the barge that deep-sixes the two-year-old vehicles too far rusted by salt air.

By the time I return to the dorm from dinner, his cubicle has been cleared, curtain half open. Won't see him again. Trying to shake the hour and a half scene; don't know how long it'll take? Never seen so much blood spilled. Sitting at the edge of the bunk am stalled recalling the event thinking, "Glad I'm off the alcohol," as just then a mellow tone; "Farrens.., you in there?" from Fitz'.

"Yeah..?" respond opening the curtain seeing him, Carmichael and a couple of others holding brews.

"Zemke's cubicle has been cleared; what's the hap's, got a clue?" from him.

"Yes..," slowly shaking my head, "around lunchtime while alone in the Comm Center he apparently cut an arm not realizing it. By the time Ellis showed, he'd bled out a bunch. Was carried out on a stretcher unconscious, don't know more after that except so much {redact}n' blood cleaned up," answer.

Slowly shakes his head, "Too bad for the guy; hope he'll be okay?" the others noddin' agreeing.

"Yeah..," from me nodding.

"You Okay..?" he asks.

"Sure.., thanks..," answer.

Smilin' he ends, "Welcome to join us anytime, comrade."

"Appreciate that, Fitz' …but think I'm gonna take bit of a walk," reply. As he's turning away, "Hold up," from me reaching back over the foot of the bunk to the side partition removing from it the largest of five jaws hanging and, "here comrade, want you to have this," with an easy smile. Taking ahold he looks at it with likened smile.., then to me and a brief bob.

Am setting foot on the sizeable square concrete wharf for docking supply ships. The naval pier for the tug, barge and few skiffs is off to the right. Both the wharf and pier are on the north length straight across from our dorm. I'm seeing ahead breakers splashing the reef across the shipping channel. Halting at the ledge, just stare out trying to shake the image of poor 'ol Zemke earlier, and all the blood.

Looking side to side of where I'm standing, thought drifts to how much alcohol's probably offloaded each time a freighter docks. Then a relieving encouragement, "Oh well, gonna keep the tradition alive and jaws for a few other comrades." Deep sigh; "Which way from here?

Believe I'll head for the BX before it closes," turning about having seen there Canned Heat's double album "Living The Blues," with "Going Up The Country," track.

Fifteen minutes 'til closing am scoping out other vinyl's seeing on Gary Puckett & The Union Gap's album "Woman, Woman," the tracks, "By The Time I Get To Phoenix," and "Kentucky Woman", so it's bought with Canned Heat's. Mellowing to those.., lastly, "In my mind I'm goin' to Carolina...," --ending, phones to the floor drifting out.., rectangle angled eleven o'clock.

Ellis is given the next day off to chill, Supervisor Keith filling in. Nothing's said by him about Zemke, nor do I ask. So it goes.., and a Thanksgiving dinner two days later. So good, almost remembering Mom cooking them up.

Next evening Milton stops by to visit me fishing but will be the last for a reason out of our control. From then on will see him out 'n about time to time with his tripod, usually at the pier or wharf. Times be out at those in inclement weather when the sea is heavy taking pictures of the massive curls upwards to forty feet!

Also the week since Wynnewood left, more evenings than not I peered out with feet propped on the flattop merging solitude with the environment; rippling's of water.., the subtle sounds of them greeting the seawall.., infrequent passing's of gulls.., the rod at my side wedged in the sidewall hole, ice chest full of Coke, and out of the small transistor radio bought during the week low volume contemporary vibes piped in from Hawaii. But when darkness settled.., preferred myself to be known simply by three, "Sea, sharks and stars…"

Also along then Pickler and Zemke's cubicles are reoccupied with indulgers, fitting right in. Another also rolled over, the occupier too acquiescing to dosin'. From them hardly a response to my passin' toting rod 'n reel and tackle, hook-pole and spear. Since the moment I took up the sport with Wynnewood, others have been seen in skiffs heading out between the channel's outer buoys. Surprisingly with guys rotating through JA is how many names at any time are memorized, a third of all if not more.

On the heels of Thanksgiving something's afoot. More heavy-duty construction equipment's being added to the existing fleet, dozers and the like, mucho building supplies offloaded from a freighter with another docking two days later as if to erect a few more JOC's. Then we get the word, JA's becoming a chemical weapons storage site, later coined "toxic-dump." Great, that added to the radio-dump..?! ...and there goes shark fishing..!

Evening after the announcement am passing the jetty turning for the slide and see two-thirds ahead a chicken-wire fence crossing the road, the east-end perimeter of a hefty construction site. Slowing up to its gate a sign on it reads, **"Construction Traffic Only."** I turnabout and this will be the beginning of staring at the hook-pole and spear leaning against the locker-closet.

As Christmas approaches, decorations are popping up and most guys receiving gift packages, an extra hundred to me from Pop. The time of the season is shown bit more festive by the Hawaiians although they're always a smiling bunch with the thumb/pinky-finger tweak given when passing opposite direction, likewise returning it.

To me it all seems pretentious, flying in the face of preparations for receipt of mustard and nerve gas-readied munitions soon to be seen, mostly fighter jet mounted projectiles. The rapid influx of construction workers not only to build bookoo number of storage bunkers but also more dorms to house the hundred or so incoming Army responsible for containment of vapors. Rumor has it that the Okinawans are fed up living with the {redact}.., want it gone.

Last two weeks of the year, Christmas coming 'n going, countermeasures are taught to the entire population should all {redact} break loose! Classroom training watching a film of guinea-pigged chimps inhalable-exposed to blistering mustard gas or spasmodic convulsing VX or Sarin!! The latter two chimps then injected with Atropine to calm them back down acting as if they've been kicked in the side of the head by the ordeal. Revolting, repulsive, sickening.., seeing the unaware innocent subjected to such suffering; the twitching.., flailing.., foaming at the mouth from the VX or Sarin!! If was not quickly neutralized, instant death!! For the one mustard gassed no way avoiding it by the bloodletting out of the mouth from ulcerating lungs!!! ...the ugliness of blistered nose and lips!!! Thankfully we're spared seeing the poor creature's finality!!

Why evolve such an arsenal to achieve victory? That insanity kills indiscriminately, blowing in the wind not only wiping out enemy combatants but also innocent infants, children, men and women too frail to fight or not wanting to..! ...anything with flesh and breathes..!!

...even our troops if the wind turns..!!! The sense of guilt just being a cog in the wheel.

Sure, we're gonna be threaten by it. The inherent danger in storing so close to a runway. Our dorm shakes whenever jet engines go full reversal..! ...distant farther from the flightline than the plot of bunkers that'll occupy the southwest quarter. Over time the salt air with daily vibrations won't weaken munition seals and bunker door seams?! Have heard that Army will be toting caged rabbits and fully adorned in hazmat apparel when entering the bunker zone; "What..?!"

The fact that from the moment-on the insanity-ship is seen coming over the horizon, a belt-holstered gas mask at one hip and two pouched auto-injecting Atropine syringes the other must be strapped about the waist at all times outside the dorm, and reachable all times inside; that doesn't emblemize a constant threat of harm..?! ...added to that of chicken-wired acres of radioactivity already?! There are no reasons to fear existence here..?! How smart Uncle Sam is flooding this place with alcohol devoid of telling us whether or not our lives are at risk, turning his back leaving us in constant fear while he commands the nearest base eight hundred miles away, resort Hickam in Honolulu. "Let's dose to that..!!!"

Relying here on mask and syringes doesn't emblemize liken to an M-16 in Nam? ...to any degree..?! If my tour is acknowledged at all in the future, will it be as a serviceman sacrificed but still did the work required of him not speaking out? ...or as trash blown off here. A squeezed grunt best ignored..? ...or a figure carved in effigy to be shunned...

Setup outdoors is a dense smoke-filled tent to emulate real-time exposure; groups of fifteen of military or civilians every forty-five minutes drilling through challenged to adequately don gas masks. Holding a deep breath am stepping through the slit-entrance closing the eyes.., halting three paces in and spun around two times by the hazmat-suited trainer, then stopped trying to whip out from its latched holster the mask …and on… striving to purge fumes! Grope to find the one of two slit-exits which is unzipped to pierce out!!

Such calamity.., everybody bent over coughing 'n gasping for clean air removing our masks! What a joke!! After seeing the chimps' sufferings and going through this, with a whiff of gas bend over and kiss the {redact} goodbye..!!! Soon to float around will be unsubstantiated word that about six hundred body bags have been crated in, speculating fifty-percent fatalities…

Three weeks into January of '71; having to go through the survival course, how bent Carmichael is, being short having one left and observing with a bunch of us from the opposite-end landing the insanity-ship's docking, all holding onto looped gas mask/Atropine belts! Fitz' is subtly shaking his head not far behind with five weeks left.

Strategically positioned back some are the Atoll's two flightline firetrucks pointing their fixed cabover firefighting nozzles at where the {redact}'s gonna offload, to shoot forth dispersing foam seen practiced.

Also postured all around standing back some are the five emergency trained hazmat dressed Air Force volunteers, and as many fully uniformed Army shouldering M-16's; "What? …what are they thinking..?!

...that a bunch of us flyboys and civilians are gonna be charging flingin' soda and beer bottles in revolt?!! Hey.., we are friendly's..!!!"

Then the offloading of Phase 1 {redact} from dawn to dusk..,
Operation Red Hat beginning as pertaining to JA.

Nonstop, pallets lowering onto the concrete, forklifts loading them onto lengthy flatbed trucks heading for the USARHAW Red Hat Storage Area.

What am I gonna do in place of my off duty main thing? The sludge truck now travels counterclockwise taking the same route as did the {redact}'s flatbed's, down the angled road passing the radio-dump, then connecting with the frontage road circling the landing end of the flightline going along water's edge after and paralleling the storage area's west perimeter coming upon the slide's corner. Except to outrun MP's down the flightline distancing pass nuke-rays, it's the only path to it.

Dosing's been putting a try on me for the last month as more {redact}'s been arriving, Carmichael say-la-vee out of here and Fitz' ...short... having a good 'ol time letting loose about the {redact}, "This one's for you, Uncle Sham..!" hind end blowin' raunchy loud followed by, "Masks..!"

"Good grief, Fitz'..?!!" from adjacent cubicles but still laughing with the rest.

Sometimes sweet girly tone offering's by him; "Mustard on your spam sandwich anyone..?" bringing laughter! Time's quickly popping off; "Farrens..? ...you got a lot of nerve, gas..," gut busting the floor! Spreads the charm around but still am laughing when it's my turn. "Helping's of rabbit tonight's cuisine..! ...oh boy, can't wait to get to it..!" on 'n on...

There's weekend basketball, and there's the gymnasium; what else? Work is what it is, nothing more nothing less ...well almost. First Tuesday morning in March, my turn to change out crypto codes. Stepping up to the teletype to handshake the swop with Hickam, the one at the other end has already printout greeted, "Good morning," as is the procedure awaiting my reply of, "Good morning, go."

It being first, the spaghetti-wired block for the one crypto device is swopped out waiting for a few teletype keys to chatter-sync, then the code-card for the other device is swopped waiting again for the teletype and the other end to ask; "Ok?"

Happening I reply, "Yes, {redact}," the acronym, "{c}see {u}you {n}next {t}time." Okay..? ...not, anymore..! Second morning after, fifteen minutes 'til my turn again --when the Serg at his desk, I at mine, says; "Awe.., Farrens..?" slowly shaking his head tilted down and chuckling, "You can't be signing off sync-up's with '{redact}'."

"What..?" by me.

He, "Hickam's got a new Crypto Tech that's a WAF."

I'm frozen.., not knowing how deep I'm standing in it?! "Serg.., I never consciously used it to be vulgar or degrading. Good grief, haven't ever shortcut with that in mind..! There are women Crypto Techs..?!"

The Serg, "Relax Farrens.., snafued..."

All I can do is bust out laughing..! …didn't see that one coming.

He tries to hold back but, not…

Stepping up to the teletype, there it is.., "Good morning." Going through the swop am thinking most likely a pretty little WAF is at the other end waiting for my signoff? Ought to be contritely charming but; what if it's a dude..? …so I go middle of the road replying to; "Ok?" with, "Yes, see you next time, have a good day." If was a WAF, probably kept her a bit raw. If a dude, he might've been thinking, "Got cha..!" With a slight puff …think, "I don't care.., they got it cush in Hawaii," leaving the clicker behind.

After dinner I decide to take a walk to the 'ol fishing hole not needing the truck anymore. Sitting on the flattop facing out am wondering what to do with the hook-pole and spear? Walking away think, "Tomorrow I'll take them over to the boathouse, donate. The tradition dies with only three jaws left hanging on the wall." Fitz' left out yesterday to much fanfare.

Climbing the stairs, the landing door is shut with a large-print note taped to it reading, "Blocked on other side, use middle stairs." Doing so starting up the last run, can hear all kinds of ruckus coming from the ward! Topping the stairwell and before a quick bend into my cubicle, catch sight of a dozen-plus guys lining the aisle halfway to my curtain cheering on the porn flick emitting from a reel-to-reel projector onto a white sheet spread tautly across the door! With beers and other drinks in hand are the gesturing's to ram hard in concert with her wailing's of pleasure!

Tempted somewhat to join in but more so flop back donning the phones delvin' into tunes high volume. Won't shower tonight, for if I do …another'll be with me rising from the bottom dresser drawer. Shouts of, "Go… go… go… go… go..," above the vibes in the phones bring remembrance of the Long Beach triple-X theater visited not long ago. Twenty more minutes pass then it quiets. Canned Heat, Gary Puckett & The Union Gap, CCR then James' vinyl lastly mellowing to, "In my mind I'm goin' to Carolina...," …phones to the floor next to the mask 'n Atropine belt …drifting out, rectangle angled eleven o'clock.

Days go by pretty much doing the same few things but not with the guys on the floor. Get along okay but maintain a buffer; the degree of drunkenness by half of them, and now hardcore mags from the mainland but not yet another porn flick. Pickup basketball, workouts at the gym and taking the truck infrequently to the jetty an hour before sunset stretch downtime. Backing to the flattop putting the tailgate down, sit peering out. Though miss shark fishing, two out of three is still fairly decent, "Sea and stars..," as night takes over listening to Hawaii on the transistor.

So many stars looking like they take up more space than that between. Too populated to distinguish constellations. Flat speck of coral-sand in the middle of nowhere being dwarfed like this, still can't grasped all their sparkling's, trying as they might to check ingoings' of loneliness. Seemingly am the only one out of eleven hundred this night to occupy the northern eastmost quarter.

The middle of March, going over six months without taking leave. Two weeks again at a Gardena motel, prostitutes coming 'n going, and hanging out a bunch with Pop in his poker club parked camper, or inside the casino where there's alcohol mixed with gaming; sound like R 'n R..? ...this to that?! Made it this far trying to cope with the two threats, and so many Army boozers around thinking they're hardcore shouldering M-16's; which Palm tree is Charlie hiding behind..?! ...better yet, maybe they'll unload into the radio-dump liberating us from the nuke-emissions..! Bunkers still being built but no more {redact} a month now. Can't get any worse than this; right..?

Two weeks later; "Farrens..?" from the Serg at his desk, I at mine, "Some good news, then again one that's not so. Which one be first?"

"Might as well the first," answer.

He, "We've been allotted another DSTE Tech arriving out of school in about a month, much earned relief for you."

Respond, "Neat, Serg..! ...now the second..?"

"The transmission tower on Sand Island has to be manned 24/7;" wheels beginning to turn inside as he continues, "There's the Coast Guard Tech to keep it up 'n running but stays over there only one day of the week for preventative maintenance, rest of the time here in Comm Operations monitoring. Six others rotate through each day but one has TDY'd off. You've been assigned to take his place starting tomorrow. I know it's your birthday but I couldn't get a change soon enough, I'm sorry."

Reply; "But I wouldn't know what to do if it goes down..?"

He, "That's okay, a phone's there. You'll be called if it has gone down and taken through steps to restart it. If doesn't, then the Tech will immediately be ferried out. You've noticed the hut at the base of the tower..?"

"Yes," answer.

He, "Been told that a bunk, small refrigerator and hotplate as well as a bathroom is there with the transmitting equipment silently lining the wall across from the bunk."

Ask; "What will I do to pass time, stare at its blinking bulbs..?"

"Read.., there's a stack of magazines, some with a lot of photos; if you know what I mean..? Take your rod and tackle but no radio because of interference," instructing while I with gradual nauseate nods. Goes on, "In the morning be at the mess when it opens for a good fill, at the pier by 7:30 to be ferried. Request at the mess food and drink provisions to carry you through the day, they know if it ...routine. The one you'll replace will return in time to have breakfast, and so forth for you. There'll be a change of bedding, travel soap and towels in the skiff. No shower out there."

Still gradually nodding, "Okay.., Serg," by me.

"Oh yeah..one last thing. Don't walk the short narrow's to the other small pad. A secured decommissioned facility is there and off-limits," he concludes, I still the nauseate nods slightly squinting.

Next morning …**The Speck of Speck**.
<u>JA dubbed The Rock, this is solitary confinement..!!!</u>

Food and drink provisions in a small no-iced cooler setting a few feet from the subtle surf, rod 'n tackle box next to that and a bundle of bedding under one arm, soap and towels straddled by the other, I stand with gas mask and Atropine strapped around the waist staring at the low-down situation as the skiff pulls away behind with the guy replaced. Sixty to seventy feet to the front wall; maybe thirty from its back to surf..? …staring, "Happy Birthday, Mic'," conjoining echo's between the ears, "<u>One …is the loneliest number that you'll ever do…</u>"

After stashing the provisions, making the bunk and gawking a moment at the transmitting equipment, I head back out toting the looped survival belt to the rod 'n reel and tackle still left there. For bait have torn bits of beef from a sandwich, and after casting am standing gazing across the channel to JA musing, "Leaving out of there this isn't the Island I had in mind. Just another turn of events, Airman First Class." And it won't be but for many years into the future that I discover what else here I'm standing on.

Puff …shaking my head; "How neat it would be seeing wee guys over there keeling over from gas..? …and me a castaway..?! …the phone ringing off the hook over there, not an answer..?!! Can't swim the channel with sharks drawing straws seeing which'll have me for a snack. How long existing on caught fish before anyone asks; "Seen Farrens around..?"

Catch a few throwbacks then try to make it through the day staying away from Centerfold's but …not, and without talking to myself but …not. Am finally drifting out whispering, "In my mind I'm goin' to Carolina..." …mask 'n Atropine belt on the floor and despite being a half-mile from it facing a different direction …still, rectangle angled eleven o'clock.

Day later Carmichael's cubicle has a newly, sociable type and right off guys are gathered around him hearing the latest Stateside. How the peace movement has grown. College campus sit-ins, protests daily just outside military bases. Music festivals, long hair …the love generation and wow, flower girls..!!! But we the so-called Military Establishment? …hated back home by them.

With passing days I draw down isolating more in my cubicle, other's also. Dual threats always in sight stepping onto the landing exiting, shark infested sea a backdrop. Remarkable stepping into the aisle looking both directions when the end doors are open, nothing but water 'til walking midway to them; not able to garner any sense of community. Hard to keep from dosing with the next stint of solitary confinement tomorrow.

Visits to the jetty are no more because of what's seen across the channel waiting for me. Have found though a small fishing spot near the boathouse, a white ten by ten storage shed nestled behind it just four feet from the pier's drop-off within a brief dual ninety degrees zigzag, the path circling behind the shed narrow and obscured by it, ideal for sitting on the ledge daggling legs over holding the rod between. Provides secrecy to prolongate palm-pressuring the eyes without caught as crying.

First time to fish there didn't have bait but knew of a Hawaiian who sat outback the mess peeling garlic and onions. What a neat, so friendly, guy who was happy to accommodate by going back in retrieving a raw T-bone! ...outrageous!! ...but apparently due to the sludge fishmeal, fish take to beef. So here I sit in civvies' shorts with legs dangling, tennis shoes four feet to water and am piecing steak. Can hardly believe the success gonna have. Small hook with bait plopped straight down is submerged just out of sight six feet or so although the water deep.

Woe, instant take..! ...though the rod not much of an arc it's fun anyway with the frantic dance at the other end! Hardly any weight to it slowly reeling up, and as it's coming into view, a four-inch brownish-orange pufferfish ballooning.., funny..! A ridge of short spines runs its back, so lightly gripping the bloated belly I gingerly finagle the deeply lodged hook out, bait left behind.

Back to water it goes, a moment floating --then thinning sinks swimming out of sight. Another piece of beef and plop. Instant take..! ...a similar tug but lesser dance. What's coming into view..? ...another one or..?! Bait left behind in it, into the water that one goes. Beef and plop, instant take..?! ...lesser tug, lesser dance. Now just a slow ballooning drift upward, got to be the same one. Used to the routine, it's gorging on beef; "Smart critter but how much repeat pain from the hook can you take?!" ask it. Hook out, bait left behind, hold up eye to eye and; "What's with you..?! ...but if can keep on with the pain of being snagged, I'll keep on feeding you, tuffy..!"

Beefed hook in the water, takes quite a while and yep after the last must be full. Been a moment from when believed I saw a shadow cruising below much larger than any of the whitetips caught. Rising, don't want to lose balance and fall in..! Calling it a day flinging the remainder of meat out far, walk away smiling about the gluttonous companion.

Middle of April the Serg receives his next TDY assignment finishing up his second hitch, is heading to Mountain Home AFB in Idaho, just an hour away from home, good for him..! For sure won't take advantage of the swops option which allows for any time before the thirty-day point prior to departure to request an exchange of assignment with someone elsewhere requesting one. Haven't seen him indulge in alcohol or even fish any, has been residing in the apartments. His replacement is scheduled to arrive a week before he leaves. Has really been good working for Leland, gonna wish him well.

The next day Ellis walks into our office, "Something's amiss with the cardpunch." I follow him back into the DSTE room and he's right, IBM cards are jamming, metal support arm for a tracking pinch roller is cracked midway and wouldn't you know it..? ...don't have a spare! Advise him that it will be down for a while, gonna have to rely on the tape punch 'til fixed.

Back in the office showing the damaged part to the Serg, "Don't know how long it'll take for a replacement but I have an idea. Pay a visit to the Hawaiian machine shop to see if a copy can be fabricated. It's precision but what the hey..?"

"Worth a try," he affirms.

I meet with a cool stocky little Islander, and he nodding, "Sure.., no problem, come back tomorrow this time," leaving the flawed sample with him.

Walking back into his shop, amazing.., spittin' image right down to the make of metal! Smiling, "Hey thanks; awe..?"

"Jimmie," he responds smiling.

"Bill the Air Force," I remark.

"No charge, happy to do..!" he replies with bit larger smile.

Back at the office; "Serg..? ...check this out!"

He nods, "Decent, can't wait to see how it flies..!" A half-hour later I call him into the DSTE room. "Looks like they're a movin' right along," he says.

"Yep," with a nod adding, "though probably best to still order in a backup."

He nods affirming.

I, "Also would like a big thank you sent Jimmie's way, the Machinist; from Command if possible?"

"I'll see what can be done," the Serg returns.

April ending, I've been showing the new DSTE guy, A1C Henley from Seattle, the ropes having arrived two days ago. It'll be some time before he does the Sand Island gig, first got to get passed the shock of being stranded on the Big Island! Haven't yet clued him in on the signoff protocol to Hickam, am disgusting grinning to myself ...but I cave. He dwells two dorms down and will be more fortunate than me with his OJT course, I having completed mine being available to help him. Ends up boding well on my second review even though the boss wrote me up quite nicely on the prior. Just more time in rank needed for promotion.

Things keep going along, four more cubicles on the floor having turned over and coming to know of another leave taker gone AWOL. Immoderate Trinity-J dosin' on the rise since the arrival of mustard and nerve gases, and another gathering for a porn flick. No getting into each other's face though, the persistent dual threats the common denominator keeping everybody semi-comatose lying around in our cubicles, the same dark humor about the gases tossed about. And as always, "<u>In my mind I'm goin' to Carolina...</u>," ...mask 'n Atropine belt on the floor, rectangle at eleven o'clock going under...

Then I get glimpse of encouragement, advance tip that a bowling center is coming to JA, not that I'll bowl but work at. Early bird scoping the possibility and it'll happen for the first two months of the three remaining in my tour, most evenings off duty and weekend splits with one other hired, but working alone operating the center accountable to the Recreation Liaison. Henley will kindly assume my on-call schedule with me backing him up if unable to effect a repair. The center is gonna have six lanes housed in a Quonset, be patronized mostly by Hawaiians and man.., loose with money..! ...the tips when paying for games and brewskies! Its "Grand Opening" projected mid-June.

Third week ending in May, Leland's replacement arrives, Ackerman another Staff Sergeant. It's kind of neat, group of four now chowing dinner most evenings, the call of Mountain Home louder 'n louder in Serg's ears. Table talk always evades the two dumps although rumor afloat has it that completion of the bunkers has fallen behind Operation Red Hat's phase-two mandated delivery date of the remaining {redact} from Okinawa, enough so having to commandeer Air Force laborers! How did I dodge that one? Maybe due to the bowling center job now set for two weeks from Leland's departure tomorrow.

Off into the sky blue yonder he goes, and Ackerman in his place is okay, giving me on-the-job seniority latitude to come and go with ease. Thank goodness for the bowling center work that'll fill much of the dead time. Extra money will be great, any tips in addition to minimum wage, going to write Pop to holdoff sending more money. He's been true to form.

Seeing wealth ahead, I've begun eying the Pioneer stereo system on display at the BX that can be ordered in. Neat reel-to-reel mag' tape player, AM/FM receiver-amp and two thirty-inch tall-box standalone floor speakers, all wood-grained incased. Going to leave the current system with vinyl's behind as part of the furnished cubicle for the next lucky..! I'll begin ahead of the new purchase collecting taped albums.

July ending I get my next TDY assignment, Myrtle Beach AFB, South Carolina, the third choice on my dream sheet! It didn't come to mind back then that another might've also been listening in on the phones to J.T.'s song repetitively ending my days; got to the guy on high..? Who knows..? Definitely won't take advantage of the swops option.

Am also ending my sixth week at the center, easily in the groove 6:30 to 9:30 p.m. Closing then and after reconciling money into the safe, I restock the two large refrigerators with beer and take inventory headin' out a half-hour later ready for quick to bed with a shower in the morning. Only the one song, "In my mind I'm goin' to Carolina...," thinkin' right on.., going unconscious, mask 'n Atropine belt on the floor, rectangle at eleven o'clock, and also in the way of freedom another Sand Island gig two days from now.

Awe.., what's being said..? ...being brought out of deep sleep by some, maybe two, low voices --then quickly upsurge wailing by another! Shock awakening evolving into unfamiliar territory! Forced discerning the unimaginable lament, "I got to get to my wife!!" is loudly despaired by the one, the other two exchanging, "She's okay..," softly saying.

"Oh God, I got to get out of here!!!" cried out with the sound of bodily ricochets off furnishings in the cubicle directly to my left the other side of the stairwell.

"You will.., she's okay, being cared for..," bit louder by the two in effort to subdue.

"Got to get to her!!! She needs me!!!" over 'n over the resonating anguish of fear amid helplessness.

"It's being arranged, please calm down.., she's okay, please calm down..," from one trying to comfort.

My poor hurting neighbor, sounds like he is but not the constancy of his crying outpour. In spite of lowering volume, the relentless fettering of sorrow remains disturbing.., "My wife...oh my wife; why..?" again 'n again as the otherwise contrite silence owned by the rest of the ward is bereft of an answer. Likewise the two comforters except for, "Don't know..," failing to keep the lull and momentary is the calm as his torment starkly rebounds out of control, clumsily bursting from his cubicle instantly slumping to the floor against the Latrine/Showers' wall just the other side of my curtain! ...the two quickly following trying their best!! Dark is densely all about and nonstop are his terrible yells thrusting through it unmercifully into my ears!!!

Bringing me down with him is trying me to put together what's horribly wrong?! But his loud woeful persistence doesn't allow for an image of just a woman harmed, but he as well at that shocking moment!! This traumatizing witnessing is also annulling movement of time, arresting me on one count of having no perspective and another of not feeling secure, an accessory to stopping hours, minutes and seconds from passing!!! How long this'll go on has no place of interest, trauma on JA is a still-shot!! ...constant fear of radiation compacted on JA a traumatizing snapshot!! Days ahead, will there be any other than those who had to endure a year here that understands that?! ...distinguish us as atomic exposed servicemen without turning a back to us..?

Sounding like another has showed, low voicing, "He's not gonna make it here like this. Let's get him to the dispensary for the rest of the night. Gather up a change of underwear and his dress blues, then secure the cubicle while I notify the Base Commander," ...the poor guy still travailing.

As he's being escorted away, the same voice diminishingly says, "Hey, hey.., she's safe now, comfortable with family and the guy has been apprehended." Phased into calm as his moaning's disappeared down the stairwell.., the abandoned space left just outside my cubicle is too {redact} quiet!!! Looking at the clock, five minutes to midnight!! In no-man's land wondering; "Can I get back to sleep..?!" All the things circling in mind as to what might've happened to his wife but one that's appalling keeps settling. Trying to overcome the thought of it I mindfully pray for his burden to be lifted ...then muster, "<u>In my mind I'm goin' to Carolina...</u>," humming lightly to myself the melody slowly drifting back out, rectangle eleven o'clock...

Saturday morning next day, returning from breakfast word circulating is that my neighbor's wife was brutally violated. Though not hearing it firsthand from Medics or MP's, no other mentioning's are to surface offsetting and the next afternoon sitting surf's edge fishing on Sand Island am feeling guilt that I'm becoming inclined to skim pages of Playboy's while imagining her ordeal. Can't dispose of the magazines because of other guys day's here. I don't look into them but defiantly do not withhold imaging such an intrusion heading back outside to ludicrously run laps around the hut putting forth to the one above the transmitting tower; "Why have I become this way..?!" having yet to kiss a woman except on the cheek of mom.

Aloha Airlines now also does a JA stop before landing Honolulu but doesn't linger long enough for the Stewardesses to stand atop the stairs waving because of the chemical weapons. Probably for the best, don't need to be seeing them in this frame of mind.

Beginning of August, here we go again but what the {redact}..?! ...still not enough bunkers built to store the sizeable amount, nearly half, of Phase 2 {redact} offloaded completing the entire transfer from Okinawa. This time a large number of gas-readied wing-mount armament is needing a bunker to call home but, not..! The remedy, "Let's stopgap erect a bunch of metal sheds to house them..!" brainstormed by the Generals, "We won't have to worry as will the grunts inhabiting JA about fumes breaking loose in the breeze due to all the jet turbine vibrations combined with salt air weakening shell casings and storage shed seals." What a sight looking out from the top landing at their comically pitiful metal farce situated with stompin' concrete bunkers next to a runway!

Some of the Army stationed in advance to receive the {redact} have let slip their displeasure of being left out of the celebratory pageantry put on by their cohorts back on the dock in Okinawa where an Army band marched passed the Red Hat Boss who led off the parade standing upright tall in a jeep, and a big rig flatbed trailer carrying an enormous red baseball cap with "Red Hat" and their "Company" designation embroidered on also having trundled by. Metals were conferred for a job well done! Okay..? ...why don't they bring the marching band and big red hat to parade down JA's flightline stopping at their job well done..?! Out of sight...out of mind..? ...or indifference to those now with the {redact} in the toilet in the middle of the Pacific.

That sort of uppity conviction will keep future generations from knowing about us, or acknowledging that there was such a sacrifice, a legacy of experiencing prolonged constant fear, and the Military's alcohol smutting to pervert any consideration of service connection resulting from. Does it take seeing the face of the enemy, or carry a rifle, or be bracketed with an instantaneously debilitated comrade to be commemorated a war hero? How afar from those great men and women will I be in the future if suffering relatively delayed but as profound an incapacity brought on by yearlong exposure to radiation?

Four weeks left 'til rotating off this place, and that many days from when the swops option expired, I'm visited while at the office, the Serg in the crypto room, by a clerk from Administrative Support handing me an envelope. Opening it and unfolding the sheet pulled from am seeing that my next TDY has been changed from Myrtle Beach. "{Redact}..!" let out loudly but apparently not enough for it to be heard beyond the office walls. I fold it up and stuff in my right shirt pocket remaining silent about it but thinking, "So much for the Dream Sheet."

Later in the evening after dinner, am at the bowling center working and finding myself unable to keep from a brewski having refrained for so long, plopping a quarter in the cash register and pulling a cold Coors from a frig. If caught by supervision would be fired, but taking the first sip ...Porterville, "I don't care..!!!" mindfully for I'm resigning right after breakfast tomorrow, then a trip to Administrative Support.

Meeting there with the Second Lieutenant in charge, paths not before crossing, I delineate that due to the underhanded sidestepping around my swops option, I see myself not reupping. "I'll see what I can do," he returns.

Week later staring at the new unboxed Pioneer stereo components and the only six-pack of Coors drank, am recalling conversations with Wynnewood. Although stressed out about this place, anxious to get the {redact} off it being uncertain of where my next TDY will be, "I gotta stay away from the alcohol the radio-dump, chemical weapon's dump and two more Sand Island gig's be damned..," coming to terms. A day later at the office I'm ordered to meet with the AS Second Lieutenant. "This is what the Air Force responded with. I don't need to know, open it the other side the door," handing me another envelope.

"Thank you, Lieutenant," reply.

"Dismissed, Farrens..," by him.

Standing outside his office am seeing, "Travis AFB, Fairfield, California." Back through there taking leave, then returning for TDY.

Two weeks passing with one left, I've gotten everything except that which'll be carried in the duffle over for crating to ship on to Travis. Am glad to have remaining in the cubicle the small stereo system to listen to, the one last largest jaw to give to Pop, and the aquatic calendar that replaced the Playboy's having only the say-la-vee date circled bigtime. There's one other item that's hidden beneath the mattress. Next, I head on over to the Terminal to book the flight out. "I can get you out mid-morning on a 141 or.., there's Aloha Air stop 'n goin' couple of hours later showing three seats unfilled as of this morning's dispatch," the fairly new A1C Clerk avers.

"Humm ...don't know. Two hours longer than I have to," I respond.

"There'll be windows to look out ...and, gorgeous Stewardesses to look at..!" he opines.

I; "What's the chance of getting bumped?"

He, "Trust me, if I get you booked by day's end, you're locked in. If not by day's end, you're on the 141 two hours earlier but let me know now what chu want."

"Alright, Stewardesses..," by me.

"Cool.., stop back early tomorrow to see if booked," by him.

I, "Thanks, my friend…"

A long…long week gone by, September 10th '71, after breakfast am moseying back to the cubicle to kick back to what will be the final hour to listen to tunes …lastly with, "In my mind I'm goin' to Carolina..," despite it being back to California. Placing the duffle on the bunk, I then reach beneath the mattress and slide out the sheathed Bowie tucking it at the beltline under my full length fatigue pants for no one to see. Leaving the duffle for now, I head for JOC with mask and Atropine strapped to the waist to say goodbye to Ackerman, Henley and Ellis. There'll be an MP at the base of the plane's stairway to take the {redact}-belt from me right before the first step up finally off this hellhole.

Leaving JOC after bidding farewells, I leisurely stroll to the jetty going all the way to its tip to peer out over the ocean to horizon …gradually scanning right in the direction of Hawaii. Funny.., seems for the first time in a year that I'm without any thought, just feeling the warm subtle salt breeze…

After a few minutes, I lower my sight and turnabout. Approaching the shark fishing spot off to the right, I pullup turning to stare at Sand Island and am still without thought except for how I felt the first moments sitting in the far right dorm's downstairs lounge upon arriving JA.

Everything else between seem to want to bury but for one thing now, all the times loosening here fishing, sitting on the tailgate with feet propped on the flattop ledge. Begin to reminisce how great a friend Wynnewood was.., what he did for me. Squinting at Sand Island with slow breaths, I remove my sight from it down to the washer notch carved in the flattop still remembering Wynnewood --then, continuing to.., slowly pull the sheathed Bowie from my back beltline and paralleling the ledge …gently rest it atop the notch. Gaze at it a dozen seconds then turn away…

Toting my duffle, twenty paces to the 737's stairs seemingly oncoming slow motion. Fifteen paces, ten handing off the duffle to a baggage handler to load. Five, four, three, two, one then halting at the MP. "Name..?" he asks.

"Farrens..," answer, handing over the {redact}-belt.

He tells me my seat assignment also offering, "Take care.., Farrens…"

With a slight smile and couple of nods I reply, "Thanks, I will.., you too…"

As the plane comes out of the tight taxying U-turn, I slowly close my eyes likewise taking a deep inhale …and, bit quicker exhale as the turbines begin high revving, eyes kept shut. Starting down the runway I'm quietly into, "In my mind I'm goin' to Carolina...," …with, rectangle eleven o'clock.

[Viewed from the dorm's fourth floor landing, the jet is accelerating to the future song "After The Garden" by Neil Young, lifting off and a steady gradual climb, banking right continuing the gradual ascent, steady straight… …fading into]

Epilogue

California, 1971 …coming to the end of
the causeway to Travis's main entrance.

The bus as the year prior pulls off into the turnaround just in front of the gate after passing through a gauntlet of a hundred or so antiwar demonstrators lining both sides of the road right up to it. Mid-afternoon, it's the ninth day back Stateside cutting leave short for it was as before with Pop.

Stepping off the bus walking the gap created by the Berkley love generation adorned as flower children sitting and chanting, "Peace.., peace.., peace..," with some hand gesturing the peace sign while others hold signs projecting varied colors of the peace symbol …there's one quite unsettling in contrast reading, "Baby Killers!"

Upon reporting in I'm assigned overnight quarters pending permanent residency. The dorm's exterior has a look similar to that of on JA, but inside are rooms instead of cubicles. After meandering lightly through dinner I rest back in a lounge chair in the dorm's downstairs television room as a commercial's airing on the tube, and am unable to shake that one disturbing sign.

Next after the commercial is apparently the channel's evening news coming back on beginning a segment with the demonstration outside the gate profiling all the love and peace --then, in the blink of an eye are scenes from Nam of our soldiers in battle!! Sitting here alone watching this crude counterpunching choreography being aired by these unsparing newscasters is bringing me to again feel Sand Island confined but rather thinking, "The alienation being in the middle of divergent creeds; whom can I relate to, or be accepted by..? ...the desperate drafted soldiers I'm seeing, or the Berkley love children passed sitting comfortable..? Relate to now and in the future, accepted by now and in the future..? ...how the past year I came to feel expendable. Is true now..?

I decided not to lookup Chaplin Malone no longer wanting to remember that experience, and our paths wouldn't again pass. My coworkers never asked about the prior TDY, nor did I mention it... ...burying... ...until...

A week after my flashback I was seen by a VA Psychologist touted as an exceptional PTSD Doctor by the Clinical Intake APN who assigned me him. Until then I hadn't heard of the initials or what they stood for. He seemed to be a compassionate guy, displaying empathy about my isolated tour of forty-three years before.

At the initial visit and subsequent sessions he patiently waited for my crying to stop first off after the door was shut, my head lowered. In the midst of one at the fourth I looked up to see him staring at me with his eyes watered red. The following visit two weeks later he asked after the sobbing ceased how I was doing paying my electric bill. I answered it is tight but getting paid. He then said that he could help, turning about to his desktop computer entering something while I lowering my head sat quiet.

The morning of the next visit two weeks passing, I got a call from a Mental Health Clinic Clerk just an hour before it informing me that my Doctor is no longer seeing patients, the phone going silent for ten seconds 'til I said; "And I'm supposed to be saying..?"

The young woman's voice replied; "Oh...I don't know..?"

Five more seconds silently passed and; "What happened to him?" by me.

She, "We're not allowed to give out that information," phone going silent five more seconds.

Then I, "Oh; now what..?"

She, "Well.., you can start over again with a new Doctor."

Me, "Hum."

"What do you want to do?" by her.

With a slight puff shaking my head, "Guess so."

It is scheduled for a week later to again visit first with the same Clinical Intake APN.

Put off befuddled, I decided to make my way anyway to the VAMC to pay a visit with the Patient Advocate if possible. Was told that the former Doctor's credentials were in question as to one of the colleges attended.

Week later sitting across the desk from the Clinical Intake APN was told that he had been promoted to a supervisory position overseeing all the other Psychologists. Which of the two had lied, the Patient Advocate or her? I retrieved my medical records and began monitoring the newly assigned Doctor's remarks infuriating him and the APN when discovered. What a turnabout in the profiling of me; and if the former Doctor was supervising, why then the ball dropped regarding help with the electric bill? He seemed to have disappeared from the VAMC grounds during the next couple months seen. All the changing up of medications made me sick and I ran from their professional treatment…

I solicited help from my then Senator and District Congressman for service connected disability recognition only to be ignored.

Shortly after uncovering what the new Doctor had begun loading into my medical records, I went looking for information to exact reasoning for the depth of my anguish and discovered on the Internet just that. In the early sixties, three nuclear armed rocket launch tests had to be aborted shattering their warheads grossly contaminating the Atoll and Sand Island, where I also slept and stood fishing, with plutonium.

In the years since 1962 contamination problems surfaced on a number of occasions. In 1964 the U.S. Public Health Service conducted an alpha survey at which time about four hundred 55-gallon drums of contaminated debris were disposed of at sea. A second survey performed in 1965 yielded another 50 drums of contaminated material. Then two years following my departure from there, the Nevada Operations Office of the Atomic Energy Commission (AEC) conducted a survey using newly developed radiation detection instruments that found radioactive contamination throughout one launch area extending to the second. Eight "hot spots" were detected on JA outside the launch complexes and nine on Sand Island.

Searches for new "hot spots" continued after 1974, and during the timeframe from June '75 to March '80 over five hundred radiation emitting spots were found and removed. In relevant part to other radioactive elements, Americium 241 (^{241}Am) was found to be distributed over the ground surface with no soil (coral-sand) barrier. In short, ^{241}Am contamination was lying on top of the surface constituting an inhalation threat when air suspension occurred! We had been put in the position to breathe airborne radioactive dust!!

The account of this contained in the U.S. Defense Threat Reduction Agency's "Johnston Atoll Radiological Survey (JARS)," unclassified public domain, reveals on page 6 therein that readings taken inside the two launch emplacements identified Plutonium 239 as well as Americium 241 gamma ray peaks. Two measurements taken outside the launch emplacements also showed ^{241}Am. These were in the packed coral field south of emplacement-1 between the inactive taxiway (angled road) and flightline, and in the field across the flightline from emplacement-1. **The area between the angled road and flightline was closed to vehicle or personal access by the JA Radiation Safety Officer as a result of these measurements. A barrier was placed there, also at the Redstone Pad Area at the end of the main road on the way from the mess hall and dorms to the Joint Operations Center (JOC)**, places walked several times a day while on tour there.

The picture would come clear thirty-five years later with the U.S. Government's January 5th, 2016 tidy closing of the matter dossier repudiating any radio-pathogenic culpability, a well befitted 237-page handwashing…

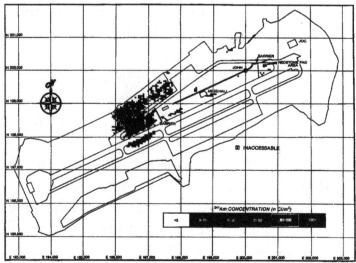

The Final ²⁴¹Am In-Situ Measurement Results (Jaffe and Tipton 1982), Figure E-11 shown on page 176 of the HEADQUARTERS, AIR FORCE SAFETY CENTER's January 5th, 2016 Final Report (Unclassified) on **Plutonium Exposures to Personnel Assigned to Johnston Atoll.**

Note: The rectangle at the end of the main road (thick straight line) was the swimming pool virtually surrounded by the massive radiation field (**black cluster**). One would be hard pressed to find online a picture of it being utilized.

Upon rotation off Johnston Atoll, servicemen and later women assigned did not receive psychological debriefing or were tested for radiation markers.

The End

19 YEARS TO JOHNSTON
And The Knife Left Behind.

Acknowledgments

obert M. "Doc" Campbell, Jr. (deceased), the 2003 - 2004 Vice Commander of the National Association of Atomic Veterans, Inc. Reading about Doc left me motivated to write the story. Clearly he was a very caring compassionate man who was very dedicated in helping Atomic Veterans striving to gain the recognition and benefits deserved. He testified on behalf of us Johnston Atoll Veterans in the matter of HR3236 to be recognized as Atomic Veterans. I regret not having the opportunity to have met him.

Also, I wish to acknowledge the many gracious employees that sat at the Reference Desk on the second floor of the Fayetteville, Arkansas Public Library, whom from the onset of this work patiently tutored me in the use of word processor software. I hope all are well, doing okay and are happy. They will be cherished friends, always...

And Seth, who exceeded all the expectations I desired to see in a son. He will be loved, always...

About the Author

H e is a seventy-year-old Caucasian residing in NW Arkansas and as of the publishing of this work is unwed. Spends his days with one foot situated there and the other on JA. The after-effect of the flashback is that his two nightmares mentioned early in the memoir have been supplanted by a view melding the immediate landscape with coral-sand flatness encircling an area of radiation. No longer though lets the walls of his abode entrap him as did the isolation of that speck. He takes one small pill daily not prescribed by VA Mental Health that enables him to go a cruisin' peaceful easy down the road. Comments about the story are welcomed at gentleharmony2@gmail.com.

Songs Location Reference:
(Each appearing as partial underlined lyrics.)

Within Chapter 5
It's All In The Game ~ Tommy Edwards
The Lion Sleeps Tonight ~ The Tokens
Venus ~ Frankie Avalon
It's Now Or Never ~ Elvis Presley
409 ~ The Beach Boys
Where The Boys Are ~ Connie Francis
There's A Rose In Spanish Harlem ~ Ben E. King
Travelin' Man ~ Ricky Nelson

Within Chapter 6
I Get Around ~ The Beach Boys
You're So Fine ~ The Falcons
Wild Thing ~ The Troggs

Within Chapter 7
The Sound Of Silence ~ Simon and Garfunkel
Good Lovin' ~ The Young Rascals
Eve Of Destruction ~ Barry McGuire
We've Gotta Get Out Of This Place ~ The Animals
He's A Rebel ~ The Crystals
Be True To Your School ~ The Beach Boys
The Game Of Love ~ Wayne Fontana and The Mindbenders
Searching For My Baby ~ Bobby Moore & The Rhythm Aces
I Will Follow Him ~ Little Peggy March
Up On The Roof ~ The Drifters

Baby, The Rain Must Fall ~ Glenn Yarbrough
I Dig Rock And Roll Music ~ Peter, Paul and Mary
For What It's Worth ~ Buffalo Springfield
Time Has Come Today ~ The Chambers Brothers
I Can See For Miles ~ The Who
Turn Around, Look At Me ~ The Vogues
Porterville ~ Creedence Clearwater Revival
Groovin' ~ The Young Rascals
One ~ Three Dog Night

Within Chapter 8
Love Can Make You Happy ~ Mercy
Time Is Tight ~ Booker T. & The MG's
Chug-A-Lug ~ Roger Miller
Time Of The Season ~ The Zombies
Walk Like A Man ~ The Four Seasons
The Wanderer ~ Dion
Where Have All The Flowers Gone? ~ The Kingston Trio
Summer In The City ~ The Lovin' Spoonful
Sloop John B ~ The Beach Boys
Sugar, Sugar ~ The Archies
Duke Of Earl ~ Gene Chandler

Within Chapter 9
Easy To Be Hard ~ Three Dog Night
Whole Lotta Love ~ Led Zeppelin
Don't It Make You Want To Go Home ~ Joe South

Within Chapters 10 thru 12
Carolina On My Mind ~ James Taylor

CPSIA information can be obtained
at www.ICGtesting.com
Printed in the USA
BVHW071834110521
607042BV00002B/172

9 780578 904962